Acclai…

Companies With A Conscience

"*Compa…* … *y* CEO (and concerned citizen) in this country."

—Peter Mathiessen, Author

"A 21st century look at the...inner workings of innovative companies that strive to put real meaning and practical effort behind the concept of sustainability."

—Elaine Lipson, *Boulder Daily Camera*

"Business is the most powerful force in the world. As business supports the community, the community supports the business. The companies profiled in *Companies With A Conscience* are proving it every day."

—Ben Cohen, Co-Founder, Ben & Jerry's Homemade Inc.

"*Companies With A Conscience* is a book that's right for our times."

—Barry R. Weingast, Senior Fellow, Hoover Institute

"*Companies With A Conscience* is required reading in my 'Corporate Governance, Power and Responsibility' class. It fulfills the need for experiential examples of companies that seek to be socially responsible. Business persons will benefit from it."

—Constance Bagley, Lecturer of Law and Management, Graduate School of Business, Stanford University

"Smoothly written and inspiring."
—Gene Ulansky, *California CityWoman*

"Plus, it's fun to read."
—Lynn Bronikowski, *Rocky Mountain News*

Companies With A Conscience

Intimate Portraits of Twelve Firms That Make a Difference

3rd Edition

Howard Rothman
and Mary Scott

A MyersTempleton Book

Published by
THE PUBLISHING COOPERATIVE
Denver

A MyersTempleton Book
Published by The Publishing Cooperative
P.O. Box 480151
Denver, CO 80248
ThePublishingCooperative@TheLightningFactory.com

Front cover, clockwise from top right: America Works founders Lee Bowes and Peter Cove (photo by Deborah Lopez); Tattered Cover founder Joyce Meskis (photo courtesy Tattered Cover); Ben & Jerry's founders Ben Cohen and Jerry Greenfield (photo courtesy Ben & Jerry's); Patagonia founder Yvon Chouinard (photo by Doug Tompkins); Kansas City Chiefs founder Lamar Hunt (photo by Hank Young).

Back cover, clockwise from top right: Celestial Seasonings founder Mo Siegel (photo by Stephen Collector); Birkenstock USA founder Margot Fraser (photo courtesy Birkenstock USA); Interface founder Ray Anderson (photo by Janet Amundsen); Greyston founder Bernie Glassman (photo courtesy Greyston); Stonyfield Farm founder Gary Hirshberg (photo courtesy Stonyfield Farm); Shorebank founders Mary Houghton, Milton Davis, James Fletcher and Ronald Grzywinski (photo courtesy Shorebank).

MyersTempleton/Publishing Cooperative books are available at special discounts for reprint editions, bulk purchases, sales promotions, fund raising and educational purchases. Contact: Sales Department, The Publishing Cooperative, Finance Station, P.O. Box 480151, Denver, CO 80248; ThePublishingCooperative@TheLightningFactory.com

Library of Congress Cataloging-in-Publication data pending

Printed by John-Phillip's Printing, Inc., Denver, CO
Cover by Scott Idleman/Blink Design

The paper in this book meets the guidelines for permanence and durability of the Committee on Production Guidelines for Book Longevity of the Council on Library Resources.

Printed on Recycled Paper

To all those who strive to operate their companies—and their personal lives—with a conscience.

Table of Contents

Preface

Oh well a Touch Of Grey
Kind of suits you anyway.

—Robert Hunter and Jerry Garcia

It's rare for any of us to really get a chance to revisit our past work, to dig deeply one more time into some long-completed project in search of new insights and old acquaintances. That is, however, exactly the opportunity we were handed when we decided to update *Companies With A Conscience* for the twenty-first century. Originally published in 1992, the book launched us on an odyssey of discovery that wound up introducing us to some very interesting businesses and some truly enlightened business people. Now, a decade later, it has thrust us yet again into this eye-opening and inspiring universe.

As was immediately obvious to both of us, the time was definitely right for an update. Almost from the moment we first sat down together with a dog-eared first edition to discuss the roads that our subjects had traveled, and how the movement they exemplified had evolved over the past ten years, it became apparent that an essentially new book was on the horizon. So many changes had taken place that we decided from the start to retain just eight of the dozen companies we originally profiled, and totally reorganize the way we told their stories. We also decided to replace four of the original company profiles with different corporate examples in order to provide an updated perspective that was more attuned to the start of a new century with new demands and new expectations. However, those parameters took on a vastly different meaning when September 11th forever changed our worldview, and they shifted yet again as fallout from the Enron collapse incontrovertibly changed the way we look at commerce and industry. If ever there was a time for a business story that was truly positive, we felt this was it. And, as we were pleased to discover once our revision had gotten fully underway, true companies with a conscience continued to be the real deal.

To prepare this new edition, we looked into all of the companies as if we were examining them for the first time. We read everything we could get our hands on about the firms that were new to us this time around before setting out to visit their main offices and some of their satellite sites. We discussed the businesses in detail with people on the shop floor, in the CEO's office, and at many places in between. For the firms that we were retaining, we likewise dove into the printed record of their last ten years while personally going back to the same range of personnel—including founders and current top executives—for the analysis and perspective that only they could provide.

So what, exactly, did we find? For one thing, we learned that there is a good reason why a popular saying about transformations over time—the more things change, the more they stay the same—has become a well-worn cliché. We soon found, for instance, that two of the firms that had been leading the charge in the past toward corporate responsibility in the public arena (Ben

& Jerry's and Patagonia) were still in the forefront and still pushing the envelope. We discovered that two of the companies that generally operated out of the public spotlight (America Works and Greyston Bakery) had continued along essentially the same paths as before but were taking far bigger strides to impact the communities in which they operate. We noted that two companies that had long been cult favorites (Celestial Seasonings and Birkenstock) were now established as major household names. And two companies that catered to highly specialized audiences (Shorebank and Quickie Designs) had become the top players in growing industries that they themselves virtually created.

There have been significant changes, of course. When we prepared the 1992 edition, Shorebank had 350 employees and Patagonia had 525; now, respectively, they employ 525 and one thousand. Two regular guys from Long Island who cranked out the world's finest premium ice cream, as well as a Buddhist abbot from Yonkers responsible for an array of incredibly popular gourmet desserts, have moved on from the day-to-day operations at Ben & Jerry's and Greyston Bakery. Celestial Seasonings merged with the former Hain Food Group. The owner of Quickie Designs faced—and then faced down—a major financial scandal at one of its other subsidiaries. Employees at Birkenstock became its owners and a former warehouse employee became its president. Patagonia named a new CEO, marking the first time that anyone other than co-founder Yvon Chouinard has run both entities. James Fletcher, one of the four visionaries behind Shorebank, died in 1998. Jerry Garcia, co-author of the song lyric that begins this Preface and co-founder of the Grateful Dead rock band—one of the four original companies with a conscience that do not appear in this edition—died in 1995.

The biggest change, though, is our inclusion of exciting new examples of socially responsible businesses that produce positive bottom-line results in every area that matters. We're pleased to introduce old and new readers alike to all of them: Stonyfield Farm, a natural yogurt-maker that uses its company to promote environmentalism; the Tattered Cover Book Store, one of the preeminent independent book retailers in the U.S. and a staunch supporter of first amendment and privacy rights; the Kansas City Chiefs, the professional football team that takes community relations to a new level; and Interface Inc., the largest industrial floor covering company in the world that is trying to mitigate the negative impacts of its industry. Getting to know these businesses and the people behind them has been every bit as enjoyable and informative as becoming reacquainted with the eight businesses retained from our first edition.

Now that the re-visitation process is complete, do we feel companies with a conscience offer a socio-economic cure-all for these confusing and turbulent times? Certainly not. But do we believe that they provide a viable alternative for an Enron- and World Com-weary world? Absolutely. When we sat down to analyze this project the first time, we discovered that there are no better corporate models than those firms that can lay claim to impressive records of community contribution along with a consistent history of corporate achievement. Ten years later, our conclusion is the same.

In this third edition, *Companies With A Conscience* again features in-depth profiles of a dozen of the best of these businesses—of various sizes and types, in assorted industries and geographic locales—to illustrate the diverse possibilities inherent in this way of doing business. We bring them to you once more in a format that allows them to be read consecutively or in any order, and in a way that allows their collective message to come through. Toward that end we've also updated a concluding chapter on the universal lessons that these firms hold out to us, and included the original Introduction verbatim because it still provides a perfect description of what we are trying to do and how we are trying to do it.

Finally, we still feel—and feel compelled to say once more—that we consider ourselves incredibly fortunate to have been presented this opportunity to reexamine these provocative and inspiring people and places a full ten years after our first encounter. Perhaps we'll look into them again in 2012. In the meantime, we have created a web site to continue the dialogue that we began in 1992. Please join us at www.companieswitha-conscience.com and tell us what you think.

Howard Rothman and Mary Scott
November 2003

Acknowledgments

Communication is key at any company with a conscience. We are therefore indebted to those people who so personally and professionally convey their company's message on a regular basis, and thank them sincerely for working with us to make this book happen. They include Lee Holden of Ben & Jerry's, Heather Duncan of Tattered Cover, Alexia Hall from Shorebank, Lu Setnicka from Patagonia, Jamie Hill of Hain Celestial, Brenda Sniezek, Pete Moris and Suzette Cox of the Kansas City Chiefs, Karen Tumelty at Greyston, Janet Amundsen, Joann Bachman and Donna Birdyshaw of Interface, Mary Jo Viederman, Cathleen Toomey and Mary Townsend of Stonyfield Farm, Sheri Ketchum and Marc Cowlin at Birkenstock USA, and Carey Winkel at Sunrise Medical.

We additionally want to thank those who offered invaluable assistance for this and the prior editions of *Companies With A Conscience*: Linda Schwartz, Deb Nastaj, John Kirk, Jim Brown, Brian Hanson, Susan Spencer, Paige Boucher, J.J. Yore, Suzanne Nakasian, Linda Woodwell, Anne and Gracie Scott, Pat, Anna and Melanie Rothman. Finally, we would like to acknowledge the person who inspired the original book, the late John G. Scott, who lived a life full of love and integrity.

Also, thanks to our long-time agent Richard Curtis for taking this ride once again; Kendall Bohannon for ushering our words into print; and Scott Idleman of Blink Design (www.blinkdesign.com) for designing our cover. Finally, thanks to Pat Cochran, Lew Goodman and, of course, our ever-loving families.

Introduction to the First Edition

It's much easier now, in hindsight, to explain why we wrote *Companies With a Conscience* than it was to articulate the fine points of the project when it first came up early in 1991. At that time, the two of us began talking about the way corporate America seemed to be resetting its moral compass. We marveled at how the greed-is-good, house-of-cards economic engineering of the 1980s was no longer in favor. And how the Michael Milkens, Charles Keatings, and Gordon Gekkos of our world—real-life Wall Street money men and cinematic West Coast power brokers alike—were suddenly and decisively out of fashion.

Because our professional and writing careers had been spent concentrating on topics like progressive business management and our personal lives had been marked by a long-standing commitment to a variety of social causes, we were more than a little interested in the trend. We decided to find out just what was going on.

From the start, evidence of this newfound ethical standard appeared everywhere. Companies like Apple Computer and Wal-

Mart were actively encouraging their employees and customers to recycle. Campbell Soup and H.J. Heinz were among those offering on-site day-care programs. Avon Products and General Mills were developing policies to help female and minority workers. Coca-Cola and 3M were investing heavily in community outreach efforts.

We also discovered that the environment really had taken center stage and that corporations of all persuasions were jumping over one another to initiate "green" policies. Candice Bergen told us how US Sprint was pledging a portion of its receipts to environmental groups. The WD-40 Co. announced a Preserve Our Parks foundation to be funded with proceeds from the sale of its household lubricant. Even General Motors released a packet of information called "General Motors and the Environment."

We knew that something important had begun to happen when McDonald's Corp. announced a far-reaching plan to eliminate polystyrene sandwich boxes, introduce recycled paper bags, and implement large-scale food- and paper-waste composting as a means of dramatically reducing trash at its eighty-five hundred fast-food franchises. We also remained skeptical until we learned more.

What we eventually found was a still small—but steadily growing—movement toward "caring capitalism," as one of its major proponents describes it. The basic tenet is that business doesn't have to be a negative force in society and business people don't have to be the "bad guys." We determined that enterprises that buy into this concept are part of an increasing network of companies with a conscience. We decided to find out exactly who these companies were. And just what they were doing that was so memorable from a business, and socially responsible, point of view.

Although giants like Wal-Mart, Heinz, 3M, and McDonald's receive the bulk of the publicity for their actions in this area, we quickly discovered that smaller, often-unknown companies really were the leaders in the nascent movement toward corporate responsibility. What's more, we also discovered that many of the small- and mid-sized firms were actually making a regular and substantial profit. Armed with statistics that told us some 1.3 million new businesses—primarily in this category—had opened their doors in 1991 alone, we felt an examination of such leading-edge entrepreneurial efforts would offer the most in the way of lessons and appeal.

Even with that much of a background, our search still took us in some unexpected directions. We met regular people from Long Island who crank out the world's finest premium ice cream and a Buddhist abbot from Yonkers who bakes incredibly popular gourmet desserts. There were health-food aficionados in the shoe, grocery, and clothing businesses. Tea makers and welfare recipients existed side by side. So did bankers and rock and rollers.

The short-term result of our search is the collection of profiles contained in the following pages of *Companies With a Conscience*, a book that identifies and then examines a dozen socially responsible—and successful—businesses in America. These are the firms that are changing not only the way they do business but the way it is conducted by all of us. And they are the firms that treat all people within their influence—employees, customers, and residents of their communities—with the utmost respect, without losing their focus on the bottom line.

As we moved more deeply into the subject, we encountered a lot of business people interested in the way our leading-edge companies were combining a commitment to the planet with one for the balance sheet. We noted the mushrooming number of business schools requiring classes on environmental or ethical issues for an M.B.A. degree. And we watched as companies like IBM and Coors began supporting major conferences on business ethics for their peers across the United States.

So how did we choose the companies we eventually decided

to include? We started by talking to people at a few of the benchmark businesses we already knew about. Ben & Jerry's Homemade—founded by two Long Island ice cream men—was a natural because of its major social agenda; Patagonia and Celestial Seasonings were two others we were aware of right from the start. Workers at these companies told us about employees at others, who recommended people elsewhere, who knew somebody worth interviewing at still another firm. Eventually, we researched hundreds of businesses and spoke with dozens of business leaders and business educators.

We then established a firm list of criteria for potential candidates, two of which were most critical.

First, we wanted only companies with a proven record of conscientious business practices over a significant period of time. While the McDonald's Corp.'s recent environmentally based actions are certainly laudatory, we sought businesses that were longtime leaders in this area rather than merely followers. We looked, therefore, for corporate structures that contained a well-articulated social mission interwoven into their basic fabric.

And we wanted only companies that had been consistently profitable over this same time, with all indications of continued success. So we looked for a clearly defined economic program as well. It was easy to find superb examples of conscientious nonprofits, along with well-meaning, new for-profits that were poised to advance from fledgling to full-fledged. But we wanted companies that could truly serve as viable role models for the corporate America that is taking shape. For that we needed businesses that proved you could have your cake and eat it, too.

Sometimes our search provided some unexpected insights. Always it offered an intriguing look into the many different ways that businesses are choosing to demonstrate their combined social dedication and fiscal commitment. One constant we uncovered among prospective subjects was an entrepreneurial bent; another was a general reluctance to "blow their own horns" by even participating in a project of this nature. But all of this ran second to a genuine desire to serve as a role model to other companies interested in adopting such a route to responsibility and success. All of the companies we selected were therefore happy to provide us with the access and information we needed to help inspire others with their stories.

We eventually settled on the twelve firms profiled in the following pages and believe our choices are interesting as well as informative. Some of the companies carry names known to the general public, for example, Birkenstock and Ben & Jerry's. Others, such as Quickie Designs and America Works, serve a much more specialized audience.

But all of these businesses are included enthusiastically because they fulfill our criteria as well, or better, than any of the other candidates.

We also included a final chapter in which we distill the factors common to these companies with a conscience and note characteristics that make them the companies they are. Foremost among these, as we've already suggested, is a concern for people. The way each enterprise exhibits it, though, is always somewhat different.

Other recurring traits—and the way these businesses go about helping their various communities—are less easy to categorize. Most are deeply dedicated to environmental issues. Many give away money. Some only employ the people they are trying to help. Others continuously sponsor a wide array of fund-raising events. Taken individually, they represent the cream of the crop in today's new business world. Taken as a whole, they offer tremendous insight into the wide-ranging ways that companies can earn money while making the world a better place.

Chapter One

From Welfare to Work

Company Name: America Works
Primary Business: Employment Agency
Type of Company: Privately owned
Headquarters: New York, New York
Number of Employees: 100
Founders: Lee Bowes, Peter Cove
Year Founded: 1984
Web site: www.americaworks.com

Mission

We change peoples' lives by lifting them from welfare dependency into the productive world of employment.

It's been four months since Eugene, a New York native, started his job as a maintenance worker at a mid-town communications firm. After his full-day shift one afternoon, Eugene stopped in to see Phil Jones, America Works' long-time sales manager, at the firm's headquarters. When the fifty-year-old eyed Jones, he went over and first shook his hand, and then wrapped his arms around him in an embrace. "Thank you," he said.

Convicted of a petty crime years before, Eugene had since struggled to hold a job. He would work a few weeks, and then find himself back on welfare, repeatedly, for years. It was a cycle he was only too anxious to break. But he needed support.

And he got it from America Works.

Formed in 1984 by Peter Cove and Lee Bowes, America Works is a for-profit employment agency that is responsible for removing more than thirty-five thousand welfare recipients like Eugene from public assistance. A profitable company with offices in New York, Washington D.C., Baltimore, Albany and Yonkers, New York, it takes in $14 million annually by finding jobs in the private sector for more than fifteen hundred welfare recipients each year.

After a one-week training program, America Works placed Eugene into the entry-level position. Once there, an America Works caseworker monitored his progress, checking with both Eugene and his supervisor. Was Eugene prompt? Did he fulfill all expected duties? Were problems at home impacting his performance? For long-term welfare recipients like Eugene, it's finding both an opportunity and support that is the greatest hurdle.

Since the 1996 federal Welfare Reform Act, the number of welfare recipients has declined dramatically, thanks to programs like America Works. Indeed, America Works, a favorite of both former President Bill Clinton and the Democratic leadership, is a key reason why the legislation passed. Lawmakers were able to point to America Works' longevity and success to prove that the welfare- to-work notion is viable. Since the legislation became law, welfare rolls have plummeted 40 percent, from 12.2 million people to fewer than 7.5 million. As many as two million adults have abandoned welfare; about two-third of these got jobs, according to the U.S. Labor Department. In New York City, the number of residents collecting welfare has declined by nearly 80 percent, according to the city's Human Resources Administration. In 2003, less than two hundred fifty thousand people collected welfare, compared with 1.6 million people at welfare's peak in March 1995.

America Works attracts job candidates through word-of-mouth testimonials, active recruiting, direct-mail solicitation, classified ads, and the extensive television and newspaper coverage it has received since its 1984 founding. A required orientation and training period, ranging from one to three weeks, teaches applicants to write a resume, learn how to best fill out a job application and sharpen their interviewing skills. Further programs provide an overview of different workplace situations that are in acute need of workers, including home health care, security, food preparation and retail service jobs. As the job candidates are working on their presentation, America Works' aggressive sales staff reaches out to potential employers who are looking for entry-level employees.

Once a match is made, most of the newly hired employees work on a trial basis for four months. America Works pays these placed workers a modest hourly wage, while billing the employer a small markup to cover salaries, benefits and monitoring expenses. Typically, the cost to employers during this period is about a dollar an hour less than the ordinary payroll cost for that position. The employee, meanwhile, also receives reduced welfare benefits during this period.

If the tryout proves successful, the employee then goes on the company's payroll at its going rate and the welfare payments stop. If they remain at the job for a year, their employer can also qualify for a federal tax credit amounting to about $2,500 over a two-year period.

America Works, on the other hand, makes its money from both the state and from the companies that hire its clients. Each time one of these clients is fully weaned from welfare, the company charges the state. Columbia University's School of International and Public Affairs recently found America Works' method costs around $5,500 per trainee. This compares with $29,000 for standard public programs in New York, which includes an $11,000 administration cost, a cash grant, Medicaid and food stamps. The state's return on the investment to America Works is almost five to one. "For $5,500, we guarantee the state doesn't have to pay $24,000," says Peter Cove, the sixty-one-year-old founder. Cove started the company in 1984 and has been running it since then with his wife, former sociologist Lee Bowes, fifty, who serves as CEO. "I've always been involved in community action programs," says Cove, a passionate dark haired man who favors bow ties. "I was at the University of Wisconsin in 1963 when the country was going through a great deal of turmoil," he says. "Kennedy was shot, and the civil rights movement was in full swing. This undoubtedly influenced what I've devoted my career to."

A veteran of several nonprofit ventures, including President Lyndon Johnson's War on Poverty, Cove eventually took over a Massachusetts not-for-profit agency funded in part by the Ford Foundation. "Our organization was the prototype for this kind of activity and proved to me that 'supported work' for the disadvantaged could work, and that it could move to the private sector," Cove says in his midtown Manhattan office. "It was at this point of my career that I began to understand my own mission. I learned that what is important in a person's life is work and employment; work is therapy, and helping to provide a job is perhaps the central most important thing I or society could do for a person. I also learned that the majority of people on public assistance would rather be working. And that's what America Works is all about."

In the beginning

After eight years in Boston, Cove was ready to take his concept on the road. "The only way to grow and expand was with capital, which was needed to fuel the expansion," he says. With $1 million from his own savings and various bank loans, Cove launched

America Works.

There were three motivating factors in the decision, Cove explains. "First, I wanted to spread what we were doing, and you can't grow a not-for-profit organization, because you need capital to expand," he says. "Second, I wanted to accumulate money for myself. And third, I knew how we operated our non-profit and that it was possible to do the same thing on a for-profit basis."

Since its launch, America Works has continued to provide valuable learning experiences to its founders. Cove's first client was the state of Ohio, whose governor had been aware of Cove's success in Boston. Cove proceeded to set up offices in both Cleveland and Dayton and found local people to run them.

Though he successfully placed welfare recipients in full-time jobs, Cove and America Works had a short-lived stay in Ohio. "We were creamed politically," he says. "We were brought in by the governor who pushed us past the state's welfare department. There was the perception that we were outsiders, and the fact that we were a for-profit company made us very threatening. We pulled out after two years."

America Works experienced a far more positive response in Connecticut. A program already existed to get welfare dependents—primarily mothers—into the work force. Seeing the success in Boston, several key state officials and the welfare commissioner brought America Works to Hartford. "We had a lot of support from the various government layers. This allowed us to establish the company to do something that was not done before." In 1988, America Works was invited to New York to salvage a similar, but unsuccessful, job placement program. "The state recognized that we had the management capacity to rescue the program, and we did," Cove notes. At this point, Bowes became head of the company. But as the company evolved, so did its challenges. There was an ever-growing need for more capital. In 1987, the pair created a partnership with Abe Levovitz, a retired manufacturer from Boston, who provided a significant capital infusion. During this early period, Levovitz taught the entrepreneurs the importance of daily accounting, and demonstrated the need to emphasize that the firm is paid only for proven placements. After a thirteen-year partnership, Cove and Bowes bought out Levoitz in 2000, again making the husband-and-wife partners the sole owners.

How it works

America Works' New York office hums with activity. On any given day, dozens of job candidates, as well as the hundred-person in-house staff, move about the classrooms, telemarketing headquarters, sales department, and conference rooms that make up the company headquarters. Still, Bowes and Cove describe their organization as being very personal. "We don't have a lot of layers, even though at any time eighty to one hundred workers are on our payroll, plus our own staff," says Bowes.

The company is divided into five divisions: Pre-employment, Business Lab, Sales, Job Match and Corporate Representatives. Duties are well divided, though the interaction between workers is apparent and vital to the company's ongoing success.

The process starts in Pre-employment, where job candidates spend their first week. In this orientation class, the candidates are introduced to both America Works and to what is expected of them once they walk out the doors.

In a bright, sunny classroom, Paula, a thirteen-year company veteran, is an instructor, mentor and inspiration to the eighteen primarily African-American and Hispanic men and women in attendance. "The whole purpose of the Pre-employment week is to prepare our candidates for interviews," she says. "We work on communications skills. Half of the battle," she adds, "is to get the candidates to effectively express themselves."

According to Paula, a former schoolteacher who was once on welfare, many of the candidates have completed high school or received an equivalency diploma; others dropped out after the ninth or tenth grades.

"On Mondays, we talk about public assistance programs and

what they were originally designed for," Paula says. "Most participants doubt the system; they don't understand that it is there to provide the tools for them to pick themselves up and move on," she says. Yet, according to Paula, many of the candidates have been welfare recipients for many years. "A woman here recently told me she was a fourth-generation welfare recipient," Paula adds. "No one in her family had taken care of themselves in decades. Recently, her son made reference to her 'never being able to work.' She felt ashamed and decided to give America Works a try. Within two months she landed a job as a clerk in a retail store.

While America Works actively places candidates in jobs, Paula encourages participants to seek out employment leads on their own. The candidates come to these meetings professionally dressed, with the men in collared shirts and the women in skirts and dress pants. "When you go to a potential employer, use the powers of observation, your eyes and your ears," Paula says to the candidates. "Dress as if you would fit in. When asking about potential jobs," she adds, "don't ask questions that can be answered with a 'yes' or 'no.'" Rather, Paula suggests inquiring with a specific request, such as: "When you are hiring, what kind of position are you most often looking to fill?" In addition, she says, use flattery. "Let the employer know that this is exactly the kind of place you want to work," she says.

The lesson is briefly interrupted when Rosemary, one of America Works' sales representatives, appears at the door. "I have an immediate job opening with a company in Jersey City, in the copy department. Applicants must have copier experience and there is heavy lifting involved," she says. "It starts at $8.00 per hour and a Metro Card will be included. Is anyone interested?" Four of the men stand up and follow Rosemary to learn more about the position.

Paula, meanwhile, addresses the importance of job applications. "The application is a tool companies use to screen you out," she says with a touch of drama. "They know your resume could have been written by a professional. But with the written application, an employer can learn many things about you. They can see if you follow instructions well, if you are neat and if you are detailed-oriented. Now," she adds, "there are some of you who were very careless with the practice application you filled out yesterday. I'll go over each of these with you."

Later, Paula explains both her thoughts and her own inspiration for initiating a new class through the orientation procedure each week. "Many of the candidates have been wondering from one day to the next how to make ends meet," she says. "They have their downs. I feel that if in this time I have a chance to influence and to build their self-confidence, and to provide some valuable tips, then I have to give it my all," she says. "We make the best of the situation, and we laugh and joke a lot. I try to reach them with a bit of humor. I know what it's like to be on welfare, and I know what it's like to get off of it. So they understand me." The encouragement Paula delivers to her classes is a reflection of the enthusiasm she receives from America Works management. "Everyone here is wonderful, and I've received nothing but support from Peter and Lee," says Paula. "There is always another challenge, and I like that."

Practical knowledge

The rows of computers purr as participants in the Business Lab, a second stop for applicants to brush up on some skills required to fill the entry-level positions that are available. All candidates must come to the workshop from 9:00 a.m. to 4:00 p.m. daily, Monday through Friday.

Laverne is the director of training at America Works and runs the Business Lab, where the day is divided between classroom workshops and independent training. "We're filling a broad range of jobs, ranging from retail sales clerks to security guards to some clerical jobs," she says. "Candidates come here to practice their skills, and they must treat it as a job," says the spirited three-year America Works veteran. "They don't get a paycheck for coming here, and they work independently on improving their skills. They must sign in. And it's also a time for candidates to work with the job match representative and to be on call to go out on interviews."

Pansy, a thirty-five-year-old single mother of four, is about to become a grandmother for the second time. Until a year ago, she was an office manager at a real estate company; then her employer went out of business. Now hoping to reenter the workplace, Pansy sits at a computer honing her word processing skills. She is called out of the lab by Risa, a corporate representative, who tells her about an interview for a receptionist position at a lingerie company.

In a small office, Risa further explains that the prospective employer is a small, family-owned manufacturer. Risa and Pansy practice a mock interview. Following the ten-minute session, Risa reviews Pansy's performance—her eye contact, her voice, her grammar—and mentions the importance of asking questions about the company and the available position.

In this, as in all settings, America Works employees treat job candidates with the greatest amount of professionalism and courtesy. "Our candidates are valuable to us in many ways," says Risa, who has worked at American Works for more than ten years. "We expect them to look and act professionally at all times and to do a good job in representing us. It's essential that they are treated with both respect and compassion."

This attitude is integral to the company's success. Cove believes that the company's equal emphasis on sales, marketing, and on-site follow-up is what distinguishes it from other employee placement firms. "When you look at where the money is spent at most government-sponsored employment programs, you see it goes primarily to training and education, to supporting the candidates with counseling, teaching, and classroom training. We are not as training oriented," says Cove. "Rather, we believe in on-the-job support.

"Our candidates have dignity," he adds. "Many of them have

been in classrooms for way too long, and they've been failed by the education and training systems. Our belief is that people need jobs, not training."

Accordingly, America Works has installed a complete post-job support program. A major part of it involves bi-monthly visits by America Works corporate representatives during the four-month trial period that starts once candidates are placed.

"We're here to deal with the issues that may keep our people from doing a good job," says Phil Jones, who has been involved in both sales and client support. On any given day, Jones visits up to ten different locations to check on America Works employees. "I'm there to interact both with the supervisors and with our workers," he says. "If there are day-care problems, or employees are late, or there is a problem at home, we can interact. Any situations that require outside help, we're there to support them." Having been involved in America Works sales effort for fourteen years, Jones estimates he's helped place more than twelve thousand employees in jobs. And while the most plentiful jobs ten years ago were for clerical office help, Jones says today's employment situation has changed. "We work with security companies, food service, telephone telemarketing firms and social service agencies primarily," he says, noting that about half of today's candidates are men.

Though he's had other job offers over the years, Jones says that he continues to enjoy his job at America Works. "Peter and Lee are the best possible people to work for," he says. "I believe in what they do and I've been here fifteen years. It's like it's my company."

Selling the program

Russell worked for several years at one of New York City's top-name employment agencies before he started as a salesperson with America Works. After no less than five interviews with Bowes, Cove and other personnel, he was hired on as a full-time sales person more than ten years ago.

"A strong sales effort is essential to our success," says Bowes. "We don't do job development, a staple of employment programs. We, like any successful job placement agency, rely on cold calling and contacting every company we know to sell our service." Bowes further emphasizes the point that "selling means you don't give it away. Our attitude is not 'take our poor welfare recipients, please.' Rather, we sell something they need and are willing to pay for." Once a sales call is made, a company that is interested in the service places a job order listing the requirements and requesting an interview with candidates who qualify for a particular position.

Russell enjoys promoting the firm. It is also immediately obvious to everyone that he is a polished salesperson. Meeting with the recruitment office of a security guard firm, he efficiently and thoroughly reviews all the particulars: that there is a trial period; that the company pays America Works, which then pays the candidate's salary during this period; that a corporate representative who will visit regularly is available to help manage the new worker. In addition, he notes that a thorough job match program ensures that all candidates sent for interviews meet all company requirements. Then Russell discusses tax benefits and the fact that his company will handle all necessary paperwork and cut through any red tape.

The most interesting part of Russell's sales pitch, however, is what he doesn't say: the words "welfare" and "public assistance" never come out of his mouth. "No, it's certainly not part of the pitch, because it has very little relevance to the outcome," he explains after a meeting where he received two job orders. "We're selling a service here, and we stand behind it. We certainly don't deny the fact that our candidates are on welfare, but we are working with people who truly want to work. That makes all the difference."

Interestingly, Russell's own mother was on welfare for several years when he was a child. "Sure, I know what it's like," he says. "I know being on welfare doesn't have to have such a stigma and that most people on welfare don't want to be. Understanding this helps me to do my job."

America Works relies primarily on cold calls to companies throughout its base cities to sell its service, and part of its sales program includes a telemarketing effort. Bowes says that because America Works differs from other employment agencies, it's often a challenging sale. "The whole four-month trial period, plus working with welfare payments and eventually rolling salaries over to the company's own payroll, can be confusing. Employers are either very open to it and willing to give us a try, or they just don't want to deal with anything that is different."

New York-based Lowes Hotels has had more than a dozen America Works candidates over the past several years. They include Georgia, a Jamaica native and mother of two who had been on welfare for two-and-a-half years. After completing the America Works program in early 1999, she signed on with Loews Hotels to be a corporate office clerk and receptionist, earning $10 per hour. Georgia quickly moved to the mailroom and onto senior clerkship, doubling her salary within two years.

Bowes and Cove say the company is poised for growth in the years ahead. While Bowes oversees much of the day-to-day operations, Cove is involved with opening additional America Works offices. Since its founding, America Works has had varied success branching to cities beyond its New York home base. "When we go to another city, we are considered outsiders, and local governments are not used to working with new people from beyond their jurisdiction. Secondly," Cove says, "we are a for-profit company, and that doesn't always sit well with many people. They don't trust our motives. This is common when the private sector works with government."

Yet, America Works has surged ahead, having opened offices in Baltimore, Washington, D.C., Yonkers, New York and the Bronx since 1998. At the same time, Bowes and Cove have had to close offices in Hartford and Indianapolis. They cite reasons including a very high unemployment rate creating an inflated employee pool in Hartford, and an unsupportive political environment in Indianapolis, as the reasons for the closures.

Recognizing a new employee

In 2000, America Works launched a new venture placing ex-offenders in jobs in its new criminal justice program. "Lee and I noted that more than six thousand people were coming out of New York State penitentiaries each year, with about double that number coming out of city and county prisons. We knew the recidivism rate is about 50 percent within three years. This is costing the government huge amounts of money in terms of the cost of the crimes committed and the cost of having these people in jails," says Cove. The partners also noted that one of the unintended consequences of welfare reform, which primarily empowers women, was that men have been neglected. "The men have been going off to jail or have disappeared," says Cove. "We wanted to get to the men to help solidify more families."

Indeed, correction officials nationwide say the number of prisoners being released nationwide will continue to increase in the years ahead. This trend is due in part to tough sentencing guidelines launched in the 1980s and 1990s. Many of the prisoners who received prison sentences at this time are or will soon be released.

Cove and Bowes compare this newest effort to their pioneering work of getting welfare recipients into jobs. "Eighteen years ago there was nothing out there for welfare recipients; today, there is very little support for ex-convicts. Lee and I decided to invest in this program," says Cove. After meeting with New York's commissioner of probation and commissioner of parole, America Works launched its criminal justice program in New York in 2000.

In the past, employers would do anything to avoid hiring ex-convicts. This is no longer the case with today's labor-needy companies. Employers at construction firms and manufacturing facilities recognize that they are hiring workers who may have committed serious crimes and served long sentences. Yet, the employers also recognize that these same people may be ready to prove themselves and were taught valuable job skills while incarcerated.

In a small classroom at America Works' headquarters, Juan, dressed in a suit and tie, addresses the twelve men seated in front of him. "I served ten years upstate, for manslaughter," he says. "I got out when I was twenty-six. I remember thinking that I would never get a job, never contribute to society," he says with evangelical zeal. "But that was fourteen years ago. I got my degrees and pursued a career as a therapist. I've worked in the Department of Probation, and now I'm here, at this criminal justice program, to help all of you get a job," he says.

Juan asks each of the candidates how old they are, what their education has been, and what are their short- and long-term goals. Pablo, who served twenty years for murder, wants a job in construction. Earl, sixty, also served more than two decades for a murder conviction. He is a trained barber and tailor. Javier, twenty-eight, just served a five-year sentence for selling a controlled substance. He went to vocational school while serving, and is looking to work with an electrician.

"I learned the hard way how to respond to the inevitable question on all applications, and that every employer asks: have you ever been convicted of a crime," Juan tells the group. "I've had the door slammed on me. People would not hire me because of my criminal history. It's a big red flag. But," he continues, "there are employers out there who need good workers and are willing to give ex-convicts like you and me a chance. But we have to earn their trust." Juan tells the candidates that employers look for people who arrive on time for interviews, are clean and are dressed appropriately.

Juan recommends that the candidates approach potential employers just as they did the parole board. "You will, inevitably, be asked about your case. Take responsibility. Explain your circumstances, and then emphasize what you have done to rehabilitate yourself."

Using his own situation as an example, Juan says, "I was in prison for a manslaughter charge. I was young, foolish and under the influence of alcohol when I committed the crime. While incarcerated, I became very involved in education and self-help programs. I earned my high school degree and got involved in vocational training. I eventually became a tutor to other inmates."

One by one, each candidate presents his own story, as Juan encourages the participants to focus on the future, rather than the past.

Later, Juan admits that many of the participants come to the America Works program reluctantly. "They don't want to be here. But they are mandated by parole or probation. But we go around the room, sharing stories and goals, and the ice is broken. The defense mechanisms drop, and they become engaged."

Juan knows too well how important it is for ex-convicts to find a job. "It's the major stipulation," he says. "With a job and a stable home, most guys can stay out of prison. Otherwise, they may go back to selling drugs, or whatever, and the cycle begins again."

Since the division's inception, America Works has placed more than two thousand of these ex-convict candidates into positions, ranging from construction to food service, and the retention rates are even better than with the welfare recipients. "Employing ex-convicts benefits society as a whole," says Cove. "We find many employers appreciate workers who have overcome their faults. We're very excited about this program and its initial success. We look forward to expanding both in New York and in other markets as well."

People are the key

America Works' success is largely the result of a strong and caring staff. Bowes feels that the selection of a diversified and thoughtful group of employees is essential to the growth and development of the company. "We are proud of our staff; everyone enjoys working together, and in that sense it makes it very enjoyable," Bowes says. "I typically have a mixed staff, both racially and ethnically, and an age balance so that we don't have one predominant group. I need extremely intelligent employees. Past job experience, on the other hand, is not as critical. What's important to me is what I look for when I hire employees—strong self-awareness, and how attentive they are of their own selves. And I also pay strict attention to the analytical skills that help them understand other people. They are therefore bound by life awareness and come here in the morning happy to be here."

The obvious enthusiasm of the workers tends to be a motivating factor for both Bowes and Cove. Furthermore, Cove is inspired by the fact that an antiestablishment person like himself can prove there is something more to business than the conventional wisdom of corporate America. "I want to show that there is a different way of doing things," he says. "What I love about us being a private company is that our philosophy is not just a theory; it's real, it exists, and it's successful. We are demonstrating something here."

The company typifies this. In 1988, America Works placed 125 former welfare recipients in private positions. Today it is up to more than one thousand per year. Ninety percent of these workers remain at their jobs one year after they are hired, and 80 percent of the employees are with the same companies after two-and-a-half years.

Bowes and Cove credit a couple of key situations that have helped America Works prosper over the past decade. "The Family Support Act, which changed welfare as we know it, has been the most significant event impacting our business," says Cove.

Indeed, America Works has been cited as being a key reason why the legislation was signed into law. Throughout the late 1980s and into the 1990s, the firm was constantly touted by the Progressive Policy Institute and President Clinton's think tank. "The Democratic leaders pointed to us and said, 'see, welfare-to-work can work.' Look at America Works," says Cove. The idea that built their business was the reason for key—and ultimately successful—legislation to be signed.

"Secondly," says Cove, "the strong economy in the 1990s provided a fertile ground that has allowed us to prove our theory works." The partners also say that the ability to buy their partner out has been significant. "Abe was our partner and our bank. In this role he restricted our growth, and that was hard for us," says Cove. "Now we don't carry debt in the company and have bank financing to spawn future growth." The partners also credit their ability to exit a situation before it becomes too draining on the company. "We've had to leave several markets because the work or political environment wouldn't support us. It's been important to see the writing on the wall and to exit promptly," says Bowes.

In retrospect, Bowes says the company didn't need to hire many of the high-priced consultants it used over the past decade. "It's the assumption that someone else out there knows more than you do. But, in every instance, we had all the answers right here, with our own people." Bowes says business people should trust their own instincts and make rational decisions. "Find the right people and put them in the right places," she says.

As America Works seeks out future growth, it is inspired by the people it employs and helps. People like Dawn, who secured her first-ever job through America Works. In a letter she sent to America Works following her successful job search, she wrote, "Thanks to all of you, and especially Peter and Lee, for giving me the opportunity. My son and I both thank you from the bottom of our hearts." Bowes and Cove may not say it in so many words, but it is apparent that such reactions are the real motivation behind America Works.

"It's our life work," says Bowes of the career she and her husband have shared for more than twenty-five years. "It's more than a company or a business. We believe in the foundation that makes this work. We will continue to run America Works and continue to take on new challenges."

Chapter Two

Covering the Environment

Company Name: Interface Inc.
Primary Business: Manufacturer of carpet and fabrics for commercial and residential applications.
Type of Corporation: Public
Headquarters: Atlanta, Georgia
Number of Employees: 5,100
Founder and Chairman: Ray Anderson
CEO: Daniel Hendrix
Year Founded: 1973
Web sites: www.interfaceinc.com
www.interfacesustainability.com

Vision Statement

To be the first company that, by its deeds, shows the entire industrial world what sustainability is in all its dimensions: people, process, product, place and profits—by 2020—and in doing so, we will become restorative through the power of influence.

Mission

Interface will become the first name in commercial and institutional interiors worldwide through its commitment to people, process, product, place and profits. We will strive to create an organization wherein all people are accorded unconditional respect and dignity; one that allows each person to continuously learn and develop. We will focus on product (which includes service) through constant emphasis on process quality and engineering, which we will combine with careful attention to our customers' needs so as always to deliver superior value to our customers, thereby maximizing all stakeholders' satisfaction. We will honor the places where we do business by endeavoring to become the first name in industrial ecology, a corporation that cherishes nature and restores the environment. Interface will lead by example and validate by results, including profits, leaving the world a better place than when we began, and we will be restorative through the power of our influence in the world.

Jim Hartzfeld remembers the moment all too well. "It was August 31, 1994, at 10:15 in the morning," he says. As a vice president in the research and development division of Interface, the world's largest manufacturer of commercial carpet products, Hartzfeld had assembled a handful of employees from throughout the company to help figure out how to deal with nagging questions about the company's environmental policies.

"Green building," meaning building with minimal impact on the environment, was just developing. Interior designers and architects who often choose a new building's floor covering were, for the first time, asking about such things as recycled content and environmental policies. At the time, company salespeople didn't know how to respond, and inquiries were directed to the firm's research and development department. In order to come up with a suitable response to the growing number of questions,

Hartzfeld gathered seventeen colleagues from various Interface businesses for a two-day brainstorming session. He also invited the company's much-admired founder and chairman, Ray Anderson, to kick off the meeting with an inspirational welcome and an environmental mission.

Unbeknownst to the meeting's organizers and participants, Anderson had been "sweating it out," as he says, for the weeks leading up to the gathering, ever since he was first invited to talk about the company's environmental policies. He didn't have an environmental vision. Up until that time, the company was certainly compliant with all U.S. and international environmental laws. But Anderson also knew his multi-million-dollar business was based on taking huge quantities of petroleum from the earth and turning it into multi-colored carpet tiles. Along the way, the company also caused air pollution, and discarded carpeting piled up in landfills. Doing things differently had never been a concern for Interface. Like most U.S. corporations, it had focused solely on its purpose: to earn a positive return for shareholders while complying with the law.

It was while Anderson was trying to figure out what to say at the upcoming meeting that a colleague gave him a copy of *The Ecology of Commerce* by Paul Hawken. The book, a favorite among environmentally conscientious companies, details how businesses can radically reduce their negative impact on the environment and still remain profitable. Reading the book proved to be an epiphany. "It hit me right between the eyes. It was a spear in my chest," he told the gathered employees that August morning. Interface had soiled the earth, he said, and he charged his employees to convert the firm into a sustainable company and then to become restorative by putting back more than it takes. Hartzfeld remembers that there wasn't a dry eye in the room. "We realized we had it all wrong," he said. "It was time to fix our ways."

Anderson writes in his book, *Mid-Course Correction*, that, "for the first twenty-one years of Interface's existence, I never gave one thought to what we took from or did to the earth, except to be sure we obeyed all laws and regulations." All of that would soon change.

Hawken's book gave Anderson the motive for not only the speech to his colleagues, but a whole new course for his company to follow. "Ray came in and spoke for twenty minutes. He dropped the bomb and walked out. We were dumbfounded," remembers Hartzfeld. The goal? To make the Georgia-based company a totally sustainable enterprise.

Following his own course

For the first six decades of his life, Anderson had been living the American dream. As the son of a postmaster and teacher, he grew up in rural West Point, Georgia, and went on to play football at Georgia Tech in the 1950s. After graduating, Anderson worked his way up the corporate ladder with one of the nation's leading carpet makers, Callaway Mills.

Though successful, Anderson yearned to start his own business. "The man I worked for often spoke with such great reverence of his father, Fuller Callaway, who had founded the company, and of the creative act of starting a company," says Anderson from Interface's headquarters right outside of Atlanta. "I was persuaded subliminally that real success comes from entrepreneurship, from the person who starts a business, versus someone who takes over an existing one." After seventeen successful years at Callaway, and its successor, Milliken, Anderson left to launch Interface in 1973. "It was like I cut the corporate umbilical cord and was stepping off a cliff," he says.

Before founding Interface, Anderson discovered the concept of carpet tiles in Europe. Introduced first in Britain, carpet tiles offered an alternative to traditional broadloom by using squares of commercial carpeting that can be laid down and replaced inexpensively. The concept of carpet tiles became popular with the ever-growing needs of corporate America. Interface grew at a rapid clip throughout the 1980s, having survived start-up, and prospering beyond anyone's dreams during the decade. By the early 1990s Interface dominated the carpet tile marketplace with thirty manufacturing plants throughout the world, and it was closing in on the $1 billion per year market.

But it wasn't always smooth sailing for the publicly traded company. Three times in its first thirty years Interface has, as Anderson says, "hit the wall." First, in 1982, it stumbled when its primary market, new office construction, ground to a halt. The company then increased its customer base by expanding to office building renovations and healthcare facilities, as well as beyond the U.S. market. In addition, it added other products, including commercial textiles used to make modular office furniture, and high-end broadloom carpeting.

Business then prospered until, once again, Interface had an abrupt downturn during 1991-1993 due to similar economic trends. Corporate downsizing, a worldwide recession, and increased competition all contributed to an abrupt slowdown in orders. The most recent blow started in 1999 with the Y2K panic when companies began investing billions into computer upgrades, and continued on through the dot-com crash. This latter period, which has lasted well into the new millennium, was debilitating enough to unravel a less committed environmental mission. "Yet," Anderson says, "there was never a thought of turning back."

Success at a price

Carpet making is a toxic business. Its components, including nylon and adhesives, are created primarily from oil and chemicals. In 1994, Interface was consuming more than five hundred million pounds of raw material each year and emitting more than nine hundred tons of air pollutants, six hundred million gallons of wastewater and ten thousand tons of garbage. It is estimated that 3.5 billion to 4 billion pounds of carpet are discarded each year, becoming solid waste in landfills.

Paul Hawken's book predicts the demise of humanity if

multinational corporations, like Interface, continue to exploit the earth's resources. "I was part of the problem," says Anderson, now in demand as a speaker at business, government and environmental conferences. "My company has been a plunderer of the earth. Some day they will put people like me in jail."

After being given the mandate from their "born-again-green-industrialist" boss, the group assembled that August day hurriedly read Hawken's book and then led other Interface managers through twelve months of developing ideas to turn their polluting company onto the path of a sustainable one.

It was, indeed, a challenge, especially considering the need to shift the perspective of more than five thousand Interface employees. Fortunately, most of the employees had already participated in a company-sponsored motivational series that promotes team building. In addition, the company simultaneously launched its QUEST (Quality Using Employee Suggestions and Teamwork) program. The first goal of QUEST was to help work out problems on the factory floor, including waste reduction.

All of these efforts left the thousands of employees more receptive to Anderson's new goal of sustainability. In 1995, Anderson assembled a group of consultants to help steer the company down its new environmental course. The group included book author Hawken; David Brower, founder of the Sierra Club; Bill McDonough, an architect known for his green designs; construction consultant John Picard; Amory Lovins, a physicist and resource efficiency expert at the Rocky Mountain Institute in Colorado; Hunter Lovins, also with the Institute; and their associate Bill Browning. The group, considered by many to include some of the world's most progressive thinkers on sustainability, worked with Interface to create its goals. With them, Interface developed the "Seven Fronts to Sustainability." They are:

- Eliminate waste. This is the first and most important step towards sustainability;
- Generate no harmful emissions. Eliminate all toxic waste;

- Use renewable energy sources. Reducing the energy used thorough efficiencies while replacing non-renewable sources with sustainable ones;
- Closing the loop: Redesign the processes and products to create goods and byproducts that are recyclable in closed loops;
- Resource efficient transportation: Develop methods to reduce the transportation impacts of both products and people. This involves plant location, logistics, information technology, video conferencing, e-mail and telecommuting;
- Sensitivity hookup: Create a community within and around Interface that understands natural systems and Interface's impact on them;
- Redesign commerce: Redefine commerce to focus on the delivery of service and value instead of the delivery of material.

Anderson equates this road to sustainability to climbing a mountain higher than Mount Everest. These Seven Fronts represent the mountain's seven faces that must be scaled. Interface employees, called associates, faced a daunting task. It was up to them to turn the rhetoric of their evangelical, far-sighted founder into reality. Hundreds of employees developed thousands of solutions. In fact, there isn't a production plant or department in Interface's huge structure that can't boast a success story.

Small steps to big rewards

Interface continued to expand its QUEST program, with the notion that any "waste" represented a lack in its own resourcefulness. At Interface, "waste" represents anything that does not provide value to the customer. It is far broader than the conventional definition used throughout the industry.

From 1995 to 1996, sales at the company grew from $800 million to $1 billion. During this time, every division from the factory floor to the company's research and development department worked to develop new procedures and plans to reduce waste. Thanks to thousands of "small" steps and the ingenuity of a motivated workforce, the value of the waste decreased by almost 15 percent in its first year.

At Interface's La Grange, Georgia plant where it makes its trademark carpet tiles, Billy, a fourteen-year company veteran, takes visitors on a tour of the cavernous facility. Walking by the large machine that trims the carpet tiles, Billy explains that just a few years before, more than six tons of these trimmings went to the landfill every day. These included scraps of brand new carpet, trimmed and discarded. By reducing the unneeded comfort margins from several inches to less than a half-inch, however, the factory has greatly reduced its scrap. Any remaining frame scrap is now recycled. The backing is separated from the nylon fibers, and some of the components are used to make additional carpeting. This effort alone means more than 2.5 million pounds of carpet scraps are not being sent to the dump each year.

Similar efforts have reaped huge rewards at Interface divisions throughout the world. At its Guilford of Maine facility, where the company makes commercial panel fabric, new computer controls on the boilers in the plant have significantly reduced CO_2 emissions. The computer controls also improved the efficiency of the boilers by minimizing human error and by monitoring temperatures more precisely.

Producing more than fifteen million yards of fabric per year, Guilford partnered with a bottle recycling plant to obtain raw materials for recycled polyester fiber that has performance characteristics equal to the virgin fiber. Now, 85 percent of the company's panel fabric is made of recycled soda bottles.

On a number of occasions, small investments have reaped huge rewards. Recently, associates at Guilford of Maine experimented to see what would happen if they reduced the amount of water they used in the fabric dying process. First, they cut the water flow from sixty gallons per minute to forty gallons per minute, and found that they still achieved the needed results.

Then, they installed an $8.50 brass nozzle to regulate the flow pattern. With the nozzle, the outflow was again drastically reduced, resulting in a rate of twenty-one gallons per minute, a 65 percent overall reduction. The nozzle and the ingenuity of employees is responsible for an annual reduction of more than two million gallons of water and a projected savings of $10,000 per year.

At the Bentley Prince Street Facility, a Los Angeles-based Interface division that makes high-end broadloom carpet, the amount of scrap carpet wasn't even monitored until mid-1996. When employees there first measured the scrap, they discovered they were discarding two yards of carpet for every hundred yards they tufted. According to Interface, that equals operating the factory two days a year, three shifts a day, and throwing all that carpet away. Now, the scrap carpet has been reduced and much of it is recycled.

The effort transcends U.S. borders, with the company's many international divisions wholeheartedly participating as well. At Shelf Mills in Yorkshire, England, employees have reduced their landfill needs by 44 percent. In 1997, almost three hundred thousand cardboard cones, weighing twenty-one tons, went to the landfill. Now the company uses plastic reusable cones. Again, employees there note that though some of the improvements depend on sophisticated technological change, often it is the simple things that matter the most. By monitoring water intake, something the mill had never done before, Interface discovered that it had been, for years, leaking huge quantities into the river. The leak was fixed, saving the division thousands of gallons of water each month.

Other small steps have reaped large results. Interface redesigned the manufacturing process of its carpet tiles so that it needs 25 percent less nylon. The company installed a $1 million photovoltaic grid that provides a portion of the electrical power for Interface tufting machines in California. Almost one-third of its smokestacks have been removed. Since its 1995 launch,

QUEST efforts have saved volumes of water and material, resulting in more efficient operations and saving the company millions of dollars.

In its first seven years, associates succeeded in more than four hundred new projects aimed at improving eco-efficiency. Many of these have come from the factory floors, further expanding the firm's more democratic approach to problem solving, and empowering employees to both act and to succeed.

To celebrate Interface's success with QUEST, the company holds an annual "Worldwide QUEST Day." At every location around the world, teams of employees join together each December to share ideas through entertaining activities. At the LaGrange plant, for instance, workers constructed a huge maze made of the flattened boxes they normally send to recycling. At another plant, associates built holiday scenes and Christmas trees and ornaments made with recycled materials from their own plant. Employees from another plant built a huge mound of recyclable waste and held a contest asking colleagues to guess the weight. QUEST Day does a lot to help everyone at the company feel a part of the company's environmental focus.

A new dawn for design

Just a few miles away from Interface's LaGrange plant stands Pond Studios, the twelve thousand-square-foot-headquarters of David Oakey Designs, an independent firm that has been designing Interface products for more than twenty years. The two-story steel-and-concrete building features floor-to-ceiling windows that allow employees to see the rolling countryside and forests around them. It is here that David Oakey works with his team of designers to come up with the patterns that grace Interface products.

Oakey says Interface's pledge toward sustainability has proven to be a welcome challenge to him and his designers. "We have been more creative in the past several years than we ever have before," he says. "It's forced us to think and create outside the box. Before it was just subtle changes like tweaking colors. Now, the environmental focus forces us to be creative."

Undoubtedly, having such a focal point has created countless challenges for Oakey and his team. They must now take into account a huge number of factors when creating designs. They now design new products with their future in mind. Are they recyclable? How much energy will they take to make? How many natural resources will be used? Can they be made with recycled material?

In 1997, Oakey came across a book by Janine M. Benyus called *Biomimicry*. The book helped define Oakey's new ideas about design. "*Biomimicry* is about how we can learn from nature to solve the problems of the future," says Oakey. The book closely relates to Interface's sustainability goals. "The question we ask is, 'How would nature solve this problem?' When you ask that question, you move in totally new directions.

"*Biomimicry* uses lessons from nature to solve the problems of the future. It involves using the colors and concepts from nature," he says. With these in mind, Oakey and his team used nature as their guide and created a carpet tile line called Entropy. The subtly shaded carpet tiles are all unique—like stones and leaves—yet when laid down side by side, the pieces blend together, without strict patterning. Oakey says that Entropy mimics the randomness of a forest floor with different shades and patterns. Besides the natural looking appeal, the carpet tiles have other advantages. When an ordinary carpet is damaged, the whole installation may need to be replaced. Patches don't work because of dye lot differences. But with Entropy, because there are no matching restrictions, small sections can be easily replaced. Tiles can be installed more quickly, because they don't have to be set in a specific direction. "Installation is easier and there is far less waste," beams Oakey as he shows samples to a guest. Entropy has been a huge success since its introduction, and the concept is being developed into other styles.

Thirty minutes north of Interface's Atlanta headquarters is

the Interface Research Corporation, the brain center of future products for the company's manufacturing sites in six countries around the world. Anderson lured Dr. Michael Bertolucci away from an industrial fabrics company in 1996 to come and run the department. There, and at previous positions, Bertolucci admits that, in the area of environment, his job was to be sure the companies were in compliance with regulations and not as concerned with ecological footprints. The goal, he says, was to stretch the limits of what the company could produce while still complying with government restrictions.

At Interface, the purpose is far more ambitious. In the state-of-the-art biology and chemistry labs at the research site, purposefully located a respectful distance away from the day-to-day frenzy of any company production plants, technicians work to create what Bertolucci calls "the most technically innovative products that, simultaneously, will have the least environmental impact."

In an age when it is far less expensive to use virgin fibers than recycled ones to create its products, one of the division's main goals is to design carpet that, at the end of its life, can be separated, recycled and made into carpet again. The company has had some inspiring first-step successes. In 1996 Interface started using backing material containing 20 percent recycled content on certain flooring products. In 1999 it introduced Déjà Vu, its first carpet tile that used both recycled nylon and 100 percent recycled PVC backing. Numerous other products made with recycled materials have since hit the marketplace.

Bertolucci is well aware that his group is working in uncharted territory. "We work a lot with our biggest suppliers to come up with solutions," he says. In late 2001, the research division started broadcasting its efforts by publishing the company's global sustainability report on one of its web sites. It is here that they post sustainability updates, detail the Seven Fronts of Sustainability and provide global and local metrics for the company's overall efforts. It is also where the company confesses that it is still a polluter and has a long way to go. It is, says Bertolucci, "a way we can keep customers informed." More importantly, Interface's sustainability web site serves as a learning tool for other companies that, hopefully, want to pursue their own environmental vision or follow Interface's environmental progress.

"Nothing fails like success"

Interface's sustainability initiative was, by any measure, a breakthrough success in its inaugural four years. Environmental groups, socially responsible investors, even President Bill Clinton lauded the company as the great green hope for the environmental movement. After all, if a carpet mill could do it, couldn't every company? "At last, a billion-dollar, non-food manufacturing company was leading the way, proving industrial companies could change and showing that sustainability could be good business," Anderson said to a business group in 2000.

But there was a problem. As Interface became a symbol of sustainable enterprise, its sales were slowing and its stock was plummeting. After peaking in early 1998 with share prices of almost $23, shares plunged 87 percent during the next ten quarters. The bottom came in June 2000 when the stock hit an all-time low of $3. "Our credibility and the credibility of the sustainability movement have most certainly come into question because of the miserable share price performance. 'Is this what a company's commitment to sustainability does for its shareholders?' someone might ask. 'If it is, who needs it?'" Anderson said.

Anderson explains that there were many factors involved in the company's downward spiral. First, there were the extreme economic issues that impacted much of corporate America. Interface succeeds the most when corporate confidence is up. "When the economy erodes and confidence lags, carpet is the first thing not to be bought," says Anderson. As industry and governments worldwide spent more than $500 billion to upgrade computers due to Y2K concerns, budgets for other expenditures were non-existent. In fact, Y2K compliance depressed the entire commercial interiors market, though it was a boon to the high tech sector. As the tech industry prospered, price/earnings ratios fell 60 percent in the commercial interiors markets. Even with these external challenges, however, it was internal conflicts that caused the greatest amount of damage. "Interface shot itself in the foot," says Anderson, who noted that "it was a wise and experienced person who first voiced the observation that nothing fails like success."

In the midst of the company's strong performance in the mid-1990s, Interface was faced with an unprecedented challenge. Its major competitor, Shaw Industries, and its top fiber supplier, DuPont, each started acquiring the dealer-contractors who re-sold and installed the carpets for the end-users. Their goal was to gain control of the distribution system that had already been established in the industry. "Our overriding concern was to protect our route to market and maintain sufficient distribution in the marketplace," says Anderson. So, starting in 1998, Interface joined the fray, eventually spending more than $150 million buying up any contractor distributors it could get its hands on. Soon, the competition between Shaw, DuPont and Interface was intense. "We woke up one day to realize that DuPont was, all at once, our largest supplier (fiber and yarn), our largest competitor (distribution), and our largest customer (their acquired contractors were still buying and installing Interface products)."

Within two years, Interface had purchased twenty-nine contractors. Yet, it was too much too soon for the manufacturer. "We got way ahead of our ability, first with the acquisitions and then with the integration issues of trying to mold all these disparate businesses into one unit," says Anderson.

At the same time, the company was compelled to upgrade its own computer system in preparation for Y2K, which contributed enormously to the overreach that so severely stretched its resources.

With the shrinking cash flow and increasing conflict among

the company's top managers on how to integrate its newly acquired businesses, emotions ran high as Interface struggled to compete in this new industry distribution model. "Our operating management team just had to deal with too much," says Anderson. "In the clarity of hindsight, Interface suffered from insensitive and autocratic management of people, plain and simple. It grew out of overreach and resulted in frustration-laden 'my way or the highway' attitudes." Anderson observes, "It's still possible to make mistakes in the old fashioned way, just like the totally unsustainable company we once were."

The situation also tested Interface's commitment to sustainability and exposed some weaknesses in that commitment. Anderson realized that the critical missing factor in its sustainability mission was a corresponding genuine focus on its employees, what he now refers to as "social sustainability." It became particularly evident to Anderson during the highly stressful days when the company was trying to integrate sales, manufacturing and the new service component of the business. "We simply failed to properly value our employees and treat people fairly," he says.

It was then, in mid-1999, that Anderson, who had previously relinquished his CEO duties to focus on the company's sustainability vision, came back to oversee the day-to-day operations. Half of the top managers left the company, including the man Anderson had chosen to succeed him. The remaining top managers were rededicated to getting the company back on track.

Interface adopted a far more collaborative work style that encourages teamwork, empowers all personnel and recognizes employees' needs while respecting individual differences. Interface rebuilt its sales forces and put in new business systems. "Frustration has given way to renewed enthusiasm for the great company that has survived what I characterize as a largely self-inflicted ordeal. We now realize that social equity begins at home with our own people, and acknowledge that sustainability is not achievable without social equity," says Anderson.

In January 2000, 125 managers from throughout the world met in Atlanta. Anderson's objective was to reach consensus on a set of values that all company members could subscribe to. "I was personally overjoyed when, after three days of meetings, sustainability was considered the core value of the company," says Anderson. The group also concluded that "people overwhelmingly matter, and their diverse views must be respected; the environmental initiative is incredibly good business; and financial sustainability depends on getting both of the foregoing right."

It was at this time that Anderson was looking for a new CEO for the company. Over a one-year period he worked with executive placement firms and considered several candidates. In the end, he realized "the guy sitting down the hall," Daniel Hendrix, was better than the rest of them put together." Hendrix, the company's senior vice president of finance, was named CEO.

The early years of the twenty-first century continue to be challenging for Interface as the nation's economy has remained negatively impacted, first by the abrupt failures of the dot-com sector and then by the economic unrest following the terrorist attacks. Interface has been forced to close some factories and lay off three thousand of its 8,500-person workforce. Anderson says the moves were necessary to pare down its capacity to match demand. "It's always painful and we hope that those let go will land in a good place. But there are more than five thousand remaining employees today who, with their families, depend on Interface's survival." The resulting and far more agile company is set to blossom when the economy improves. In addition, it is expanding its focus to other less cyclical markets, such as hospitals, schools and libraries.

In the DNA

Through the economic downturn and an in-house crisis that foiled Interface for more than two years, the company's commitment to its fledgling environmental focus never waned. "Sustainability is in our DNA," says Anderson today. "It's the difference between a coat of paint brushed on an old warped fence, and the yeast in the bread. What we are doing is important to not only us, but our customers as well."

Indeed, Interface's sales staff acknowledges that its environmental prowess is often the tiebreaker when closing a deal. If price and quality are the same among competitors, Interface wins due to its environmental appeal. "The secret weapon is that our customers love us for what we're doing, and they're supporting us," says Anderson. The company encourages customers to come tour its facilities to see that its commitment is far deeper than the rhetoric found in the marketplace. And customers are reacting. In an early 2003 meeting among salespeople, every person mentioned landing a new customer because of Interface's environmental commitment.

Meanwhile, Anderson continues spreading Interface's sustainability message to the thousands of people who hear him speak every year. That alone, he says, has boosted the company's image. "No one would ever have heard of our company if it wasn't for our new drive, our new mission. It's the best advertising anyone can ask for," he says. In addition, the company hopes to pursue its leasing idea, called the Evergreen Service Agreement. In this program, Interface is responsible for maintaining, replacing, taking away and recycling carpet tiles as they wear out. The buyer actually "leases" the product, that is, buys its "service," and Interface is responsible for its manufacture, installation, maintenance, removal and replacement during the entire life cycle.

Interface Research Corporation's Hartzfeld, promoted to vice president of Sustainable Strategies, says leasing is more of an idea than a reality so far. He notes that the way taxes are structured on capital expenses (buying a carpet) versus operating costs (leasing a carpet) makes it less attractive for many potential buyers. Nonetheless, the option captures the imaginations of their customers and everyone wants to talk about it, he says. "It's always good to have the discussions. It leads to more fruitful relationships overall."

Interface is on course to become the prototypical company of what it calls the new industrial revolution by "doing very well by doing good." Along with its more recent emphasis on valuing its own people, Interface will also continue to invest in its sustainability practices. It is calling on its suppliers to develop products that are both made of recycled material and are recyclable. As such, Anderson is inviting Interface employees to help realize the vision to become the first sustainable industrial enterprise in the world. "You can't beat that for bringing people together," he says.

Chapter Three

One Step Ahead

Company name: Birkenstock Footprint Sandals, Inc.
Primary Business: Footwear distributor
Type of business: Employee-owned company
Headquarters: Novato, California
Number of employees: 250
Founder: Margot Fraser
President: Matt Endriss
Year Founded: 1967
Web site: www.birkenstock.com

Mission

Our purpose is to share our heartfelt belief that comfortable, healthy footwear contributes to happiness and well being.

Through our distribution of high quality footwear, we strive to create positive, harmonious relationships with employees, customers, vendors and the environment, emphasizing honesty and integrity in all we do.

Within our company, our goals are to provide an atmosphere that stimulates growth and creativity among employees and to reward and encourage contributions.

Back in 1999, a salesperson at Birkenstock's flagship San Francisco store approached management with a unique proposal. The employee, named Bodhi, asked if he could create and fill a new position called "environmental sustainability coordinator." Bodhi recognized that Birkenstock already was embracing a plethora of conscientious business practices, many championed by the U.S. company's German-based partner and manufacturer. As an operations manager, Bodhi focused on making his retail store more environmentally friendly and knew that every department at the company already had incorporated a number of environmentally conscientious programs. Yet, Bodhi felt that in this new position, he could consolidate these programs and improve upon their already stellar accomplishments.

Bodhi knew it was a lot to ask for. After all, the position would not directly contribute to the bottom line of a company that imports and distributes a popular line of sandals and shoes. But, as he says, everyone at Birkenstock wanted the position to exist. And his proposal drew a great deal of support.

Rather than being patronized or ignored—as he might have been in another multi-million-dollar enterprise—Bodhi was encouraged to expand upon his idea. He drafted a job description and a more complete proposal, which included a cost-benefit analysis of the new post. After several months, the position was approved. And that single job has since grown into two, with a colleague eventually joining Bodhi as Birkenstock's community relations manager.

Together, their department developed a waste analysis audit in order to improve its recycling efforts. It has also launched a composting system for the company's in-house cafe, and is responsible for a shift to geothermal and solar power to supplement its traditional fuel sources. In addition, it bolstered an existing community relations program. Bodhi himself has also initiated conversations with Birkenstock's German manufacturer, discussing how their shoes could be produced in a more environmentally friendly manner. Ideas that have been bantered about include developing and employing alternatives to the chemical compounds traditionally used in shoe manufacturing.

Lenore, a ten-year company veteran, coordinates the company's volunteer program. This provides paid release time to employees who volunteer their time to various non-profit organizations in the community; about a third of the two hundred fifty-plus on staff now participate. In addition, the company has initiated a matching gift program for employees who donate cash to qualifying non-profits, many of which have maintained long-time relationships with Birkenstock. Both Lenore and Bodhi agree that they have their "dream jobs," and that it took a progressive management to recognize the value of creating their positions and department.

People first

While such activity by employees and encouragement from management may be unusual at other firms, at Birkenstock it is mainstream. Since founder and former president Margo Fraser launched the company in 1967, Birkenstock has exemplified a business that views people—employees, dealers and customers—as its greatest asset. And despite its consistent growth, the firm continues to focus on its people. Employees are encouraged to expand beyond their day-to-day duties and contribute ideas concerning areas in which they have a particular interest. Sharing in the total efforts remains as important as sharing in the rewards.

"We recognize that people have a need to contribute, to feel enthusiastic about what they are doing, and we try to create an atmosphere where this happens," says Mary Jones, who, as a part-time bookkeeper, was the company's first employee. She retired in 2001 after being its sole vice president for more than three decades. During her tenure with the company, Jones was a counselor to hundreds of employees. "I was really there to help out, to motivate, and to encourage workers to strive for higher and greater opportunities," Jones says.

The people-oriented philosophy follows that of the company's driving force, Margot Fraser. Another example of this is Kerry, who first worked in accounts receivable.

"Kerry reported to me," Jones recalls, "and she once came to me and said, 'Mary, I really think your correspondences could use some help.' I had no idea she liked writing, but I said 'Sure, please take a look.' I saw she was a beautiful writer, and then she told me she always dreamed of being a writer. She started writing my letters, and Margot sent along her own letters to write. She was doing all of this in addition to her accounting job, but like a lot of people here, she reached the point when she had to move one way or another. She chose to become our full-time company writer. But it started with her pursuing her dream.'" After several years in that position Kerry decided to further utilize her keen organizational skills, and in the mid-1990s she moved on to the company's inventory department.

In fact, moving to various departments is the norm at Birkenstock, where it's not unusual for an employee to have worked in two or more. The opportunity has also kept the employee turnover rate significantly less than at other companies in its Marin, California, community.

Different from the start

The dreams of Margot Fraser, now in her mid-seventies, never included owning and operating a company that distributes more than two million pairs of sandals each year. It all started with a vacation trip to her homeland in 1966. "I was living in California, and my husband and I took our annual trip to Germany," says Fraser, who at the time suffered from chronic foot problems. "Every year while in Germany, I bought a new pair of shoes that were good for the feet, since they were then unavailable in the United States. At a health spa in Bavaria, I saw my first pair of Birkenstocks." She bought them, took them home, and was quickly hooked.

After three months of wearing the chunky sandals, Fraser noticed a dramatic change. "I looked down at my feet and said,

'My God, my toes have straightened out,'" she recalls with a laugh. "At that time some of my friends wanted to get pairs, so I wrote to the company and ordered several." But Fraser was a busy housewife, with no intentions of getting into the shoe business. "I was a former dress designer and much more interested in the arts than business," she says.

Even if she had been interested right from the start, Fraser still faced a formidable obstacle that might have scared her off. In those days, Birkenstock sandals were a brand-new product, even in Germany, where the Birkenstock family had been making custom shoes for more than two hundred years. It was not until Karl Birkenstock entered the business in 1954 that the idea of mass-producing anatomically correct shoes was conceived. In 1964, a year before Fraser's trip to Bavaria, Karl's dream finally took shape with the creation of a single-strap sandal designed for post-operative wear. This sandal was just beginning to gain a following in Germany when Fraser bought her first pair.

Fraser's involvement, from the beginning, was motivated by more than pure profit. She wanted to sell Birkenstock sandals simply because she hoped to provide comfortable, beneficial footwear to women who suffered through the day's fashionable but tight, high-heeled shoes. "I immediately thought of other women when I started wearing my own Birkenstocks," she says. "They had suffered long enough in pointy shoes!"

Despite Fraser's enthusiasm for sharing her discovery, her first foray into the shoe market was a failure. "I brought the shoes to two California shoe stores, one in Berkeley, and one in Santa Cruz, in 1966," she says. "Both owners looked at me and said, 'Women will never wear those things!' Interestingly," she adds, "both eventually signed on and are still strong dealers today."

After these initial visits to shoe stores, Fraser turned instead to friends who were connected to the then-burgeoning health-food industry. They advised her to show the Birkenstocks at an upcoming trade show in San Francisco. She took their advice and set up a minimal display. "There we were with only a table, a tablecloth, and a few sandals displayed on top," she remembers. "What happened was that women began trying one pair at a time, mostly for themselves." But something else happened, too: Slowly and surely, the company began developing a strong and growing following. Fraser now believes that this initial entry into the health-food market was critical to her eventual success.

"The health food store owners were a dedicated group of people," she says. "They also had a clientele that they communicated with easily, and they recommended products. This was a hugely effective entry into business. Remember, I was quite naive. If I had grown too fast, I wouldn't have known what to do."

If the shoe fits

In those initial years during the late 1960s and early 1970s, Birkenstock experienced limited sales. "I would buy a few dozen pairs at a time from Germany and sell them to my tiny network of health food stores," says Fraser. But it was during those early times that she also cultivated her refreshingly compassionate philosophy toward business and developed the people-oriented practices that would later serve her so well.

"I started selling Birkenstocks from the closet of my college dorm in 1972," says Melanie Grimes, one of Fraser's early vendors. "When I eventually opened a store of my own and ordered eighty-seven pairs of shoes, the shipment arrived with a letter from Margot saying, 'If the shoes are not for you and your customers, please send them back for a full refund.' That letter is still on the wall." Grimes now owns three Birkenstock-licensed stores in the Seattle area, and she likes to keep reminding Fraser of that long-ago promise. "I keep threatening to send back my entire shipment."

Grimes also remembers her initial business relationship with Fraser as being both supportive and nurturing. "When I was planning on opening my first store," she says, "I was choosing between two locations. One was in town on a busy street. The other was way out of town, in the back of a friend's health food store. When I asked for Margot's advice, she said, 'go where you are happy, because if you are happy, you will sell shoes.'"

Grimes decided to join her friend at the out-of-the-way health-food store, a decision she now considers vital to her eventual success. "I would have been overwhelmed at the Main Street location," she admits. "At the health-food store, I was small. Yet I grew at a rate I could handle."

Margot Fraser's business grew slowly, too, and she believes it helped her mature at a manageable rate. "I didn't know a thing about business," she says. "I didn't realize it took money to make money. I didn't understand financing, didn't make projections or sales reports. I was just trying to get people into Birkenstocks."

Previously, Fraser had worked as a dress designer for a Canadian manufacturer, and that, more than anything else, helped her form the pro-people views that would ultimately shape her firm. "It was there that I experienced many of the frustrating aspects of being an employee," she notes of her stint at the dress operation. "I was designing dresses, but I didn't know a thing about the rest of the company. I was in my own bubble."

Stll, it was Fraser who initially decided to sell exclusively to health food stores where, she now says, "people were tripping over vitamins while testing our shoes." It was also her choice to import, rather than manufacture, shoes that allowed the self-professed "housewife with sore feet" to launch a business that, in 2002, had an estimated $110 million in sales. And it was her sincere concern, both for the people who worked for her and those who bought her product, that created the growing legion of loyal dealers and customers springing up around the country.

In 1973, shoe-store owners approached Fraser asking to see, and carry, her line. In addition, a number of entrepreneurs opened "concept stores" shortly thereafter, presenting the sandals in a highlighted position as the primary product they offered.

But even after broadening her dealer network to include these mass-market options, Fraser never lost sight of the basic ideas and philosophies that had taken her so far. "We attracted a number of bright, motivated people who perhaps felt they didn't fit into the established corporate world and wanted to start their own business," she says. "This was a way to earn a living while also providing a beneficial service." She readily accepted these new dealers and enthusiastically invited them to grow along with her company.

In the mid-1990s, feeling pressure to grow more rapidly, the company expanded its distribution to more than six hundred department stores throughout the country. Birkenstock brought in an outside sales force, and soon enough, the sandals were showing up in many of the mid-price department stores. Before too long, the company's managers realized it was the wrong way to go.

"It was a huge mistake," Fraser says now. "Birkenstocks require a knowledgeable and interested sales effort in order to be successful, and we didn't get the support we needed at these more mainstream stores." After three years, the company closed the accounts, and let go of the outside sales staff. "We ended up taking back a lot of merchandise and took a hit in 2000 because of this. It was a big learning experience," she says.

Indeed, as Fraser watched many Bay Area firms—particularly dot-coms and high tech companies—explode during the 1990s, she said she often felt as if her company was "like a dinosaur." But after seeing many of these companies "grow so fast, and crash just as quickly," she is even more convinced that slow, sustainable growth is the best path for any company. "With growing slowly and staying within your means, you know that you will be around in the next decade, and the one after that, as well," she says.

For that reason, the company plans to continuing fostering its relationships with trusted customers. By the early 2000s, the distributorship base had blossomed to more than one hundred independently owned "concept stores" and three thousand dealers throughout the United States. In addition, some department stores, including Nordstrom's and Parisian stores in the southeast, do a good job selling Birkenstocks.

Correspondingly, her line grew from one style in one color to more than four hundred styles, colors and materials. And the product has grown dramatically from the original offering that still includes the quintessential two-strap, suede Arizona sandal. Today, there are snakeskin thongs in hot pink and bronze, strappy slip-ons and a sandal that features the artwork of Jerry Garcia. Children's sandals are available with multi-colored buckles and clogs are in green and yellow. Men's models include fancy lace-up office-style oxfords and hiking boots. And though some of the shoes cost a lot—up to $240—their longevity amazes many customers.

Over the years, Fraser and her team of designers have provided valuable input into the market here, resulting in a strong growth in product offerings geared toward the American shoe buyer. "We understand the U.S. market, and they have always listened to our ideas," says Fraser of her German colleagues.

Additionally, the Birkenstock shoe line has gained unprecedented acceptance from trend-setting celebrities; its passionate supporters include well-known names like Madonna, Gwyneth Paltrow, Uma Thurman and Leonardo DiCaprio. And while "Birkies" have often been associated with granola-eating, Volkswagen-driving ex-hippies, the shoe has developed a strong following among mainstream Americans—men, women and children alike.

In 2003, Birkenstock took a giant step toward becoming more "hipster than hippie" when it introduced its Architect collection. The $240-plus priced shoes were designed by San Francisco industrial designer and brand developer, Yves Behar. Behar had previously designed an art exhibit on athletic footwear design at the San Francisco Museum of Modern Art. Birkenstock approached him to bring out a totally updated collection. "The resulting shoes focus on the elements Birkenstock is known for: that the shoes are recyclable, are made of natural materials and are extremely comfortable," he says. The updated Birkenstocks feature the standard cork foot bed with more new materials for the sole. While the standard Birkenstock philosophy remains, the Architect collection, sold only at select high-end shoe stores, exceeds what has been considered green design. And though the prices are high, the company notes that many people wear their Birkenstocks for years at a time, an end result of the product's high quality.

The conscience remains

Today Birkenstock exhibits many traits that qualify it as one of America's most socially and environmentally responsible companies. For example, it continues to donate cash, as well as product, to a variety of causes, mostly concentrating on local environmental and human needs efforts near the firm's Marin County headquarters. Recipients include the Marin Conservation League, the Marin Agricultural Trust and Draw Bridge, a local art program for children living in homeless shelters. "Our goal is to develop long-term relationships with non-profits, so that they can count on our support year-after-year," says Lenore, the company's community relations manager. In addition, Birkenstock provides gift certificates for non-profits, in order to help them raise funds. It also donates shoes to the National Odd Shoe Exchange, a non-profit that provides single shoes to people with disabilities. In addition, about one-third of the employees participate in the company's three-year-old matching gift program. With this program, Birkenstock matches donations of up to $250 made by employees to either environmental or human services non-profits. "We draw the line at political or religious organizations, but otherwise, employees are free to support groups that they are most passionate about," says Lenore.

An atmosphere that encourages internal communication as well as employee appreciation is emphasized in the company's offices. This, staff members agree, has been evident and integral to the operation since its founding. "When I started out and hired

Mary Jones as the part-time bookkeeper," says Fraser, "I said to her, 'Look, this is what we want to achieve. Now, how do you think we can do it?' I learned much later that this is called participation management.'

Before her retirement in 2001, Jones was in charge of the company's human resources, a position she felt carried a special imperative. "Being Margot's first employee, I understood what her philosophy of caring for people is all about. I was the one to ensure that it all happens," she said. Now, after carefully laid plans, Jones and Fraser have both retired from day-to-day operations. Yet, their people-oriented approach to business remains a company mainstay.

This attitude has a central role in its employee handbook. Rather than the negative "don't do this, don't do that" tone common in such volumes, Birkenstock's handbook emphasizes the firm's belief in individual growth.

One passage reads:

> Birkenstock has a strong commitment to staff development. We want to help you succeed. We also encourage you to strive for your own individual growth and advancement in the company. You are encouraged to plan a growth program for yourself, take responsibility for it, and work closely with your manager and the personnel department on monitoring your growth. Decide what your own talents and abilities are and what can be accomplished as a result. Decide on the skill you must develop to achieve your goals.

As the company grew and departments became more segmented, Birkenstock created greater avenues for the managers to communicate with employees. Once a month, there are company-wide meetings where one department, such as advertising or shipping or the environment and community department, will update the others on current activities they are working on.

Ten years ago, a shipping department employee said, "It's the awareness of knowing exactly what is going on throughout the company that keeps us on our toes. There are twenty-two of us responsible for shipping more than a million pairs of shoes a year. It could be tiring and thankless work, but because we are included in so many parts of the business, we feel we're really an important part of the whole picture."

Birkenstock also believes in paying for productivity. For years, the company determined its compensation packages by informally canvassing neighboring businesses and others in the industry. As sales grew, however, Fraser and her managers realized there was a need to hire consultants to help them determine pay structures for the various levels. "We looked at our location, our industry, and the positions," says Jones. "If there was a job we felt was especially important to us, then we provided extra compensation." Among those positions considered essential is warehouse shipping clerk. Indeed, the company pays above the industry norm for all warehouse employees. "They are our vital link between the company and the customer," she noted.

Upper-management salaries are also essentially in line with comparable positions at other local industries. Despite the firm's increasing sales and solid growth, its directors and managers receive fair but not excessive salaries. "We always wanted to ensure managers were not making enormous amounts of money," says Jones. "We are competitive for the job everyone does; we are fair for the market rate."

Even more importantly, perhaps, upper management does not receive the type of perks—like car and clothing allowances—that tend to alienate rank-and-file employees. Instead, in 1978, the company launched a pension and profit-sharing program in which all employees benefited from the success of the company.

And in 1992, Fraser—until then, the sole owner of Birkenstock—decided to launch an Employee Stock Ownership Plan (ESOP). Under such programs, stock is allocated continually to employees while the companies that offer them derive various tax advantages. "We didn't have a lot of cash that first year, and realized we wouldn't be able to make a contribution to the pension plan. And though we didn't have cash, we did have stock, so that is how we started the program," says Fraser. Within a few years, employees owned 10 percent. By the end of 2002, Birkenstock became entirely owned by its employees when Fraser gave up the remaining shares of her stock to the company's two hundred fifty employees.

The ESOP was, for Fraser, the natural next step for Birkenstock. "It was not hard for me to give up sole ownership," she says. "I never considered this to be 'my' company. One can't really own anything. Rather, it's lent to you for a short while. You can't take it with you." Over nine years, Fraser sold off her stock in blocks, but only to her employees.

Over the years, many companies approached Fraser to see if she would consider selling her business, a plan that she easily rejected. "Selling the business would not have been a good thing," she says. "If we were acquired by a larger competitor, they would squash us. Everything we worked so hard for would disappear. My sole ownership, and then passing it on to the employees, has allowed us to stay true to our goals, without financial pressures of a parent company or stock holders pressuring us to forsake what is truly important to us."

Stepping back

In the mid-1990s, Margot Fraser, then in her late sixties, decided it was time to consider retirement, and to start planning for her successor. She looked no further than her own ranks, and in the fall of 2000, Matt Endriss, a twenty-two-year employee who first worked in the company's shipping department, became Birkenstock's new president.

"I've grown up at this company, " says the now forty-six-year-old Endriss. "My rise through the ranks is testimony to the opportunities available here at Birkenstock." When he started, there were only a dozen employees. After twelve years in the shipping department, Endriss became director of operations, and then the head of the company's sales department. Asked why he was invited to become president, Endriss says that Fraser knew him, trusted him, acknowledged the contributions he had made and recognized he had a strong relationship with their Germany partner.

In his new position, Endriss has no intention of reinventing the company. "My role is to create a business model for a shared vision, and to continue to grow the company in sustainable ways." In addition, he says, he plans to recognize the talent within the company's own ranks, and to further create an atmosphere where growth and opportunity are day-to-day mainstays.

Meanwhile, Fraser, who still comes to the office most days, has more time to devote to other interests. "I hope to have more contact with the outside world, and to encourage more women entrepreneurs to make their start," she says. She also plans to get back to her designing roots. "I look forward to designing new Birkenstock models," she says. "And I want to continue to be a motivating force to our employees, our dealers and our customers."

It is this type of attitude—when individual achievement and corporate generosity take center stage—that has been key to Birkenstock's growth, maturation and success. Since Margot Fraser initially discovered that first pair of sandals in Bavaria some four decades ago, she and her staff have developed a company that communicates with each other and those they do business with on a continuing basis. Because of that, as well as a revered product that virtually speaks for itself, Birkenstock has remained a step ahead of its competition.

Chapter Four

Ice Cream & Integrity

Company Name: Ben & Jerry's Homemade Inc.
Primary Business: Manufactures and sells ice cream and other frozen desserts
Type of Company: Subsidiary (of Unilever)
Headquarters: South Burlington, Vermont
Number of Employees: 800
Founders: Ben Cohen and Jerry Greenfield
CEO: Yves Couette
Year Founded: 1978
Web site: http://www.benjerry.com

Mission Statement

Ben & Jerry's is dedicated to the creation and demonstration of a new corporate concept of linked prosperity. Our mission consists of three interrelated parts. Underlying the mission is the determination to seek new and creative ways of addressing all three parts, while holding a deep respect for individuals inside and outside the company, and for the communities of which they are a part.

Product

To make, distribute and sell the finest quality all natural ice cream and related products in a wide variety of innovative flavors made from Vermont dairy products.

Economic

To operate the company on a sound financial basis of profitable growth, increasing value for our shareholders, and creating career opportunities and financial rewards for our employees.

Social

To operate the company in a way that actively recognizes the central role that business plays in the structure of society by initiating innovative ways to improve the quality of life of a broad community—local, national, and international.

Underlying the mission of Ben & Jerry's is the determination to seek new and creative ways of addressing all three parts, while holding a deep respect for individuals inside and outside the company, and for the communities of which they are a part.

When word first leaked out about Ben & Jerry's new flavor for 2002—a typically wild blend dubbed One Sweet Whirled that consisted of caramel and coffee ice creams, marshmallow and caramel swirls, and coffee-flavored fudge chips—it didn't appear in the dairy trade press or a national business periodical. The buzz was started instead by MTV, and few inside the entertainment or food industries were surprised. After all, the tempting concoction drew its name from a song called One Sweet World by the Dave Matthews Band, and it was being produced with the active support of the popular group. Ben & Jerry's, which in years past linked other cool new flavors with other hot rock artists, had once again combined the elements that made it hip, must-have, and talked about.

More significantly, perhaps, this entry from the unconventional ice cream company conveyed another unmistakable message aimed far beyond the MTV crowd. Like other personality-flavored offerings in its past, the newest from Ben & Jerry's was also central to an ambitious advocacy campaign—this one an effort to fight global warming. A portion of each sale was earmarked for an all-star alliance of major environmental groups called SaveOurEnvironment.org, and the packaging itself urged consumers to "reduce their CO_2 emissions with simple, easy actions and share those commitments in political messages to Congress."

And while this distinctive mix of showbiz, politics, philanthropy and fat-filled temptation has been dispensed many times over the years by Ben & Jerry's, it showed loudly and clearly that the company—despite being purchased less than two years earlier by the $46 billion global consumer-products giant Unilever—had not lost any of the quirky feistiness for which it became known under the ubiquitous duo that gave it their names and their personalities.

Ben Cohen and Jerry Greenfield may no longer be part of the company's day-to-day operations, One Sweet Whirled seemed to shout, but the business they started in an abandoned Vermont gas station a quarter-century earlier was still striving to be a leader in corporate social responsibility. Even as it tallied $237 million each year in sales. Even under the ownership of a global conglomerate that respects, but doesn't necessarily see eye-to-eye with, the founders.

"Unilever wants to let Ben & Jerry's be Ben & Jerry's," says Yves Couette, a French native installed as CEO by the new parent firm just twelve months before the Dave Matthews-global warming combination. "And I'm delighted to say that it is."

No one would have predicted such a thing in the early years, which are now the stuff of business legend. Ben and Jerry, then both twenty-eight, opened their first ice cream shop in 1978 with the hope of remaining in business for a year. They managed to not only survive but thrive by churning out superior ice cream, treating employees like family, purchasing as many ingredients as possible from suppliers that adhered to their principles and philosophies, and supporting worthy causes in both their adopted home state and around the world. They even institutionalized these latter efforts by eventually creating a non-profit foundation to give away 7.5 percent of their pre-tax profits.

The firm faced various challenges and problems over the years. And like any growing business, it had its ups and downs. But as an example of "caring capitalism," which is how the founding pair has long described their corporate vision, Ben & Jerry's remains hard to beat. The company produces an excellent product, helps its suppliers, aids its community, and supports its workers. It is precisely everything it purports to be.

The same could always be said about Jerry and Ben. The only thing that changed as the two old friends and their company grew, in fact, was their ability to help more of the causes they deemed worthy of support—and to keep enjoying themselves while doing it. Unlike many of their peers, the enthusiasm they showed for these dual principles only increased over time.

"In the past, people who consciously decided to go into business usually did so because they saw it as a way to make a lot of money. People who were motivated by social and humanitarian values tended not to go into business because they saw business as valueless," Cohen says over breakfast in a Waterbury, Vermont, inn several years before the Unilever purchase. "But some of those people with strong social and humanitarian values—like Jerry and me—got into business by accident and were not sorted through that grid. So, through some quirk of fate, instead of ending up in a non-profit social service agency, we happen to be trapped in a for-profit business."

Cohen laughs heartily at the image and reiterates two quotes that have guided his company since it survived that first year—an unexpected accomplishment commemorated then (and now on each anniversary) by a massive ice cream cone giveaway. One is from Jerry: "If it's not fun, why do it?" The other from Ben: "Business has a responsibility to give back to the community." And even when it was hard to do, Cohen recalls, the company adhered diligently to both.

"I think it's always difficult to do anything right," he muses. "It's like that song by Jethro Tull, 'Nothing is Easy.' If what you are trying to do is produce the highest-quality ice cream, that's difficult. If you're trying to make a lot of money, that's difficult. And if you're trying to run your business in a way that benefits the community, that's difficult, too. But I don't think any of those things are difficult to the point of not being possible," he adds. "I think it's really just a matter of priorities."

At home in Vermont

The town of Waterbury is just a blip on Vermont's Interstate 89, nestled in a scenic valley about halfway between the state's capital and its largest city. Despite this prime location, Waterbury had been essentially unremarkable for most of its history. It is home to a few cozy shops and restaurants, a couple of quaint country inns, the Vermont state police, and some spectacular views. But it wasn't until the arrival of Ben and Jerry—and their decision to locate an ice cream plant in this community of about five thousand—that Waterbury really showed up on the map.

The forty-three thousand-square-foot facility the pair built began operation in 1985, and faithful ice cream lovers from around the world have been flocking to it ever since. Company officials were astonished when forty-one thousand came through its doors during the first six months, but by the time an entire episode of the hit TV sit-com "Everybody Loves Raymond" was built around a visit there in 1999, they had come to expect such pilgrimages. Some two hundred fifty thousand now take the plant tour each year, and the more than 3.4 million who have trekked through its corridors since it opened make Ben & Jerry's the number-one tourist attraction in this very tourist-oriented state.

But visits were not the only thing to skyrocket once the plant opened. An employee named Mary, who was hired to drive a Ben & Jerry's truck in 1982 and later asked to organize its tour program, recalled working with only forty-two others when she moved inside from the road. Sales were just $9 million at the time, but the company was initiating an ambitious nationwide expansion thanks to funds raised through a special stock offering open only to Vermont residents and a second traditional one for investors across the country. These would help boost the employee ranks and corporate revenues more than tenfold in just five years.

The company strove to make the various internal adjustments necessary for this rapid growth, however, without altering any of the counter-cultural business practices on which it was founded. Even more ice cream and money was given away, traditional advertising was still avoided, and the unique management approach remained in force. The key was the purposeful direction of Cohen and Greenfield, who never deviated from the unorthodox path they chose long before. But problems did arise.

"For a while, we were growing at about 100 percent a year," says Cohen. "Our outside sales were expanding faster than our internal organization and our infrastructure. We knew we were growing too fast. So we made a very conscious decision to slow our outward growth and devote a large amount of energy and resources to improving the quality of our organization—the way we work together as a team and the way we develop each of our employees."

Because of the company's structure, the partners could immediately and dramatically change the way they did business. Movement into new markets was immediately slowed; expansion of franchised "scoop shops" was instantly curtailed. This allowed the company to breathe and get back on track. Growth was then resumed in an organized fashion that evolved to meet the times, whether it was the 1990s or the new century that brought new ownership.

But none of this is really surprising when one considers the history of the company and the background of its founders, two boyhood pals from Merrick, New York, who first really bonded as outsiders (and lovers of food) in the seventh grade. Neither could find their niche as young adults, either—Greenfield tried his hand as a lab technician while hoping to get into medical school; Cohen studied pottery, drove a taxi, and taught crafts—and their drift to Vermont was as aimless as their career paths.

But then serendipity: The two discovered a correspondence course on making ice cream that was offered by Penn State and only cost five dollars. They took it, Greenfield and Cohen say, because they could afford it and they liked ice cream. And after achieving a perfect score on the open-book final, the duo took a $12,000 investment ($4,000 of which was borrowed) and opened their first scoop shop in the college town of Burlington.

Financial success didn't come overnight—it actually took about five years before their young company turned a profit—but notoriety was theirs from the start. It came in part from their richly flavored homemade concoctions with unusual names, like Dastardly Mash and New York Super Fudge Chunk. But it also came in part from the two owners. They quickly endeared themselves to Vermonters by working hard, enthusiastically becoming part of their community, and unabashedly plastering their cheery images on the lids of new pint containers in which they began distributing ice cream throughout the winter in order to keep their dream alive. Their penchant for social activism, of course, didn't hurt either.

The seeds of giving

The summer of 1991 was a big one for Ben and Jerry. It was the season they launched Chocolate Chip Cookie Dough, still one of their most popular flavors. It was the time they started paying dairy farmers a premium for supplying milk that was free of Bovine Growth Hormone, a controversial additive that they had fervently come out against two years earlier. And it was when they first sponsored free "One World, One Heart" festivals—huge outdoor Sixties-ish extravaganzas that featured performances by musicians like Carlos Santana along with activities like Dye Your Own Tie Dye T-shirt. Those first festivals, held in Chicago, San Francisco, and Stowe, Vermont, also included presentations by a group called 20/20 Vision, which advocated military spending cuts to meet environmental and humanitarian needs. Free ice cream cones were given away to anyone willing to write a postcard or make a video on this theme and then send it to their representative in Washington.

By all measures, the festivals were a big success. As many as one hundred thousand attended in each location, tie-dying T-shirts, listening to music, and passionately producing postcards and video messages. The concept proved so popular it was continued on an annual basis, although ultimately only in the company's home state of Vermont as an adjunct to its annual shareholder meetings. But it showed Cohen and Greenfield the power that their company could yield as it grew.

"One of the nicer things about becoming bigger is that you can throw bigger parties," Jerry and Ben said in a flier announcing each of those initial events. "This festival is a time to play and celebrate together," it continued. "It's also an opportunity to take the first step in a sustained effort at working together for a more just world."

This message and the medium that carried it, though, were but two manifestations of the concern for their environment and fellow citizens that Greenfield and Cohen had been espousing nearly from the beginning.

"When we first started, our only goal was to have our homemade ice cream parlor on the corner. We didn't plan on being anything larger than that," Cohen says. "And while we had strong feelings about wanting to be a business that benefited the community, we didn't know what that meant at the time." As the company passed its first anniversary without going bankrupt, its founders expanded their commitment to the constituents who helped it survive. They kicked off their annual cone giveaway and instituted a free summer movie program and a recurring autumn festival, all natural ways to thank the community that supported them. They also began donating a lot of ice cream to local organizations. But it wasn't really difficult yet for them to juggle business and social concerns, because the company wasn't making a profit.

That all changed in 1981, when the balance sheets started to sprout black ink and the company authorized its first franchise. Two years later, it began distributing ice cream outside Vermont for the first time and the founders brought in local nightclub owner Fred "Chico" Lager to serve as president and help them expand still further. The company kept giving away ice cream and money to local charities, too, and everything looked terrific. At least for a while.

"Originally, Jerry and I were ice cream men working in this ice cream shop," Cohen recalls. "But then the business started to become more of a business, and we had a bunch of employees and were spending our time on the phone and writing letters and memos and hiring and firing. We turned to each other and realized we were no longer ice cream men; we were businessmen. And our immediate reaction was to sell the business, because we didn't want to be businessmen. But then I ran into this old restaurateur down in Brattleboro, and he convinced me to keep the business. He said if there was something I didn't like, I should just change it. That really hadn't occurred to me before."

Rather than sell, the pair decided to expand so they could make even more ice cream and help even more organizations. Not surprisingly, they also decided to fund this growth in an unconventional way: by offering residents of their adopted state a chance to buy a piece of the company. In 1984 they sponsored the first-ever Vermont in-state public stock offering with a low minimum buy of $126, which allowed everyone in who wanted a chance to participate. The sale eventually raised $750,000—

enough to finance construction of the Waterbury plant. A traditional nationwide public offering in 1985 permitted the expansion to continue, and an evolving passion for social issues also advanced as the company's financial resources grew.

A foundation for success

To keep the commitment viable—and to appease the legions of new stockholders who sometimes wanted Ben & Jerry's run more like the public company it had become—the partners created the non-profit Ben & Jerry's Foundation in 1985. Initially established through their donation of company stock, it was designed to "support projects which are models for social change; projects infused with a spirit of generosity and hopefulness; projects which enhance people's quality of life; and projects which exhibit creative problem solving."

Some of the initial beneficiaries were the Devastators, an all-children's Afro-Latin percussion band that worked to combat drug abuse, AIDS and homelessness; the Heifer Project, which provided agricultural animals to impoverished communities; and the Worker Owned Network of Athens, Georgia. Each year since its beginning the company kept the foundation going by giving it 7.5 percent of Ben & Jerry's pre-tax profits. The foundation in turn kept uncovering new causes to support by actively soliciting grant proposals that relate to children and families, disadvantaged groups, and the environment. A nine-member employee board was formed to make decisions on recipients.

But that is only a small part of the company's official philanthropic outreach. Community Action Teams—comprised of employees at each of the five Vermont sites it now runs—offer additional grants to non-profits in the state. The program was funded with half of all receipts from adult visitors who take the plant tour, and beneficiaries have ranged from the Association of Vermont Recyclers to a group of woodworkers who produce toys for underprivileged local youngsters.

Thousands of gallons of factory seconds are also removed

regularly from the plant and given to community organizations around the state, donated to food banks, or sold by special arrangement in Vermont stores—with a portion of that income donated as well to local organizations such as libraries, recreation centers, and fire and rescue squads. "Every day I come to work I feel I'm making the world a better place," says a plant manager named Don. His sentiments are commonly echoed at every level in the company.

Despite such good feelings and the activities on which they are based, Jerry, Ben and some others felt they were not doing enough. So, in 1988, they wrote a Statement of Mission that officially dedicated the firm "to the creation and demonstration of a new corporate concept of linked prosperity." It consisted of three interrelated parts: a product mission ("to make, distribute and sell the finest-quality all-natural ice cream..."), a social mission ("to operate the company in a way that actively recognizes the central role that business plays in the structure of society by initiating innovative ways to improve the quality of life..."), and an economic mission ("to operate the company on a sound financial basis...").

But this, it seems, still didn't suffice, for Ben & Jerry's was by then being flooded with unsolicited requests for assistance that it simply could not fill. "All of them were worthy causes," Cohen recalls, "and we realized we were never going to solve all the problems that we were looking to solve. Our contributions were just a drop in the bucket."

The company's response was to begin using its muscle, through the ice cream itself, to spread messages as well as raise money. Two of the first of these efforts came in 1990, when it promoted Farm Aid benefit concerts on ice cream containers and sponsored a large anti-nuclear billboard at a prominent Boston intersection. The concept evolved still further when it created a chocolate-covered ice cream bar on a stick called the Peace Pop. Additional efforts were aimed at alerting consumers to the disappearance of family farms and the destruction of rain forests. They continue today with the new Dave Matthews Band/One Sweet Whirled flavor, along with scholarships for historically black colleges and universities and donations to groups the children's playground-building organization called KaBoom!

Choosing suppliers with care

Few people outside of Maine have ever been aware that the state's Passamaquoddy Indians harvest and process wild blueberries. When Ben & Jerry's found out, they bought $300,000 worth to use in a Wild Maine Blueberry ice cream that it produced one summer. Simultaneously, the company was buying nuts from the Amazon rain forest, brownies prepared by homeless employees of a New York bakery, peaches grown by African-American farmers in Georgia, and dairy products from the five hundred-member St. Albans Cooperative in Vermont. Developing such relationships with suppliers that address otherwise unmet social needs has become another important outgrowth of Ben & Jerry's social mission and another key to meeting its multi-part mission.

"We do this on every level," Cohen says, "because we made it an integral part of our bottom line. We tried to figure out why business tends to be valueless and uncaring and, in the worst situations, actually harmful to the community and exploitative to its workers and its environment. And we found that this is because the success of its business is measured solely by the traditional bottom line—that is, by how much money is left at the end of the year."

So Jerry and Ben decided to change the way their company measured success. They developed an alternative that assesses the year by how much money is left over, as well as by how much the company helps its community. It didn't work immediately; some managers felt the two goals were mutually exclusive. But the founders convinced them to add a new variable to their purchasing decisions and taught them to pick vendors according to three factors (social benefit, price, and quality) rather than the usual two (price and quality).

And, once they began, the task became easier. Along with food products, Ben & Jerry's has been applying this philosophy to the millions of dollars it regularly spends on office and building supplies. It switched to an insurance company and a credit-card issuer that place their premiums and profits in compatible investments. And it initiated proactive programs like PartnerShops, where nonprofits around the country can offer employment and job training in subsidized Ben & Jerry's ice cream stores while using the proceeds to expand their efforts. The first of these was opened in 1994 in New York's Times Square by the Common Ground Jobs Training Corporation. It has since been joined by others in San Francisco, New York's Upper East Side, Chicago and Minneapolis. Their effectiveness is underscored by the fact that Common Ground opened two additional PartnerShops during the summer of 2000.

"Our goal is to integrate a concern for the community in all our day-to-day business decisions," Cohen notes. "Each year we find more and more ways."

This process is also evident in the company's resource-management decisions. Its environmental programs manager has led efforts to raise awareness of recycling options and find markets for recyclable materials. Its art department works with suppliers that use basics like recycled paper and soy-based inks. Solid waste, such as cardboard and plastic pails, are reused whenever possible. And the company has even developed a Solar Aquatics Greenhouse at its plant that successfully purifies the waste from dairy production by means of a natural ecosystem of flowers, fish and compost.

As programs like this came to light, the company's good name got even better and thousands of unsolicited job applications began pouring into the firm's headquarters. But it also caused something of a backlash. Some major national publications like *Rolling Stone*—which reached the youthful ice cream-loving audience then like MTV does today—ran skeptical articles asking whether Ben & Jerry's was really too good to be true.

They questioned whether the founders were truly as committed to social change as they were to increasing their own wealth. They noted the small number of minority employees at the Vermont facilities. They even pointed out the potential health consequences from eating too much high-fat super-premium ice cream.

Wearying of the criticism as well as the day-to-day grind, Jerry and Ben decided to step away from direct management. Jointly retaining about 15 percent of the company's stock, but reserving control of nearly 45 percent of its voting power and keeping their top positions on the board of directors, they announced in 1994 that they were going outside to hire a new chief executive officer. And they were going to do it, they said, in typical Ben & Jerry's style.

Movin' on up

Despite occasional forays into faddish big-time corporate programs like Total Quality Management, Ben & Jerry's has always been run a bit differently than most other businesses. It has accounting and shipping and H.R. departments like the others, of course. But the suite of rooms where flavors are created was long ago designated as the Alchemy Lab. Full-color life-sized cutouts of James Dean, John Wayne and other movie stars, each wearing the pastel hair covering required in all food-preparation areas, are known to pop up in offices throughout the organization. Huge white trash cans are everywhere, conspicuously emblazoned with bold black markings that make them look like dairy cows. Striking personalized decorations adorn practically every work space. A group called the Joy Gang regularly sponsors a variety of unusual company-wide events, like miniature car derbies and Elvis look-alike contests. Even the stab at Total Quality Management characteristically included a call for employees to "keep that euphoric feeling" by doing the "ten steps of the Improvement Boogie."

And then there was the "Yo, I want to be your CEO" essay contest, as unorthodox a competition as was ever held to find a new chief executive. The competition attracted enormous publicity and 22,000 applicants, but none in the vast pile of entries suited the board so it looked around on its own and in 1995 hired McKinsey Company consultant Robert Holland Jr.—even though he had never worked in food production and had little prior exposure to the company's rather unique philosophies.

Few were surprised, therefore, when Holland's arrival resulted in several major changes. For one, the company's highly touted "compressed salary ratio"—a key aspect of its original "linked prosperity" ideal which had prevented the highest paid employee from ever earning more than five, and later seven times the lowest full-time wage—was officially abandoned in order to attract higher-quality job candidates. For another, the crowded administrative headquarters, long housed in a pair of funky adjacent buildings near the Waterbury plant, was deemed no longer adequate and traded for a 97,780-square-foot former Digital Equipment Corporation assembly plant in South Burlington. This sprawling one-story building, one of the largest in Vermont, proved so big it was also able to accommodate the company's main warehouse functions as well as the offices of Burton Snowboards, a computer training firm, and a local Internet service provider.

Holland also initiated plans to extend Ben & Jerry's further overseas. The company had held a lucrative licensing deal in Israel since 1988 and ran an ultimately failed joint venture in Russia in 1992, but it really moved full-speed on global expansion in the mid-1990s. First came distribution in the United Kingdom, then a debut in France; then introductions in the Benelux region of Belgium, Luxembourg and the Netherlands; then an entry into Japan. Each new market was approached in much the same way as the U.S. had always been handled, too, allowing the distinctive Ben & Jerry's name and image to transfer intact as much as possible. A contest in Britain to create a new flavor, for instance, drew such entries as Grape Expectations and The Rolling Scones. The winner, Cool Britannia, was eventually served in America as well.

Despite the overseas movement—which has proven positive in the long run—overall performance stagnated. Holland's traditional management style didn't go over very well with the nonconformist Vermonters, either, and he left under some pressure after barely two years. Widespread expectations among employees and stockholders was for an immediate reversal in fortune, and spirits soared in anticipation of a new chief executive. But Holland's replacement did not initially do much to sooth those who had been skeptical.

Perry Odak, formerly CEO of the company that produced Winchester rifles, took the reins in 1997 to more than a little surprise and concern. He soon turned many of his critics into supporters, though, by displaying an incisive understanding of the company, its industry, and the relationship between the two. Not long after settling in, for example, Odak dropped a few outdated products like the Peace Pop and added some well-considered new ones that both addressed the firm's multiple missions and captured consumers' fancy. (One, called Phish Food—after a Vermont band named Phish with a strong national following and its own philanthropic foundation—remains one of the company's top-selling flavors.) Additionally, Odak ordered environmental improvements, like the unbleached paperboard containers now used for all the company's pint packaging, and marketing updates, like moving the co-founders' iconic portraits from the packages' lids to their sides. Sales ultimately climbed impressively, net income jumped 60 percent, and even the long-languishing stock began to rise.

Stakeholders were not the only ones paying attention, and Ben & Jerry's suddenly became a hot takeover target. Tension in the still-new South Burlington headquarters rose as all sorts of rumors circulated, and at one point several simultaneous bids were made by interested suitors. The leading offer was for $326 million, a hefty premium for stockholders that could not be ignored. Despite their professed reluctance the board of directors accepted it in April 2000 and Unilever, the 279,000-employee multinational in control of omnipresent brands like Hellmann's mayonnaise, Snuggle fabric softener, and Breyer's ice cream—which already made it the world's largest purveyor of frozen desserts—became Ben & Jerry's new owner.

The future is now

Unilever operates under two virtually equal parent companies in England and the Netherlands, and shortly after the sale was completed it dispatched one of its chairmen to South Burlington to address the shell-shocked troops. Basically, the Vermonters were assured, their company was not bought to be changed. Unilever recognized the merit—and the potential—in Ben & Jerry's. Give it a chance, employees were urged. You'll still be able to feel good about the work you do.

In its Anglo-Dutch bases, Unilever had fashioned itself along the "enterprise culture" lines suggested by progressive European management theorists like Charles Handy. It expresses a desire to promote employee empowerment, and follow a "multi-local" approach at its subsidiaries that "works only if we are truly part of the local culture." It prepares periodic Environment Performance Summary Reports and conducts annual Social Reviews, ultimately posting both on its web site. "In Unilever our aim is that corporate social responsibility should be managed as professionally as any other business discipline," a recent review began. "We recognize the need to be more explicit, to articulate our approach and to demonstrate our commitments in practice."

As if to underscore that obligation, Unilever pledged to institutionalize its support of Ben & Jerry's philanthropic efforts. Their deal included an initial $5 million gift to the Ben & Jerry's Foundation, and guaranteed annual contributions for the next ten years of at least $1.1 million (a boost from the existing 7.5 percent benchmark). It also provided Cohen with $5 million to start a new social venture fund that he could run however he saw fit. And it worked to attract proven socially minded executives like

Walt Freese, who developed a solid reputation after eight years at Celestial Seasonings—as well as during stints at Nestle and Casual Corner—before becoming Chief Marketing Officer in Vermont in 2001. "To me, in terms of a company that's been in the forefront of the social mission in business, Ben & Jerry's is it," Freese says. And when the head of Unilever's worldwide ice cream division came out and said that "our job was to keep them on the outer edge of their comfort zone," he continues, "we knew they were committed to not just honoring our heritage but to building upon it."

The co-founders were among those who remained openly skeptical, remembering how consumer-products giant Quaker Oats completely botched its acquisition of Snapple fruit juice just a few years earlier. Their apprehension was aired most publicly about six months after the deal was sealed, when Perry Odak bowed out of the CEO chair and an existing board member that Jerry and Ben supported to replace him was rejected in favor of a candidate from the corporate office. The two even released a press release decrying the choice, which was twenty-four-year Unilever veteran Yves Couette. But even many long-time employees were now growing anxious to see how Unilever would run the company under Couette, who had been managing Unilever's Mexican ice cream business for four years. "It's kind of nice to have someone at the top for the first time who has a background in ice cream," one commented privately.

Almost exactly a year after arriving, Couette and more than a few around him expressed satisfaction with their direction. "I knew it was difficult for the founders—especially for Ben—because it's hard when your baby has grown and you have to let it go," he says. But the company's subsequent efforts, as evidenced by the foundation funding and new products like One Sweet Whirled, prove the commitment is genuine. Still, the new chief executive, who admits his prior knowledge of the company was as sketchy as most from outside the U.S., also contends there is work yet to be done. "My objective is to make it a full success," he says. "They already had a great product, and the social mission has built tremendous equity. These won't be touched. But I want to focus on the financial aspect. I want to prove you can do this and make it work financially."

Cohen, who underwent quadruple-bypass heart surgery about a month after Couette took over, has certainly not bypassed the activism that shaped his life and that of his former company. Following his recovery he began speaking out again at gatherings of socially responsible businesses, and steering the venture fund financed by Unilever as well as another he created "to get equity into the hands of people who normally don't have it." And working from his home and an office provided for him in the Ben & Jerry's headquarters, he dove full-speed into Priorities Inc.—a far-reaching non-profit that has spawned projects like TrueMajority, its grassroots education and advocacy arm for facilitating communication on critical issues between members and their Congressional representatives in Washington. He remains as dedicated as ever to the principles under which his ice cream company was founded, but chooses not to discuss specifics there any longer except to reiterate his long-held opposition to the sale itself.

A quarter-century after unwittingly creating the standard, though, Cohen remains optimistic that socially responsible businesses run properly continue to offer a viable alternative for a world outraged by the excesses of Enron and its progeny—and he's pleased that younger people (like those who watch MTV) keep gravitating toward them. He's also still happy with his public position as an iconoclastic social activist trapped in a for-profit frozen-dessert world.

"I think I'll always be an ice cream man," he says after the briefest pause, when asked if he misses the only working life he's ever known. "You can take the fat out of the arteries, but you can't take the ice cream out of the man."

Chapter Five

Banking on the Community

Company Name: Shorebank Corporation
Primary Business: Financial services for individuals and businesses
Type of Company: Bank holding company
Headquarters: Chicago, Illinois
Number of Employees: 525
Founders: Ronald Grzywinski, Mary Houghton, Milton Davis, James Fletcher
Vice Chairman: Bob Nash
Year Founded: 1973
Web site: http://www.sbk.com/

Mission Statement:

Shorebank is a development bank holding company in the business of increasing opportunities in under-invested communities.

From Chicago's Stony Island Avenue, at a point about nine miles south of the city's fabled Loop, you can see both the promise and the peril of modern-day urban America. On one side of the wide asphalt strip is South Shore, a neighborhood that in the past several decades has seen the consistent rise of rehabilitated apartments, neat single-family homes, clean streets, and hope. On the other is Woodlawn, a section largely marked during that same period by burned-out buildings, debris-strewn lots, graffiti-scarred walls, and despair. Stony Island serves as a physical separation for these two adjoining neighborhoods in the heart of America's third-largest city, but in reality they are worlds apart. And the difference between them is Shorebank.

Formed in 1973, when South Shore and Woodlawn were suffering equally from early doses of decline, Shorebank is now an internationally recognized pioneer in community development. With a bank as its core and a group of non-bankers as its heart, it has become a multi-faceted for-profit business created specifically to bolster the fortunes of communities like South Shore. By most measures—and particularly in contrast to the atrophy that remains evident in Woodlawn—it is a remarkable success.

Since its establishment, South Shore property values have risen far more rapidly than those in other neighborhoods around the city. Unusual coalitions of "housing entrepreneurs" renovated thousands of rental units in hundreds of buildings. New shopping centers and other commercial buildings sprang up for the first time in decades. Thousands of local residents benefited from educational and job-placement programs. Dozens of new businesses received organizational support. And Shorebank—which has since replicated these efforts elsewhere in Chicago as well as in other cities—is turning the kind of profit that satisfies both banking regulators and its investors.

Perhaps even more encouraging is the fact that its successes are now widely recognized, and are even being copied by a financial community which once collectively downplayed the merits of its admittedly unconventional methods. Former President Bill Clinton was one of the institution's few early outside supporters, enthusiastically bringing Shorebank's concepts to rural Arkansas while governor of that state and then publicly praising its goals and practices while a candidate for the nation's highest office in 1992. Now, after years of being repeatedly cited as the ultimate model for effectively distributing its particular brand of residential and small business loans, there is an entire industry comprised of similar community development financial institutions based directly upon this premise.

Such accomplishments and recognition did not come easily. Money managers, developers, and even residents in the originally targeted South Shore neighborhood were openly skeptical—if not downright hostile—when Shorebank's founders purchased a failing local bank and announced plans to use it as the centerpiece for an ambitious program of community redevelopment. The commercial revitalization that they initially envisioned along with it has never matched the neighborhood's residential rehabilitation. And achieving overall profitability was a mighty struggle for the first few years.

But with the help of dedicated employees, flexible managers, innovative programs, and a little old-fashioned luck, Shorebank has indeed become a role model for other socially responsible business enterprises—a segment of the corporate world that did not even exist when its founders entered South Shore some three decades ago.

"We wanted to create an institution that would do something like what we are doing now," says Ronald Grzywinski, currently chairman of the corporation and the individual most responsible for its formation and development. "We had an idea. We had a vision. We knew that there had to be a better way to rebuild the cities of America for the benefit of the people who lived there."

The route taken by Grzywinski and Shorebank's other three founders—Mary Houghton, now its president, Milton Davis, who retired in 2000, and James Fletcher, who died in 1998—was to form a company specifically designed to revive its home neighborhood by reinstalling credit, rehabilitating self-confidence, and reestablishing a functioning market economy. It has done so by combining banks, real estate development subsidiaries, tax-exempt affiliates that attack housing and employment problems, and a consulting arm which advises other public and private enterprises involved in economic development.

These efforts helped the corporation grow from a single struggling $41 million bank to a healthy $1 billion bank holding company that has duplicated these services in additional Chicago neighborhoods, Cleveland, Detroit, the Upper Peninsula of Michigan, and the Pacific Northwest. In addition, its consulting company assists with development organizations in other locations across the U.S. and around the world.

Its roots remain in South Shore, though, and looking around that neighborhood today it is hard not to find reasons for the continuing optimism expressed by Shorebank officials. From Jackson Park on the north to Eighty-Third Street on the south, and from Lake Michigan on the east to Stony Island Avenue on the west, South Shore's two-and-a-half square miles stand as a continuing testament to their vision.

The roots of rehabilitation

People at Shorebank like to tell the story of a former electric company employee who had a vision of his own. One of the first South Shore residents to take advantage of the new lending policies introduced by Grzywinski and his cohorts, the man raised enough money to buy a dilapidated forty-four-unit apartment house for $55,000. He fixed it up, leased it out, and sold it in less than a decade for $450,000. A few years later, at the age of sixty-eight, he owned seven more refurbished buildings and had become very wealthy.

His success inspired others, like the manager of a dry-cleaning business who bought a small apartment house with money lent by Shorebank. The man repaired it, rented it out, bought a second and then a third. He eventually owned about fifty units and quit his dry-cleaning job in order to begin restoring apartments full-time.

These impressive stories are hardly unique. Hundreds of "housing entrepreneurs," as bank personnel refer to the electric company retiree and the dry-cleaning veteran, are responsible for renovating more than twenty-two thousand housing units since 1973 in some one thousand multi-family Chicago buildings. And as they raised their own standards of living with Shorebank's assistance, they also helped make their community a better place.

Those who are associated with the bank are not surprised that its unconventional plan for urban improvement—born from the social and civil rights movements of the 1960s—continues working so well in the twenty-first century. A team of complimentary talents with a unified view, founders Grzywinski, Houghton, Davis and Fletcher realized more than three decades ago that traditional non-profit and governmental efforts were severely limited in their ability to handle such complex urban woes. Though only in their thirties at the time, they understood that a new kind of for-profit attack with a social-worker orientation might be better.

Such thinking, it turns out, developed naturally. Grzywinski was a businessman before moving into the world of banking, where he pioneered the formation of a community-oriented approach later embraced and expanded by Shorebank. Houghton held a master's degree from the Johns Hopkins School of Advanced International Studies when she joined up with Grzywinski and the others. Davis, a civil rights activist and chairman of the Chicago chapter of CORE (the Congress on Racial Equality), was on the faculty of the Graduate School of Business at the University of Chicago. Fletcher was a former grade-school teacher, a veteran of Chicago's War on Poverty, and the assistant director of the federal Community Action Program.

The four, who lived near each other and often traveled in the same circles, joined forces in the late 1960s to create their new kind of bank. But they never liked being referred to as "bankers." Instead, they always saw themselves as social reformers who operated a bank as a vehicle for societal change. And they believed that their idea developed and flourished precisely because they were not "bankers" in the traditional sense.

"We were all working with various community-based organizations, and those organizations were trying to deal with a variety of problems in the neighborhoods in which they were located," recalled Davis—long considered by insiders to be the "heart and soul" of the effort—before suffering a stroke several years ago that eventually led to his retirement from day-to-day operations. "But it was like an ant fighting an elephant," he continued, "because those organizations were always consumed with raising money to pay the rent, the light bill, and the staff. They simply had no time to deal with problems they were confronting in the neighborhoods, and so there was no way those problems could ever be adequately addressed. We were convinced that we ought to take a look at designing an organization that would have a fighting chance of dealing with those problems."

The actual concept originated with Grzywinski, who grew up in a Polish-American neighborhood less than five miles from South Shore. After graduating from Chicago's Loyola University, he took a job selling computers locally for IBM. He eventually left the corporate world to take a position with a bank in the nearby city of Lockport. After rising to that institution's presidency, he returned to his old neighborhood specifically to help organize a deal to buy a struggling bank in Hyde Park, an area just north of South Shore that was changing for the worse.

Under Grzywinski's supervision, the new Hyde Park Bank formed an Urban Development Division that made loans to minority entrepreneurs throughout Chicago. The program brought major deposits to the bank from government and private sources interested in furthering the division's goals and helped the bank itself return to profitability. It also attracted Davis, an Atlanta-born African-American who was living in South Shore; Houghton, a white program officer for the non-profit Johnson Foundation who had recently relocated to Chicago; and Fletcher, an African-American who had grown up in a public housing project just five miles from South Shore.

The four immediately recognized the power that a bank could wield as a development force, but they also quickly learned of its limitations. Federal regulations at the time banned banks from most development-oriented activities, for example, including ownership of real estate not directly used by the institution. Congressional approval of the 1970 amendments to the Bank Holding Company Act and the Federal Reserve's subsequent definition of newly permissible activities soon erased that drawback, however. Bank holding companies were finally freed to invest in community development corporations—as long as their primary purpose was to benefit low- and moderate-income groups. Since that was precisely what the foursome planned, they knew a nontraditional banking structure could now best help them achieve their goals. They only needed an appropriate neighborhood in which to test their theories.

Shorebank finds a home

South Shore is one of those fiercely independent enclaves that gives Chicago its reputation as a city of neighborhoods. Developed in 1893 to house railroad workers, it evolved into a middle-class bedroom community with large single-family homes, small brick bungalows, and street after street of multi-unit apartment buildings.

Thanks in part to a choice location along the Lake Michigan shoreline, amenities like Jackson Park, and an easy commute downtown, South Shore became one of the city's most desirable residential communities by the 1930s. Its main shopping district—Seventy-First Street—reflected this status, and residents of other southern sections traveled there by commuter train to browse through its high-fashion jewelry, clothing, and shoe stores. Local public schools were also first-rate, and their graduates often moved on to some of the best universities in the country.

By the 1950s, however, a major transformation was underway. Change first rocked two nearby neighborhoods—Woodlawn and Hyde Park—as blacks increasingly moved in and whites increasingly moved out. More and more Chicagoans were opting to live in newly constructed dwellings in the heart of the city, or in newly expanded suburbs to the south and west. Existing apartments in South Shore were not properly maintained, and single-family home values there correspondingly started to decline. Gradually, many long-time South Shore residents joined other city-dwellers and began seeking homes outside the neighborhood.

As was the case at the time in urban areas across America, the situation only worsened as the years rolled by. Older apartment buildings deteriorated still further. Many were subdivided into smaller units, drawing poorer and poorer tenants. The number of welfare recipients mushroomed. Middle-class residents, both black and white, moved on when they could. Racial tensions grew. The Seventy-First Street shopping strip deteriorated. Crime rates soared. Property values stagnated. Within a few years, the neighborhood suffered an almost total decline and most of the so-called experts declared its fate sealed. In 1972, even the area's primary financial institution—the South Shore National Bank—requested permission to relocate.

Swayed by organized neighborhood opposition, though, the federal comptroller of the currency rejected the relocation application because the bank had "failed to show a persuasive reason for abandoning its service area." Grzywinski, who was seeking a home for his proposed banking-based development program, asked if the institution was for sale. He was told it was, and that its book value was $3.2 million.

Grzywinski had left Hyde Park Bank in 1969 to develop a structure for the new community development effort he envisioned. The resultant plan, which he completed with his three colleagues and help from a few others, was initially called the Illinois Neighborhood Development Corporation. It was ready to go when the existing South Shore bank came on the market, but putting the necessary capital together was another story. Not surprisingly, the group's plan to purchase a failing bank in an economically depressed neighborhood for the purpose of testing a radical new idea attracted few investors. Over the next couple of months, in fact, only $800,000 was raised from a few individuals, a couple of foundations, and the United Church of Christ Board of Homeland Ministries. To meet their goal, the founders were forced to secure the other $2.4 million through a loan guaranteed by Grzywinski and his wife.

On August 23, 1973—"vastly undercapitalized and seriously over-leveraged," as its members now readily admit—the new management team assumed control of South Shore Bank. Though it faced an array of major obstacles, the quartet decided to immediately begin the task for which it was formed.

"As we saw it, one of our chief purposes was to restore South Shore's competitiveness by rebuilding the market forces disinvestment had destroyed," Grzywinski has written. "The neighborhood was far from hopeless. A lot of storefronts were boarded up, but not all. A dozen apartment buildings had been abandoned, but not more. The trouble was that every bank in town had redlined South Shore, including the bank chartered to serve it—the South Shore National Bank. In the year before we bought the bank, it had made exactly two conventional home-mortgage loans for a total of $59,000."

Grzywinski and his colleagues aimed to change that. They planned to spark renewal by carefully and deliberately reinvesting all of their resources in just one targeted community: South Shore. Not many people had high expectations for the idea, but their conviction would prevail.

A rocky beginning

When South Shore's new ownership took control in 1973, deposits were low. (They had, in fact, fallen from a peak of $80 million to about $42 million in little more than a decade.) Existing loan officers were reluctant to accept the newly liberal-ized lending criteria. The bank building itself had not been properly maintained for years. And its only parking lot was located across a busy street and out of sight, forcing the few customers that remained to take a long and potentially dangerous walk in order to do business there.

"From the beginning, we envisioned that the bank would be the centerpiece," the late James Fletcher said in the 1990s while serving as the institution's president. "But we bought a bank that was in trouble as opposed to buying a healthy bank, and that made a big difference." It meant that the ambitious affiliate activities needed to proceed at full speed—the real estate development company, the operation to promote housing and employment, the not-for-profit neighborhood advocate—would have to wait until the bank itself regained a solid financial footing. But it didn't mean that all of the community development efforts envisioned by the new owners had to be put on hold. So the foursome set about the task of raising more capital to make it happen.

Grzywinski, Houghton, Davis and Fletcher decided that they could do this most efficiently by increasing deposits, which they felt residents would be more than willing to make once they understood that their money was going only to development activity within their community. To bolster activity they cut the minimum balance needed to open a savings account to $1, extended the bank's hours, reduced its service fees, and eliminated most paperwork. At the same time they improved the bank's appearance, built a new parking lot directly across the street, and even constructed a drive-up teller facility a couple of blocks away.

Simultaneously, the bank overhauled its lending policy. From that point on, it declared, loan officers could only deny applications from South Shore residents—or from those who wanted to buy a home or open a business in the community—after the applications were also rejected by the management committee. In addition, the bank began aggressively courting entrepreneurial borrowers, much like the owners had done with their urban development program at Hyde Park. Davis, president at the time, visited an array of neighborhood organizations with Grzywinski in order to explain Shorebank's new programs and long-range plans.

Unfortunately, not all of these moves generated the desired results. Neighbors of the new drive-up facility, for example, feared its presence could draw crime near their homes; others were angered that the bank tore down an apartment building to make way for its new parking lot. Long-time loan officers never completely accepted the new lending philosophy, and most had to eventually be replaced. Increasing the number of small savings accounts did not provide the capital Shorebank needed—and actually lost money for the institution. But the biggest disappointment of all was the small-business loan program. "When we first got here," Davis recalled, "we made noble efforts to make loans to all the businesses along these streets. We lost every one of them. They just couldn't compete with the regional shopping malls, half an hour's drive from here, that have two hundred stores."

Refusing to give up, the managers fine-tuned their efforts. They appeased neighborhood groups opposed to their construction plans as best they could. They raised savings-account fees in order to cover costs, and decided to focus their lending initiative on South Shore's true strength: residential real estate. Significantly, the program they formulated to do so eventually turned their entire undertaking around. Called Development Deposits, it was designed from the start for outside depositors—from pension-fund managers to individual savers—who wanted to open a competitively structured account at Shorebank because their money would be used exclusively for development within the South Shore neighborhood. Simple, yet radical, it reversed the usual banking practice of taking local deposits and then investing them in faraway places.

"A community like South Shore, by definition, doesn't have the resources to fund long-term development operations," explains Joan Shapiro, a Shorebank officer in charge of this reverse-redlining program for twenty years before leaving in 1997 to become a consultant. "What happens in most cases is that you have a net outflow of investable resources from the low-income communities to the more affluent neighborhoods. Development Deposits brings outside resources into our service area."

The response was enthusiastic from the start, with people from all fifty states and a score of other countries opening accounts. And since the program's inception in 1974, their funds have helped Shorebank as well as the neighborhoods it serves. Today, approximately 3,200 Development Depositors own about 5,500 accounts worth a total of $182 million. "We'd be a very different bank without it," Shapiro says.

Not business as usual

A woman named Stephanie learned first-hand how Shorebank provides multiple benefits to its constituents when she rented one of its development subsidiary's South Shore apartments in 1996. In short order she was offered a part-time job in an after-school program operated by the corporation, then a full-time position as a receptionist with the employment agency run by its Neighborhood Institute. While working her way up to secretary, then to administrative assistant, and then to placement coordinator, Stephanie decided to go to school to earn a bachelor's degree and now plans to pursue a master's. She has also purchased her first house with help from a Shorebank program that gives residents information and assistance on home ownership, business startups, and educational advancement.

Scores of banks across the U.S. have been subject to justifiable public criticism in recent times, stemming from taxpayer bailouts, federal takeovers, discriminatory lending practices, and various other missteps and improprieties. But Shorebank has remained free from any such problems despite lending tens of millions of dollars and providing uncountable opportunities for support to those in its service areas who would otherwise be unlikely to obtain it. Impressively, its core banking operation has been able to do this while recording a profit every year since 1975.

"People always ask me if what we do is risky. But where have the losses been in this industry?" Shapiro asks. "Not at Shorebank." Indeed, over the last five years the corporation's Chicago bank—its first and by far largest—has maintained a lower average loan loss rate (.37 percent) than its peers around the nation (.46 percent). And such measures have generally remained equally positive throughout the operation even as the number of total development loans has skyrocketed from one record ($146 million in 2000) to another ($233 million in 2001), reaching a level three times the corporation's consolidated average capital for the first time since it raised funds to expand to five new locations in 1990. At the same time, Shorebank also doubled its lending to churches and community organizations and tripled the amount it invested in real estate development over the previous year.

In Chicago alone, Shorebank has lent approximately $600 million to thirteen thousand families and businesses since it began three decades ago in South Shore. And most observers, Milton Davis noted before his retirement, will readily acknowledge that this investment has made the difference in the way its initial service area has developed to this day. "The prediction by a lot of people, especially in the real estate arena, when we got here was that this neighborhood would go to abandonment and demolition in five years." But Shorebank not only helped refurbish South Shore successfully, it did so without pushing low- and moderate-income residents out in favor of more well-heeled newcomers. "That is the single thing I think most of us here are most proud of," Davis added. "We have helped this neighborhood without gentrifying it. How? By developing or rehabilitating housing and then keeping rents at a level that the people who already live here can afford."

By catching the areas it serves in the early stages of decline or when improvement was least expensive, Shorebank has been able to both assist in a dramatic reversal of fortune and maintain viability for those with limited economic choices. It has also been able to attract other investors, lenders, and developers, many of whom now regularly enter these neighborhoods with affordable projects of their own.

The pieces come together

After turning a profit for three consecutive years, Shorebank was finally able to begin adding the ancillary non-bank components in 1978 that its founders had envisioned from the start. First came a wholly owned residential and commercial real estate development subsidiary. This was immediately followed by the Neighborhood Institute—the first tax-exempt affiliate ever developed by a bank holding company—which was formed to tackle deep-seated housing and employment problems. A Minority Enterprise Small Business Investment Company came the next year, created to finance small business loan requests that the bank itself could not approve. Shorebank Advisory Services, which was designed to assist both financial and non-financial institutions on issues like banking, economic development, and affordable housing, was authorized in 1987.

From the beginning, the bank was envisioned as the operation's centerpiece—but a bank, by regulation, can just do so much. It may only respond to the specific requests of its customers, for example, and so "action vehicles" like these ancillary pieces were necessary in order to really make things happen. Over the years, the interrelationship between these affiliates and subsidiaries has enabled Shorebank to put together a unique community revitalization program that works on many levels. And each organization in the corporation is now responsible for a series of impressive projects that helps the others succeed.

Today, for instance, the Shorebank Development arm employs a wide variety of funding methods to renovate large apartment houses, manage property, build low- and moderate-income housing units, and develop commercial real estate. Its residential successes have been well documented, and one of its biggest projects ever in the commercial area was the $9.4 million Jeffrey Plaza Shopping Center at the intersection of Chicago's Seventy-First Street and Jeffrey Boulevard—right in the heart of South Shore's original shopping district. As recently as 2001, this subsidiary built and sold 116 new housing units worth $24 million in the Windy City alone.

The Neighborhood Institute now restores buildings for cooperative ownership, manages neighborhood small-business "incubators," and trains and places job applicants in property-management firms, banks, theaters, manufacturing companies, and a variety of similar local endeavors. Among its many notable rehab projects are a thirteen-story apartment building in which one-fifth of the units are reserved for very low income tenants, and an innovative artist's colony called One Artists Row.

Sisters Building Bridges, a support group for women living in subsidized housing rejuvenated by Shorebank Development, is an example of how such subsidiaries function in unison. When the group's eighteen members first got together in 1989, only three were working; Shorebank helped them formally organize to "overcome their barriers to work and financial self-sufficiency," and today, thanks largely to its influence, almost all are employed full time. Some joined employment programs sponsored by the Neighborhood Institute while others participated in Shorebank's Individual Development Accounts—a wide-ranging program that helps each person involved work towards their own goals in housing, employment or education. Members now also hold block parties, volunteer in after-school programs operated by Shorebank Development, and are active in a prize-winning community garden.

In addition to its consulting operations, Shorebank Advisory Services today also supervises the distribution of loans to small businesses in other nations. During recent years it has made as many as 550 of these, totaling some $9 million annually, in a dozen foreign countries. One in 1999 was a $170,000 equipment loan made to a father-and-son team that opened a clinic called Dema Ltd. in the country of Georgia. It now employs nine doctors and offers forty-four types of ultrasound procedures to the people of that nation and Northern Azerbaijan.

On the road

Thanks to its advisory subsidiary, Shorebank has been able to enter into a variety of innovative development partnerships that help spread its ideas both at home and abroad. For example, in addition to consulting with domestic clients like Specialty Mill Products of San Francisco—a non-profit cabinet shop that trains low-income high school dropouts in cabinetmaking and mill working skills—it allowed the institution to expand its entire concept into other geographic areas. One year after opening a variation of South Shore's initial operation in the far west side neighborhood of Austin—the largest in Chicago—the Winthrop Rockefeller Foundation and the state of Arkansas (governed then by Bill Clinton) asked management to help "accelerate the pace of economic activity" in a very rural thirty-two-county area. Grzywinski, Houghton, Davis and Fletcher formed a second bank holding company, Southern Development Bancorporation, to do so; it continues successfully today and has even expanded into the Mississippi Delta region.

Following that project, Shorebank initiated its own full-service programs similar to the original Chicago operation—complete with community development banks, real estate development firms, and venture capital organizations—in the Upper Peninsula of Michigan, Cleveland, Detroit, and the Pacific Northwest. These have also grown quite large in ensuing years, and become very effective in translating the original idea onto new turf. Cleveland's ShoreBank became that city's second highest SBA 504 lender during 2001, for instance, one year after it distributed $13 million in loans to businesses and commercial real estate customers while providing office and production space for some fifty companies employing more than two hundred people through the operation of two business incubators. And in Detroit, an auto parts assembler and part-time college student named Theresa became one of hundreds of customers nationwide who was able to buy her first house after taking perspective homebuyer classes and then obtaining a mortgage. "Owning a home is a big step, but ShoreBank Detroit made it a manageable one," she told officials in a statement reprinted in their annual report.

Perhaps the most challenging of all its newer projects take place overseas, where Shorebank has been developing credit programs in countries like Bangladesh and Finland since 1983. One of the most intricate of these began in Poland in 1989, where, in cooperation with the U.S. government-backed Polish-American Enterprise Fund, Shorebank introduced the same type of programs utilized in its domestic development efforts. By the turn of the century this international work was responsible for disbursing some $9 million annually in small business loans throughout Western Europe, the Middle East, and the former Eastern Bloc. Examples of its programs in these regions include a training program for Jordanians who want to offer micro-finance assistance in Arabic, and development of an institution called Aspire in Northern Ireland that, in its first year, approved one hundred affordable loans to entrepreneurs who otherwise would not have had access to such funds.

Back in the U.S., the most striking new initiative in recent years involves Shorebank's active embrace of environmental goals into its overall corporate plan. Based on what the institution now calls its "triple-bottom line"—achieving long-term prosperity, enhancing quality of life, and helping improve the environment—it is centered at the institution's Pacific Northwest affiliate and funded in part through so-called "Eco-Deposits" made by investors nationwide. Modeled on the bank's pioneering Development Deposits, the program assists local businesses wanting to adopt more sustainable practices by turning these funds into loans that support such efforts. Almost $11 million was dispersed in 2000 through one hundred of these loans.

This is hardly the only region or program in which Shorebank's newly emphasized ecological sensitivities can be found, however. Sound environmental principles have also now been intentionally incorporated into the institution's efforts around the country, mirroring "the restoration, conservation and adaptive re-use of the built environment" that has been its hallmark from the start. Following recommendations of an employee-led task force that met throughout 1998 and 1999, the corporation developed a "conservation vision" that now sets the tone for direct actions internally as well as those it can indirectly impact among its customers and in its communities. To address Shorebank's own environmental performance, the company began tracking its energy, water and paper use, in addition to its production of waste, recycled materials and emissions. To build this ethic externally, it began offering loans to those promoting energy conservation as well as those expanding businesses involved in "green" markets. Its loans made for these purposes more than tripled from $13 million in 2000 to $42 million in 2001, making capital available to reduce negative environmental impacts, produce new products, extend the useful life of old buildings, and even restore abandoned buildings to productive use.

Today, the corporation has grown to some 525 employees—due in part to a 1995 merger with Chicago bank holding company Indecorp that immediately doubled its size—and its impacts are felt around the world. It is still occasionally subjected to criticism from those who complain that its operational costs are too high, or that some of its subsidiaries have not become self-sustainable and continue to be supported by the profitable core bank. But Joan Shapiro, the consultant who ran its Development Deposits program for two decades, brushes these complaints aside by noting that this comes from Shorebank's tenacious obligation toward community development and its unrelenting pledge to walk the walk as well as talk the talk.

"Its commitment to the development agenda has, from my observation, provided the motivation to make initiatives and endeavors work that more conventional companies would try to shut down," she says. "And this has really changed the way that those who follow these issues in the banking industry think about minority and under-invested neighborhoods." Few others are willing to do what Shorebank does, she adds, but even the biggest banks now have significant redevelopment programs that are at least partially based on the way her former employer has faithfully and passionately invested in its communities.

Some of these newcomers, in fact, now also provide Shorebank with a challenge it never expected in years past: convincing investors, granting agencies and customers to go there instead of the competition. One way it has chosen to combat this was by naming Bob Nash the vice chairman of its holding company in April 2001. Nash, who served in Bill Clinton's presidential and gubernatorial administrations—and has been connected to Shorebank through them since 1985—is charged with raising the operation's profile and planning for the future, among other duties. "Some of these things were being done," Nash says, "but with Jim Fletcher dying and Milton Davis retiring, there was a need to redouble our efforts and do some new things."

Doing new things, and making positive changes in neighborhoods like South Shore takes time. The regions didn't become blighted overnight, after all, and so there is no reason to expect that they can be turned around overnight—or even quickly. But the success of Shorebank's policies are readily apparent to all who care to look for them. To see for yourself, just go to a point about nine miles south of Chicago's Loop and stand in the middle of Stony Island Avenue.

Chapter Six

A Committed Culture

Company Name: Stonyfield Farm
Primary Business: Produces and distributes all-natural and organic yogurt and ice cream
Type of Company: Private corporation. Forty percent owned by French company Groupe Danone.
Headquarters: Londonderry, New Hampshire
Number of employees: 170
Founders: Samuel Kaymen and Gary Hirshberg
CEO: Gary Hirshberg
Year Founded: 1983
Web site: http://www.stonyfield.com

Mission Statement

• *To provide the very highest quality, best-tasting and all natural certified organic products;*
• *To educate consumers and producers about the value of protecting the environment and of supporting family farmers and sustainable farming methods;*

- *To serve as a model that environmentally and socially responsible businesses can also be profitable;*
- *To provide a healthful, productive and enjoyable work place for all employees, with opportunities to gain new skills and advance personal career goals;*
- *To recognize our obligations to stockholders and lenders by providing an excellent return on their investment.*

It was in the late 1990s that Gary Hirshberg, CEO of Stonyfield Farm, felt the urgency to respond to his shareholders and sell off part of the privately held company. With $70 million in annual sales, he needed to come up with a liquidity exit plan for the nearly three hundred shareholders who had invested in the yogurt company and helped it be successful for the prior nineteen years. The fact that many of these investors were employees, friends and relatives of the forty-eight-year old president, made it even more vital. They had helped him, and now it was time to pay them back.

For several years, Hirshberg explored every possible option. He looked into turning the yogurt company public with a traditional initial public offering (IPO). He considered a direct public offering, allowing Stonyfield's loyal customers to buy into the company with the products they so relish. Yet, he realized these options would cost him something more valuable than the millions of dollars that would be gained—the ability to control his mission-driven business.

"This is my life and this is the life of our employees. It's not a hobby," says Hirshberg from his sun-filled office in southern New Hampshire. "I want to stay and expand on everything we've achieved so far. I just don't want to hand it off." With this in mind, Hirshberg realized that a partnership was the best way to go.

Over several years, Hirshberg talked to every leading perishable food company in business. The interest in Stonyfield was keen, and with good reason. The company, which makes more than eighty varieties of natural and organic yogurts and ice creams that are sold throughout the United States, had been solidly profitable for the past decade, with the fastest compounded annual growth rate (24.3 percent) of any U.S. yogurt brand. In early 2001, it became the fourth top-selling yogurt brand in the United States, behind Dannon, Yoplait and Breyers. With 70 percent of its line certified organic, Stonyfield benefited from the explosive growth and interest in this natural food products sector. In fact, sales of organic yogurt grew almost 50 percent in 2000 alone—and most of that increase was attributed to Stonyfield.

So Hirshberg drove a hard bargain with potential suitors, presenting an exhaustive laundry list of conditions. The new owners might have a majority interest, someday, but couldn't have control. They must buy into the company's long-time pact to donate 10 percent of profits to environmental causes. They must agree to not move manufacturing elsewhere and shut down Stonyfield's New Hampshire production plant. The company would always need to retain its sense of purpose, delivering a healthy product while making as little environmental impact as possible. To realize this, Hirshberg was to remain chairman of the board and in control of all management and operations following the sale.

The potential buyers exited as quickly as they lined up. Some companies wanted to move production, other didn't agree with Hirshberg's valuation of the company. One by one, the contenders "fell out like competitors in an Olympic marathon," says Hirshberg, until only one remained. And that suitor was French food conglomerate Group Danone, makers of cereal, snack foods, Evian water, and the world's number-one selling yogurt, Danone, known as Dannon in the United States.

There were two factors that most impressed Groupe Danone's management. First was Stonyfield's dominant market share in the burgeoning organic marketplace. "The Dannon brand is good for the regular segment," said Laurent Lamaire, head of investor relations for Group Danone, following his late 2001 signing of the partnership agreement. "We have no real experience in the organic segment. We hope to learn a lot by investing in Stonyfield." Second, Group Danone's management liked the feisty New Hampshire entrepreneur. "Our best protection is that Gary Hirshberg remains," said Lamaire.

Still, Hirshberg agonized up until the last minute, trying to decide if this was the best possible solution. As the clock ticked, his colleagues with him in his Boston attorney's office weren't sure he would actually sign on the dotted line. But he did. "If it was totally up to me, I would not have sold," admits Hirshberg afterward. "But I have three hundred shareholders who deserve this. It was the best of all possible options."

Danone initially purchased approximately 40 percent of the company for an estimated $100 million. Eventually, it will have the option to purchase all remaining non-employee shares. Yet, even after this stage, Hirshberg will remain a large stockholder and will continue on as Chairman, President and CEO. In addition, he will retain control of three of five board seats for as long as he chooses, up until 2016

A kitchen launch

Stonyfield Farm began as a kitchen-stove and bathtub operation in an eighteenth-century New Hampshire farmhouse in the early 1980s. There, the then twenty-eight-year old Hirshberg and other trustees were trying to help founder Samuel Kaymen come up with ways to raise money to save The Rural Education Center, an organic farm and education center on the brink of bankruptcy. They considered selling pickles or opening a brewery. They thought about selling "shares" in their dairy herd. Meanwhile, Kaymen served the brainstorming group some homemade yogurt made from his cow's milk. They all marveled at just how delicious it tasted. It then dawned on them that the healthful dairy product could be produced and sold, and Kaymen soon launched the business to do so.

Hirshberg, at that time, was executive director at the New Alchemy Institute on Cape Cod, Massachusetts, doing field research on solar and wind systems, organic agriculture and energy systems. During a visit to Disney's Epcot Center, Hirshberg found himself in the giant Kraft's foods pavilion. "There was a display of how they thought food would be made in the future that was totally chemically driven. Thousands of people were paying to see this every day. The whole exhibit lauded synthetic food production that was the exact opposite of my organic agricultural views. And yet there were throngs of people clamoring to see it," says Hirshberg. It dawned on him that more people visited this exhibit on artificial food in one day than visited his organic farming institute each year. Hirshberg realized he could be far more effective spreading his beliefs using a commercial entity as his platform. "If I was going to make a difference, I needed to embrace business," he says. By the spring of 1983, Hirshberg joined Kaymen, now retired, in the yogurt business called Stonyfield Farm for the farm where the business was based. The partners had a lofty goal: to create and sell a healthy, beneficial product while supporting environmental responsibility. Values would be the cornerstone of the business.

Kaymen sought out initial funding, and received the first infusion of money from a $35,000 loan from a Catholic order of nuns, The Sisters of Mercy, who were interested in community economic development. This allowed them to produce, package and get their first yogurt cups to retailers in their New Hampshire community.

Growth and profitability came slowly for the company, with Hirshberg and Kaymen doing everything from milking the cows to making and delivering the yogurt to finding investors for the company. Fortunately, there was a groundswell of interest in the yogurt itself with customers clamoring to buy it. "Samuel had a world-class recipe that was better than anything else out there," says Hirshberg. "Our main goal was to get people to taste it. Once they did, they were hooked."

Keeping up with the mounting bills was always a challenge. Hirshberg says those first years were a "frantic" time, with "anyone in a tie" considered financing bait. "Our UPS guy would be afraid to show up on Thursdays, payroll day, because he knew I would try to hit him up for a loan," says a laughing Hirshberg now.

The duo's devotion to the product and strong environmental beliefs—not to mention generous loans from family and friends—kept Stonyfield afloat. Yet, for Hirshberg, this added even more pressure. "I couldn't just give up and get a real job. I had the investments of a huge group of people who were friends and family to consider," he says. "I could not fail."

Sales grew as the products became available first in New England grocery stores and natural food markets, then in the New York market, and slowly across the country. "Because there are so few local chains anymore, it was just a matter of time before we were all over the Northeast and then, eventually, the United States," says Hirshberg.

During this time, Stonyfield created the in-your-face marketing practices that still dominate the company's strategy. Rather than advertising, Hirshberg promoted the brand by giving out thousands of free yogurts anywhere there was bound to be a group of people, including nonprofit events such as Earth Day and the Walk for Hunger and at road races, such as the Tufts 10K, a popular Boston event attracting thousands of participants. The ulterior motive has always been to convert customers away from other yogurt brands, while also introducing new customers to the Stonyfield brand.

At first eschewing slotting fees, the cost most supermarkets charge vendors to carry their product, Hirshberg realized he would have to pay in order to enter certain markets and chains. But he will only go so far. More recently, when a New York chain's fees got to the point Hirshberg described as "extortion-like," Stonyfield pulled out. "I often said that slotting feels are 'sinful,' but I realize that supermarkets are in the business of making money. But, if they are too high, then we pull out, as we did with the New York chain. And it hasn't hurt us at all."

Always the product

Stonyfield's commitment to responsible practices impacts every area of the business, from where it buys its ingredients, to how it produce its products, to educating consumers on issues it deems important.

It would be the quality of the products, however, that would allow the business to grow and succeed in all areas of this mission-driven business. Since Stonyfield's inception, the company dedicated itself to using all-natural and healthful ingredients, even as other yogurt companies were seeking out cheaper ingredients in order to lower costs.

"Having a great product is the first step to success," says Hirshberg who, like every employee at the one-hundred-thousand-square-foot Londonderry offices and plant, gushes about Stonyfield's yogurts and ice creams. At its visitor center adjacent to the plant, employees encourage guests to try samples of everything from super premium ice creams to soy-based yogurts. Afterward, visitors can shop for cow paraphernalia and other New Hampshire-made goods, and thumb through a yogurt cookbook written by Hirshberg's wife Meg.

Today, Stonyfield invests 1 percent of sales in research and development, according to Kasi Reddy, the company's vice president of research and development. Under his guidance, Stonyfield became the first yogurt to contain the probiotic culture Lactobacillus reuteri and the first dairy in the United States to add the prebiotic inulin to its products. These ingredients, says Reddy, enhances the benefits of the yogurt's probiotic cultures.

"When I first came to Stonyfield we reformulated the yogurts to be less acidic, smoother and less sweet," says Reddy, whose office is next to the company's production plant. "And by using different cultures, we make a milder yogurt that consumers prefer. At the same time, the new version creates a favorable environment for probiotic cultures." By using the best ingredients possible and by rigidly controlling air quality, Stonyfield yogurts have an impressive fifty-day shelf life, as compared to the more typical thirty-two-day average of its competitors.

At the same time, new product creation is a constant at Stonyfield. Since 1995, the company has introduced a total of eight new product lines, ranging from its YoSqueeze yogurt line to a super premium ice cream. "Being number-four is great, but we would lose our market position if we didn't keep introducing new products," says Hirshberg. "If you don't grow your slice of the pie, it grows in on you as competitors move in on your territory. It's the nature of consumer products."

Hirshberg notes the "predatory" nature of the food industry, with new products given only a few months to succeed. Stonyfield has hit a few home runs in the recent past, namely, the 1999 introduction of its YoBaby line of whole milk yogurts. Hirshberg had seen similar versions while on a European trip, and gave his team the edict to produce something comparable. Within three months, the Stonyfield version was on the shelves, a testimony to Stonyfield's agility. YoBaby sales grew by 32 percent in 2001. In 2002, Stonyfield introduced its line of "drinkable" low-fat yogurts, a popular product in Europe that Reddy predicts will be well-liked on this side of the Atlantic as well.

Quality ingredients make quality products, and Stonyfield has always gone the extra mile to buy only the best. It now buys most of its milk and milk products from the St. Albans Cooperative, a member-owned collective of more than five hundred family farms based in St. Albans, Vermont. More than three-quarters of these are considered "small farms" and the cooperative makes sure that all members' animals are well fed, housed and protected from inclement weather.

Stonyfield takes it a step further by buying milk only from those farmers that pledge to not inject their cows with the recombinant bovine growth hormone (rBGH). Cows given the hormone can increase their milk production by an average of between 10 and 25 percent. Stonyfield Farm pays farmers a premium to not use rBGH.

The company's opposition to rBGH hits many levels and Stonyfield has been a leading opponent of the controversial practice. First, according to Hirshberg, common use of the hormone swells the country's milk supply, resulting in a drop in the prices paid to farmers. "Although it would be far less expensive for us to produce our products with cheaper milk, we have to stick to our values. By increasing the milk supply, small family farmers would be devastated. It would put them out of business," he says.

Secondly, Stonyfield is concerned with animal welfare, noting that a recent study found that the hormone increased the chances for cows to get udder infections, lameness and reduced longevity. Finally, there is concern that the hormone could prove unsafe for consumers. The company promotes its firm stance by stating on its packaging that "WE OPPOSE rBGH and the family farmers who supply our milk and cream pledge not to treat their cows with rBGH."

An organic move

Stonyfield's single-minded emphasis on product innovation has led it in many directions over the years that run contrary to the industry in which it operates. One of the most non-traditional, most far-reaching, and ultimately most self-defining, was Hirshberg's decision to produce his yogurts according to organic standards.

It was in the mid-1990s that Hirshberg approached his sister, Nancy Hirshberg, Stonyfield's vice president of natural resources, with a challenge: See what it would take to convert our yogurts to organic. Organic production is a complex method of farming and manufacturing that eliminates synthetic chemicals, and is one of today's most popular—though demanding—food trends.

When Stonyfield started making its yogurts, organic wasn't even an option. "At the time there weren't even organic standards for dairy products," says Nancy Hirshberg. "There was no organic feed available for cows and no companies offering the organic ingredients we need."

However, as more dairy farmers were converting their practices to organic, the option became viable. "We started with one product, our whole milk plain yogurt, because then we didn't have to worry about sourcing organic flavors," says Nancy Hirshberg. With that product successfully launched, the company then introduced more organic flavors. "At first it was just a problem finding a source for organic sugar, for instance. I found one, and we had to pay triple the cost as conventional sugar. It was a huge challenge."

Nancy Hirshberg recalls the irony all too well. "You need a market in order to create demand for organic ingredients. At the same time, you need the ingredients in order to create the market." Yet, it was a mission of the company and one that also helps family farmers, who are able to charge more for the organic milk than the conventional version.

Education has also been a key part of this program. "We realized that many of our customers just didn't understand what organic means," says Nancy Hirshberg. As a result, the company created a booklet called *A Practical Guide To Understanding Organic*, in 2000, and by providing information on its web site. According to the booklet:

> Organic refers to the way agricultural products—foods and fibers—are grown and processed. It is an ecological system of management that, at its core, relies on a healthy, rich soil to produce strong plants that resists pests and diseases. Organic farming prohibits the use of toxic and persistent chemicals in favor of more 'earth friendly' practices that work in harmony with nature and preserve biological diversity—the multitude and variety of life.

Katie Hyland, Stonyfield's manager of organic compliance and new product development, is charged with making sure all

Stonyfield products fulfill the U.S. Department of Agriculture rules and regulations. "The USDA provides us with a 150-page catalog that details everything from what kind of feed a cow must eat to how to get third-party certification," she says. Even today, it's a challenge to find organic ingredients, particularly flavorings. There are only two organic strawberry flavorings available, as opposed to one thousand non-organic, and Stonyfield needs to make sure the organic versions taste just as good, if not better, than the conventional ones. All of this brings extra challenges. By mid-2003, 70 percent of Stonyfield's line was organic. The company is fully committed to the organic cause and hopes to someday have 100 percent of its line organic.

Providing a strong market for its organic offerings is about the greatest contribution Stonyfield can make to its family-farmer suppliers. "This has saved more family farms than anything else we have done," says Nancy Hirshberg. "With organic, farmers are paid a fair price for their milk. It's been a boon to the farmers who have converted."

Nancy Hirshberg believes the move to organic has been the most important milestone for the company. "It addresses all of the points of our mission statement—to produce the highest quality products, to be environmentally sensitive, and to support family farms. The organic program achieves all these goals."

Not business as usual

Since its humble beginnings in that farmhouse, Stonyfield has not forgotten the people and places from which it grew. And this continuing commitment to those roots—manifested in the caring way it treats its suppliers and the conscientious way it behaves toward its environment—is another thing that sets it apart from the corporate crowd.

Recognizing the need to help support its milk suppliers, for example, since the early 1990s, Stonyfield has awarded up to $12,000 per year in grants to farmers who produce the milk it uses to make its yogurts and ice creams. According to the company's web site, "Grants are awarded for projects that will lessen the impact of farming practices on the environment and increase the long-term viability of farming in the region."

This, according to Nancy Hirshberg, can range from a grant of $450 to build owl boxes to help rodent control, to another of $5,000 so a farmer could buy a compost turner. Each year the company sends proposal requests to all of its dairy suppliers. Other programs recently supported include helping farmers develop homeopathic veterinarian care, and building fences for erosion control. "It's out there for everyone, and is just a small way we try to help our family farmers," says Nancy Hirshberg.

Stonyfield's sense of organizational obligation, not surprisingly, also extends to the land. In its Profits For the Planet program, Stonyfield donates 10 percent of its post tax profits (after a 15 percent employee profit-sharing program) to environmental organizations such as Oxfam America, The Sustainability Institute, Children's Health Environmental Coalition and The Rainforest Foundation. In 2001, it gave $125,000. Since Stonyfield launched the program in 1995, it has given away more than $750,000.

Naturally, the company is dedicated to cleaning up the environment. In-house operations were therefore targeted for improvement. Among related measures implemented in the mid-1990s, a solid waste minimization program was one of the most extensive and effective.

"We are constantly working to reduce the amount of waste created in the process of making yogurt," claims the company on its web site. Not surprisingly, Stonyfield recycles all of its cardboard, paper, aluminum and plastics. And instead of throwing away the waste yogurt generated from product switchovers and tests, it gives the leftovers to local hog farmers. Most of the wasteful impact, however, comes from the supply chains, whether it be farms, or flavor suppliers, or the plastic manufacturers that make the product containers.

"We did an eco-audit in 1997, and it was clear that we needed to look at both the inputs and the outputs of the business," says Nancy Hirshberg. The effort has paid off. "Reducing the volume of the packaging coming in is one of the easiest ways any company can reduce waste," she says. "It's the low hanging fruit on the tree."

Stonyfield has worked with its suppliers to come up with ways they can send product—whether it's milk or flavorings or sugar—in reusable totes rather than the buckets and pails previously sent. Nancy Hirshberg points to its vanilla supplier. Before, the supplier sent the flavoring in five-gallon plastic barrels. Now, they come in huge five hundred-gallon containers that are sent back to the supplier and reused.

For its own product containers, Stonyfield recently switched to a lighter-weight plastic, eliminating the production and disposal of more than one hundred tons of plastic per year. The company gives all of its used plastic containers—and ones sent in by customers and retailers—to Recycline, a Massachusetts product manufacturer. Recycline uses the recycled plastic to make toothbrushes. The resulting toothbrushes are made of 100 percent recycled plastic, 70 percent of which comes from Stonyfield.

In 1996, the company's management set other environmental goals, including developing a program that would offset all carbon dioxide emissions. "We tried to envision a company that was totally sustainable," says Nancy Hirshberg. "Clearly, our use of non-renewable fossil fuels such as oil and propane is not sustainable. Also, the fuels we burn to make and distribute our products release even more $C0_2$ into the atmosphere." Stonyfield set the goal to first reduce and then offset the remaining of its $C0_2$ emissions.

The company first looked to its own manufacturing facility—getting its own house in order—creating equipment, lighting and steam systems that require less energy. These included installing both efficient lighting fixtures and a hot water heat recovery system that captures wasted heat. Other changes included switching from using freon to ammonia in the company's refrigeration systems, making it 14 percent more efficient. The company also improved the air quality system in its production facility so that it's similar to what is found in a medical lab. These initial efforts reduced overall CO_2 emissions by 15 percent, and have saved the company thousands of dollars every year.

After calculating its reduced emissions, Stonyfield gathered data to establish its "carbon footprint." Using CO_2 emissions factors for New Hampshire utilities, Stonyfield came up with an estimate of the annual pounds of CO_2 for which it is responsible. The company calculated that it generated 1,928 metric tons of CO_2 through its use of propane and electricity. Stonyfield then partnered with Trexler and Associates in Portland, Oregon. "They act as a broker, and invest in projects that either absorbs what is put in the air or creates less than it would have elsewhere," says Hirshberg. One project included planting trees in the Northwest wilderness. Growing trees trap CO_2 so that Stonyfield Farm's emissions are offset, making its production zero. Other projects Stonyfield has invested in include a coal mine methane recovery project in Ohio and a home building project in China that constructs energy efficient straw bale housing that reduces household coal use by up to 90 percent.

Nancy Hirshberg says that when Stonyfield first looked into a CO_2 reduction plan she was surprised to learn that other companies, particularly large corporations, had not already put similar programs into place. As a result, the company created a booklet *Reversing Global Warming: Offsetting Carbon Dioxide Emissions* that is available to other companies on its web site. "We now get calls from companies throughout the country and the world. We hope other companies can take advantage of all of our research and development," she says.

A marketing mission

Another one of Stonyfield Farm's missions is to educate consumers on key issues and steps everyone can make toward a healthy planet. These efforts include its educational lid program, advertising campaigns, educational programs geared toward children and a web site that is as much a learning center as it is a promotional tool for company products.

One key is an ongoing program in which the lids of its six- and eight-ounce containers carry messages that focus on environmental and social issues. Every few months, Stonyfield prints a "call to action" on up to two million of its yogurt lids, bearing messages on everything from global warming to the importance of properly inflated tires to handgun control.

In mid-2001, Stonyfield's lids said: Wake Up Washington. Tell the hill not to drill. Choosing arctic drilling, fossil fuels and nuclear power over energy efficiency leaves only a legacy of waste and a warming world.

Another one read: Wake Up Washington. Did you know increasing U.S. auto efficiency by only 3mpg would save more fuel than will be procured from drilling in the Arctic National Wildlife Refuge? Tell Washington the only real refuge for our children is energy conservation.

Referring customers to its web site, Stonyfield provides detailed information on such issues. There, it notes that Washington should increase federally mandated efficiency standards for automobiles and light trucks, as well as household appliances. In addition, it promotes higher investments in cleaner and more efficient fuels in order to increase the country's dependence on oil. "The U.S. receives more energy in the form of sunlight in forty minutes than from all fossil fuels we burn in a year. Imagine if our government subsidized solar development instead of oil development," it says.

Another lid noted: "We support inflation. If all Americans inflated their cars correctly, two million gallons of gas could be saved every day." As customers were eating the yogurt with these lids, Stonyfield hosted Tire Inflation Stations in cities across the U.S. There, commuters got their tires checked, free of charge, and received information on energy efficiency, and were entered to win an energy efficient refrigerator full of Stonyfield yogurt. Afterward, Lori Handrahan, a congressional candidate in Maine, urged residents there to follow suit, and even encouraged the state's governor to establish a day for tire inflation in order to "collectively demonstrate our solidarity to fuel sustainability by inflating tires."

When the lid's strong advocacy stances cross over to non-environmental issues, Stonyfield has experienced backlash. Most notable was its lid program in the summer of 1995, when the company issued a yogurt container lid that promoted Stop Handgun Violence, a Massachusetts-based gun safety group founded by a group of businessmen. As the containers were hitting store shelves, Stonyfield was besieged by irate phone calls from both customers and store buyers. The buyers felt that Stonyfield had crossed the line by turning the supermarket into a platform for controversial viewpoints. One chain threatened to pull the Stonyfield products with the lids from all of its stores.

Since then, the company has primarily focused its lid program on environmental issues. In one, the top of the lids said, "Congress, have you flipped your lids?" Underneath, the copy encouraged consumers to mail the lids to Congress with a letter stating, "I don't support cuts in environmental funding." Stonyfield reports that during the one-month campaign, thirty-five thousand lids reached Congress.

It was only recently that Stonyfield entered the paid advertising arena. For years, the company had relied totally on word-of-mouth and an extensive public relations campaign to promote its brand. Yet, Hirshberg came up with the notion of "advitism," a medium that combines advertising and activism. Using celebrities who are also environmental advocates such as Kerry Kennedy Cuomo, Trudie Styler, actress and wife of Sting, and Olivia Newton John and Kelly Preston, the ads promoted both environmentalism and the company's products. The one of Styler, for instance, shows a photo of her against a rainforest backdrop. The copy notes that Styler is committed to: "Protecting the rain forest and the people who live there. A sustainable environment. Healthy living through mind, body and soul. Organic gardening. Organic Luscious Lemon Yogurt. My family. Business run by people who care." The small print below notes that no fee was paid to the subjects and that a contribution was made to their non-profit environmental causes.

Momentary missteps

To say that Stonyfield Farm was, from the beginning, a successful and viable company would be like lauding a twenty-year veteran actress on the night of her first Oscar as an "overnight success." With the benefit of hindsight and distance from reality, Hirshberg recounts several situations he wished he had handled differently.

First was the 1987 decision to partner with a co-packer in western Massachusetts to help make its product. "Samuel and I had known the owner for years, considered him a friend, but didn't conduct the due process any business person should adhere to," says Hirshberg later. "When the co-packer went under, he nearly took us with him. We lost a quick $400,000 in one week in October, and then $20,000 a week for the next fifty weeks due to that deal going sour on us. It nearly cost us the business."

Another costly blunder occurred in the mid-1990s, when Stonyfield invested $300,000 to build a plant in St. Petersburg, Russia. Hirshberg thought this new venture could prove to be an economical entry into Europe. He admits today that the company hadn't explored all of the hardships it was bound to face, including corruption, extortion and crime, all common business traits in the former Soviet Union at the time. Yet, Hirshberg, not wanting to give up, continued to try to work through the problems. After a $650,000 loss, as well as a reduction of focus and time, Stonyfield pulled out.

Finally, Hirshberg concedes he wishes they sold far less of the company's ownership as early and as often as they did. "We launched the business with less than $500. As we grew, I was in a position of complete desperation where I needed every nickel I could get. I could have taken steps that would have resulted in fewer losses and, therefore, less needed investment," he says. "I would not have so readily thrown money at problems because I am much more aware of the consequences today. If I had one hundred fifty shareholders versus the three hundred we did, there would have been other ways of meeting the obligations besides selling off a portion of the business."

As satisfied as he is with the recent deal with Group Danone, Hirshberg believes it will be a couple of years before he will know if "great things will happen, or if it will be a complete disaster. There's a whole pendulum of possibilities."

However, he believes the unique deal he shaped with Group Danone will prove to be a model that other entrepreneurs faced with the need to pay back their investors can follow. "My timing was good in that I was able to learn from other businesses in similar situations that chose other routes," says Hirshberg. "I am now freed of the financial demands and looking for a solution that consumed my life for the past seven years." With the deal set, Hirshberg is happy he can focus his considerable energies on the business. This includes converting all of its products to organic, reaching $100 million in sales, further reducing its packaging, and minimizing the ecological footprint of the company.

With its continued commitment to supporting family farmers and to creating healthy products, Stonyfield is in a strong position to grow, prosper and to continue to spread its goodwill well into the twenty-first century.

Chapter Seven

Twenty-First Century Teatime

Company Name: Celestial Seasonings
Primary Business: Maker of specialty teas and herbal products
Type of Company: Subsidiary of The Hain Celestial Group Inc.
Headquarters: Melville, New York; **Main Offices:** Boulder, Colorado
Number of Employees: 251
Chairman of the Board, President and Chief Executive Officer: Irwin D. Simon;
Founders: Mo Siegel, Wyck Hay, John Hay
Year Founded: 1970
Web site: http://www.celestialseasonings.com/

Mission Statement

To create and sell healthful, naturally oriented products that nurture people's bodies and uplift their souls. Our products must be:

- *superior in quality*
- *of good value*

- *beautifully artistic*
- *philosophically inspiring.*

Our role is to play an active part in making this world a better place by unselfishly serving the public. We can have a significant impact on making peoples' lives happier and healthier through their use of our products.

For observers of Celestial Seasonings and its peripatetic co-founder Mo Siegel, it was deja vu all over again.

In the early 1990s, Siegel agreed to cut short a retirement from Celestial Seasonings after only five years. His mission: to help the leading natural and specialty tea producer in North America recover from its ill-fated acquisition by a larger food company. Then, shortly after the turn of the millenium, Siegel was asked to end one more attempt to step away from Celestial—this time after just three years. His mission: to help the business he founded make its merger with another food company a success.

The basic goals were the same. The specifics could not have been more different.

In 1991, the leveraged buy-out that Celestial engineered to free itself from its mismatched relationship with Kraft Foods was seriously aggravating an ongoing cash-flow problem. Fallout from the unfortunate deal also weighed heavily on morale at the firm's facilities in the shadow of the Colorado Rockies. Siegel—who once tramped through those very hills on herb-picking expeditions before sewing tea bags, filling boxes, and hand-delivering the finished product to local health-food stores—had stepped down as president and CEO several years earlier because he was simply burned out. When those left minding the store sought his help in regaining its footing, he enthusiastically jumped back in for a few years before once again bowing out.

And then in 2001, the call went out again. Celestial had merged the year before with Hain Food Group, and leaders in the newly combined $550 million entity—rechristened The Hain Celestial Group—wanted Siegel's day-to-day help once more. Some less-than-successful attempts at diversification, a couple of disappointing licensing deals, and an increasingly competitive landscape had all combined to stymie Celestial's potential in the final years of the twentieth century. The prodigal Siegel's second comeback was, as before, designed to push a drifting ship back on course. Also, as before, its mere announcement was enough to generate tremendous excitement among the company's stakeholders.

Such reaction, of course, was hardly surprising to anyone who followed Siegel or his company. Although successful by most measures almost from its inception, the tea maker seemed to periodically reach a critical juncture that practically cried out for Siegel to step in and set things right. Passionate consumer loyalty consistently made it the top brand of its kind—"a $45 million company back then, with the public image of one that is ten times larger," recalls a former board member from his days as a director. And dozens of its herb, green, black, organic, wellness and Maté teas, all distinctly packaged and emblazoned with catchy names like Sleepytime and Red Zinger, could be found in grocery outlets and health-food stores around the world. Despite more than doubling annual sales during the 1990s to approximately $110 million, however, Celestial once again reached out to the man who had been its driving force since 1970.

Siegel's reappearance the first time was required to prod Celestial forward after the end to its tumultuous relationship with Kraft, a union consummated with great optimism in 1984—but which proved much more disastrous, and far more expensive, than anyone dared imagine until it was finally dissolved four years later. When Mo returned then, the enthusiasm, risk-taking, and seat-of-the-pants decision-making that long had marked the company as an iconoclastic beacon also returned with its well-known founder. Everyone from tea baggers to Siegel himself could feel it.

"The LBO has been hard on the company. It made us private, but it stung," the soft-spoken Siegel said a few months after ending that first retirement. "Now we're going to bring about some pretty dramatic changes. We're going to introduce a plethora of new products. We're going to redo our boxes and upgrade our art. We're going to be better."

Combining a sincere people-oriented countercultural heritage with an energetic all-business approach, Siegel seemed exactly the right sort of person for the job. He had always been a thoughtful hands-on manager who immersed himself in everything from tea recipes to packaging artwork to advertising copy, and that approach hadn't changed. His genuine commitment to both the company and its products never allowed for anything less.

Siegel's direction was clear upon that first return, but he lacked the wherewithal to achieve his goals. In order to build the internal resources necessary to boost its external reach, he decided Celestial had to go public—a move it considered, but couldn't pull off, several years earlier. But while the company's triumphant emergence on the NASDAQ exchange this time did provide critical capital and increase public visibility, it also wound up at least partly responsible for Siegel's stepping down a second time. Preparing to bow out of the roles of president and chief executive officer again in 1997, he acknowledged that meeting the quarterly demands of analysts and outside investors had been much more of an ordeal than he previously imagined.

But Siegel couldn't stay away very long that time, either. Shortly after Hain, the New York-based distributor of some of the biggest brands in the health-food business, merged with Celestial in a $390 million stock swap, he agreed to rejoin the newly combined firm as its second-in-command. At fifty-two, Siegel would answer only to his new partner's chairman, president and chief executive officer, Irwin D. Simon. As passionate as ever about his business, its people and its products, Siegel was excited about being back in the chair he had occupied for most of the past three decades.

After a relatively short return stint, however, Siegel again could not sit still and in September 2002 he retired for a third time. According to the company, this exit was planned so he could fulfill another longtime dream: to finish hiking the last set of fourteen thousand-foot Colorado mountains he has yet to climb.

"We will miss Mo Siegel," Simon wrote in the company's 2002 Annual Report. "Mo returned to Celestial Seasonings two years ago after we concluded our merger, when I saw the need to have his experience, knowledge and wisdom to help us in the transition. Mo has accomplished what he and I set as our objectives, and Mo now moves on, as he puts it so aptly, to new adventures. All of us at Hain Celestial thank Mo for all that he has accomplished, and wish him the very best in the future."

Is he gone for good this time? Probably. But only time will tell.

Cup of tea?

When visitors arrive at Celestial's Boulder, Colorado offices, everyone asks if they'd like some tea. Fancy coffees, bottled waters, fruit juices and soda pop may be available but they are seldom mentioned. Here, instead, it is Roastaroma or Chamomile? Tangerine Orange Zinger or Cinnamon Apple Spice? Peppermint or English Breakfast? Distinctive flavors and distinctive teas, all poured with pride and enjoyed across the board.

Barney Feinblum, a one-time vice-president of finance tapped to run the company following Siegel's initial departure, was no exception. In most respects, he was typical of Celestial's workforce. Hired in 1976, when he was twenty-eight, Feinblum always favored the kind of casual outdoors clothing that was chosen attire for almost everyone at Celestial—except, that is, for

Mo Siegel, who in the old days was usually the only one in the entire building with a necktie. Feinblum's appearance and quickness with the tea kettle could be somewhat deceiving, however. As president and CEO, he was responsible for keeping the company on track during its brief but unhappy alliance with Kraft. It was a responsibility he took very seriously.

"Business has to reflect the values of society," Feinblum commented during his years in the top spots. "You don't have to be a dirtball to succeed."

Feinblum, a native of New York, chose to live in the Rocky Mountain West when he was studying for an MBA at the University of Colorado. While working later for the Denver-based Samsonite Corporation, he was offered a job up the Boulder Turnpike as production manager at Celestial. Although the position paid just $225 a week—two-thirds of his salary at the luggage maker—Feinblum jumped at the chance to work for a firm that had no dress codes, no reserved parking spaces, and no artificial symbols of status or class.

When Feinblum arrived, Celestial instead reflected the values imbued by Siegel, a Colorado native who spent much of his company's early days picking wild herbs in the mountains around Aspen with his friend Wyck Hay. With help from various friends and relatives, the two gathered enough to produce five hundred pounds of their inaugural product: Mo's 36 Herb tea. Moving their base of operations to Boulder, they packaged their herbs in ten thousand hand-sewn muslin tea bags, boxed it all up, and sold it successfully through Boulder health-food stores.

Hay's brother John joined the company in 1971, and he and Siegel became co-presidents. They capitalized their enterprise with $800 realized from the sale of a Datsun 240Z, and established their first real production facility in an old barn outside of town. Owing to his personality and flair, Siegel took up Celestial's public relations, operations, and marketing arms and quickly became the company's most visible public figure. John Hay assumed responsibility for sales and finance, performing competently in the background. Wyck Hay took over Celestial's art and advertising division, and ran it until he left the firm in 1976.

As herbal teas began catching the fancy of Americans, Celestial positioned itself on the industry's cutting edge. Improved distribution put its products in stores throughout Colorado and New Mexico, and then up and down the East Coast. The partners stopped picking herbs themselves and pioneered a development-and-importation network in locales like Guatemala and China. Celestial committed to using only the highest-quality products and began working with growers around the world to ensure that its supplies of exotic ingredients, such as hibiscus flowers and lemon grass, remained both consistent and up to its exacting standards.

"The Celestial name is known worldwide for high integrity and trust," says Kay Wright, the company's Director of Botanical Purchasing. For more than two decades Wright has traveled the globe for Celestial to oversee production, meet with farmers to personally explain the company's philosophies, and ensure that crops meet its needs. Along the way, she has also helped the company offer dependable work and teach natural crop management techniques to Third and Fourth World growers in thirty-five countries. "The growers call us picky and fussy, but they know that if they produce a quality product, we'll stick with them. They trust us," she adds, "and they want to work with us."

Domestic employees always felt the same way, and young people with all sorts of backgrounds, interest, talent and education flocked to the rapidly expanding tea maker during the 1970s. Once there they found a benevolent employer who really cared for their needs. Free family-style hot lunches were served daily, everyone was presented with bonus checks on their birthdays, and a stock-ownership plan gave all a stake in the company. In addition, Celestial offered rapid advancement opportunities that were gobbled up by the very competent (and often very overqualified) workers in the Denver-Boulder area. Wright, for instance, held degrees in anthropology and English when she was hired in 1975 to straighten files. A year later she became responsible for buying domestic herbs. When the firm's chief herb buyer resigned shortly after, she moved into one of Celestial's key jobs. She still holds it more than a quarter-century later.

Consumers and the environment were treated in much the same way. All-natural ingredients, grown without pesticides, always comprised the entire formulation for everything Celestial produced. Wasteful packaging components—such as individual foil envelopes, strings, tags and staples—were never found on any of its products. Even unrelated activities that matched the company's overall vision were promoted to the public. The primary example was cycling, which got its first significant U.S. race in 1975 when the firm created the renowned Red Zinger Bicycle Classic. That event no longer exists, but the tradition continues today: the company is now the lead sponsor for the Bolder Boulder, Colorado's premier foot race.

Barney Feinblum was one of the many young workers initially attracted by this staunch commitment to corporate responsibility, personal growth, and employee camaraderie. When Celestial finally took off in both name recognition and sales he was also among those who took off with it—and later among those who worked to ensure that it remained the kind of place that people like him would want to work.

"The family feeling keeps people here," agreed an employee named Kathy a few years after the Kraft debacle. Kathy was initially hired to brew tea, part-time, for consumer testing panels; six years later, as part of the Consumer Services Division, she was overseeing the personalized replies that are sent to any correspondent who takes the time to contact the company. (Those days it was twenty-three thousand phone calls and letters a year; today, with the addition of emails, the annual count has risen to roughly eighty thousand.) "Everyone is treated fairly—employees and customers," she says. "Without them, we wouldn't have a company."

That tenet, more than anything, was the primary reason the ill-fated relationship with Kraft "forever changed the history of this company," as Mo Siegel says today.

The cheese stands alone

Business-wise, Siegel initially felt very good about the deal that put Celestial under the Kraft Foods umbrella. Personally, he liked it because he was frankly tiring of the enterprise that had by then totally consumed about half his adult life. He honestly felt it was time for both him and his enterprise to move on, and this was the best way to do it. "I started this company when I was twenty," he explained, "and I just had enough."

Since the late 1970s, Siegel had recognized that his firm needed a fiscal transfusion as well. Supermarkets were stocking its teas by then—taking them mainstream and away from the exclusive domain of the health-food stores that first championed them—but rising sales were not matched by corresponding increases in profits. To compound matters, the cyclical nature of the hot-tea business, in which three-quarters of all products are consumed during the colder months, was hammering the firm's resources every summer. A ten-member strategic planning team, created by Siegel and including Feinblum, searched desperately for ways to end the company's persistent inability to get on its financial feet and fund infrastructure improvements that would take it to the next level.

The idea of a buyout was never really broached until General Mills suddenly offered to purchase Celestial for $8.3 million in 1979. Feinblum, then in charge of finance, convinced his colleagues to first explore other options like a proposed public stock offering (which failed before getting off the ground). Around that time co-presidents Siegel and Hay were also finding that they no longer could work effectively together, although they remained close friends. So when the two became acquainted with H. Keith Ridgway—a senior Kraft executive regularly in Boulder to visit a son who was living there—they all began exploring ways to combine their enterprises that would allow Celestial to grow and its founders to gracefully exit. The buyout offer came soon after.

The deal, as deals always do, took much longer to consummate than anyone suspected. But by the time Celestial finally became a part of Kraft's Retail Food Group in July of 1984, the price tag had also grown far beyond original expectations: Kraft eventually paid a reported $40 million for the tea maker, and shelled out $4 million more to purchase employee stock. When every worker received a check equal to approximately one year's salary, most of them thought, like Siegel, that the match was made in heaven.

At first, it appeared as if this were true. In addition to the sorely needed capital that Celestial required to expand and increase efficiency, Kraft provided market-research expertise and doubled its new acquisition's annual advertising budget to $4 million. Soon, Celestial also doubled its share of the booming herbal tea market and moved ahead of all competitors.

Almost as quickly, however, there were signs of trouble. Kraft did push the development of new products as it promised, but saddled them with bland names like Celestial Seasonings Herb & Spice Cooking Blend that alienated employees and consumers accustomed to teas called Red Zinger and Morning Thunder. The new parent company also moved more slowly and cautiously in research and development than Celestial had hoped, reining in the aggressive nature that marked its culture from day one.

"It was frustrating because we couldn't implement changes fast enough and Kraft didn't understand why we had to make changes that we knew we had to make," noted a botanist named Trish hired two years before the acquisition. "Mixing up a blend of tea is nothing like making mayonnaise," she continued. "Mayonnaise has a recipe, and you use exactly the same ingredients each time. But botanical ingredients change every single time you order them because of different climactic influences. Batches have to be adjusted every time. You have to be flexible, and Kraft wasn't."

Feinblum, one of the few at Celestial who publicly opposed the deal from the outset, watched with alarm as his unique, innovative company began to change. Kraft was building market share, to be sure, but it was spending way too much on ill-conceived spin-off ventures like salad dressings and spices, none of which ever emerged from the test phase. It was also pouring millions of dollars into a national ad campaign featuring television actress Mariette Hartley; these commercials got Celestial's name in front of the public, all right, but they also turned off many longtime customers who bristled at the company's new middle-of-the-road direction.

Siegel remained with Celestial under Kraft until 1986, when he announced he was retiring at age thirty-six to pursue philanthropic ventures and travel the world. He named Feinblum his successor and was at first turned down flat. Feinblum later said he would rather open a sprout farm than work for a Fortune 500 company, but he eventually accepted the offer and became Celestial's new president and CEO.

Before long, Feinblum would be wishing he had chosen the sprout farm. Ridgway, the Kraft executive who initially befriended Siegel and Hay, retired suddenly. In his absence, Kraft demanded even more accounting and tighter control. Its management also proposed drug testing at the Boulder plant, which Feinblum and others there vehemently opposed on principle until the issue was dropped. But the final straw came when the division in which Celestial had been placed fell behind in its performance and Kraft shifted the tea business to yet another corporate arm—where it became even more isolated, and more ripe for meddling by absentee managers.

By mid-1987, Feinblum was actively exploring ways to get the company back from Kraft. He first presented the idea of a leveraged buyout, or LBO, to the parent firm that fall, offering around $40 million to seal the deal. Kraft told him the tea maker wasn't for sale, and then turned around and announced it was selling the Boulder firm after all: but to Thomas J. Lipton Inc. When word got out that Celestial might now be owned by an archrival—and rumors spread that its operations would subsequently be moved from Colorado to New Jersey—the frustration turned to anger. This same emotion also erupted across the country in the Connecticut offices of R.C. Bigelow Inc., which produced a competing line of specialty teas called Constant Comment. Claiming the Celestial-Lipton deal would create a company controlling more than 80 percent of the market, it brought suit in 1988 to block the proposed sale. The U.S. Court of Appeals in its home state agreed, and enjoined the merger.

By this time, Kraft had become the subject of an unsolicited takeover bid itself from Philip Morris Companies (now the Altria Group). Suddenly more motivated to make some sort of deal that would shed its Celestial diversion, officials there invited Feinblum to make a new offer. Together with Vestar Capital Partners, a New York-based investment firm, he put a $60 million LBO proposal on the table. This time the deal was quickly approved, and on November 2, 1988, Celestial Seasonings was freed from Kraft's control. People at the Boulder plant took to calling that their "Independence Day."

A new beginning

Despite the financial hardships associated with the LBO, Celestial immediately set about restoring its original direction. One of its first acts was to create a board of directors and invite Siegel to join. (He accepted.) A second major step was to break ground for a new corporate headquarters on the outskirts of its home city. The sprawling two-story plant-and-office complex that opened in 1990 on those ninety-one acres consolidated all operations that had previously been based in several different Boulder-area buildings. And, as a place where all of the tea maker's office and factory workers could finally come together physically, it also symbolized the break with Kraft more graphically than anything else that transpired after the buyback.

The final piece fell into place the next summer, when Siegel agreed to take over daily management responsibilities once more.

Celestial's family atmosphere, a mainstay at the company from the beginning, had been one of the first casualties of the Kraft acquisition. Now, with the business again under Siegel's direction, the one-time parent firm's color-coded identification badges and assigned parking spaces were history. In their place was a modern, friendly, unified workplace with a spacious dining room in which everyone from a temporary receptionist to Siegel himself regularly took their midday meals. The food wasn't free like in the old days, but it was subsidized from the start to the tune of about $75,000 a year. (This practice continues today, although the dollar amount is no longer made public.)

An open-door policy which promoted private dialogue between employees and managers was also encouraged once more, and often resulted in concrete change. John Odbert, a former vice-president of human relations and long-term consultant to the firm, recalls the time a janitor suggested that owning its own trucks—rather than hiring common carriers to move herbs in from the coasts and finished teas out from the plant—would save the company money. His supervisors listened carefully and agreed. They then bought the vehicles, hired the drivers, and placed the janitor in charge of the new department. "For a lot of people," Odbert notes, "this has been a real shot in the arm, career-wise."

Such thinking additionally led to the development of an impressive internal environmental program, originally coordinated by an employee committee formed just before Earth Day 1989. To this day it still incorporates the regular recycling of products used in tea production (like paper, aluminum, glass, cardboard and burlap). In addition, it calls for the purchase of recycled office paper products whenever possible, is responsible for the installation of personal recycling bins beside most workstations, and has brought about the elimination of all cardboard and plastic from the cafeteria.

Similarly, Celestial's consumer products have always been made with predominantly recycled and good-for-the-earth materials. The company also uses as little packaging as possible, and its unique "pillow" tea bag design forgoes unnecessary fixtures that would otherwise be introduced into the waste stream. Its tea bag paper is comprised of a blend of chlorine-free fibers, and everything is packaged in cardboard boxes made of 100 percent recycled paperboard that is constructed from at least 35 percent post-consumer waste material. All of this represents quite an environmental statement, considering the company now produces eight million tea bags each day during its peak seasons.

Celestial retains its commitment to the neighboring community through ongoing efforts like Adopt A Road, a local volunteer program that encourages all employees (along with their family and friends) to clean up a stretch of land on either side of a nearby highway every year around Earth Day. It also continues its quietly effective Best Buddy Bear program, which was initiated in the mid-1980s to provide every police officer, firefighter and paramedic in Colorado with a Sleepytime teddy bear to help them comfort any traumatized youngsters they encounter in their work.

"Of the things we've done, that is what we're most proud of," Feinblum once said of the ongoing program that remains mostly unknown except to those who participate in it or benefit from it. "Like all of the extra efforts we make, we did it because we thought it was a good thing to do," he continued. "Our profit benefit is nonexistent, and even if it costs us a little money, so what? We've always tried to be good corporate citizens."

Feinblum relinquished the top spots at Celestial upon Siegel's first return and assumed the position of COO until leaving the firm a few years later. He never did start that sprout farm, but came awfully close—running the nearby Horizon Organic Dairy until he retired in 2000.

This Hain's for you

In 1997 Siegel decided that he no longer wanted to work more than thirty hours a week, and passed on the responsibilities of Celestial's president and chief executive officer to Stephen Hughes (while retaining the title and duties of chairman). Formerly a marketing executive with ConAgra's Healthy Choice and Tropicana brands, Hughes took over daily management tasks at the company and was one of the first of several outside food-industry professionals to be elevated to positions of prominence at Celestial over the next few years. With a mandate to push Celestial beyond its core—but self-limiting—hot-tea business, Hughes began looking for ways to leverage its considerable consumer loyalty in new areas. One of the first was the burgeoning market for nutritional supplements, where herbal blends and extracts like St. John's Wort could be branded with the popular Celestial name.

A public company then for about four years, Celestial's new leadership continued seeking innovative ways to deliver shareholder value while remaining as true as possible to the firm's roots. Efforts at expanding into the booming pre-packaged ice-tea market, with big-name partners like Perrier, failed miserably a few years earlier. An attempt to market herbal throat lozenges, in a licensing deal with Warner-Lambert, was only a moderate success.

Under Hughes, a television-and-print ad campaign for Sleepytime tea, still one of its best-known and best-selling products, was also launched in 1998 to try and return some sizzle to Celestial's stagnant hot-tea sales. By the following year, though, it was apparent that this would not be enough. Celestial's stock price dropped 40 percent as these marketing moves and other diversification attempts failed to produce significant bottom-line results. Even though the company now claimed a full one-third of the $305 million specialty tea market in the U.S., and eighty thousand people a year were trekking to its Boulder factory for a tour and a taste-test, observers continued to see Celestial as a potentially huge brand hobbled with consistently mediocre performance.

"Overall, Celestial is a successful, viable company with a very strong brand franchise," noted Matthew Patsky, an investment analyst with Adams, Harkness & Hill in Boston who focuses on the natural food and beverage industry. "But we see them as a dominant player in a business that isn't growing. That's problematic."

Irwin Simon, founder and head of the Hain Food Group, saw things in much the same way. About a decade younger than Siegel, Simon shares the personal drive and professional passion of Celestial's co-founder but has built his career in an entirely different way. A native of Glace Bay, Canada, he moved to New York in 1985 and set his business life in motion with stints at Haagen-Dazs and Slim-Fast. There, he realized that many consumers would reach for natural, healthy, specialty foods if given the proper selection. He began assembling the portfolio of companies that would become the Hain Celestial Group in 1993, when he took out a second mortgage on his home to purchase a kosher frozen-foods business. After taking it public he expanded by seeking out similar companies that, like Celestial, were leading their markets (or close to it) even though they were dramatically under-performing.

"I'm looking for strong brands that are mismanaged or misfocused, and brands that I can take to the next level," Simon says from recently relocated company headquarters in Melville, N.Y. "I thought Celestial was a billion-dollar brand sitting in a $100 million business."

Simon kept an eye out for just this type of company after his first acquisition, eventually gathering a diverse assortment of related brands that could capitalize on critical mass and economies of scale to reach new and bigger audiences. After purchasing what became the firm's namesake, the fifty-year-old Hain Pure Foods (crackers, cookies, oils, condiments), he acquired a litany of brands like Arrowhead Mills (cereals, grains), Westsoy (soy-based drinks), Westbrae Natural (vegetarian meals), Nile Spice (soup cups), Earth's Best (baby food), Health

Valley (soups, baked products, cereals), Terra Chips (potato and vegetable chips) and Weight Watchers (dry and refrigerated diet products). In all, more than two dozen of these natural and organic, medically directed (sugar-free, dairy-free, low-salt) and weight management companies offering some fifteen hundred items would end up under Simon's management. By centralizing many of their operations, implementing uniform quality controls, and initiating integrated marketing campaigns, the one-time $2 million business has grown nearly twenty-five-fold and now employs some two thousand people across North America.

Not long after *BusinessWeek* named Simon one of the nation's top entrepreneurs and Ernst & Young feted him as Entrepreneur of the Year, he decided that Celestial Seasonings had "conformity with all our brands" and would make a perfect fit at Hain. With its tea business continuing to provide the Boulder firm's lone spark—and its foray into the supplement market "almost bankrupting it," Simon says—Hain reached out with a proposition.

"I always call it a merger," he notes. "Celestial had been around for thirty years, Hain for eight. Celestial really brought Hain a lot of credibility. We've gained tremendously from the deal."

Shareholders in both companies saw the same benefits, and approved the merger on May 30, 2000. Hain issued 10.3 million shares of common stock and exchanged 1.265 shares of it for each outstanding Celestial share. The company was renamed, but continued trading under the HAIN symbol on the NASDAQ exchange. (Celestial's CTEA symbol was retired.) And then it once again convinced the tea maker's founder to get back into the everyday game.

"Mo Siegel is the Billy Martin of tea," Simon says now with a chuckle, referring to the iconic New York Yankees manager who also was known for periodic retirements and repeated comebacks.

Fits to a 'T'

In the spring of 2002, Siegel had just returned to Colorado from a Hain Celestial sales meeting in New York, where he once again marveled at the array of healthful natural products that his newly combined company had to offer. As much as anything, he found his connection to such breadth to be the biggest and most positive change to hit his business since the merger.

"There were so many products and ideas in so many categories. Soy milk, chips, lots of stuff," Siegel says. "And I was thinking of when I was twenty or twenty-one years old, and I drove from Colorado to Connecticut to sell my tea. It was my first real sales trip." He ran into the CEO of General Foods along the way, he recalls, and told him about Celestial while showing him the tea. "He said something like, 'This is silly, your tea idea. You need to go to a real company; come to General Foods.' He also said that within ten years all food would be produced in test tubes. Better living through chemistry," Siegel continues with a gentle laugh. "I was encouraged. If that's what people like him were thinking—save the world with Tang—we were going to be okay. And we're now the closest thing there is to being the General Foods of natural foods."

Despite the significantly larger size of its new partner—Hain's net sales were $205.9 million the year before the merger, Celestial's were $109.9 million—the tea maker's distinctive culture would not be absorbed in this deal as was destined under Kraft. Simon recognized the value that developed over three decades, he explains, and also understood that there were huge differences between Boulder and Long Island that could not be eradicated with the mere issuance of a memo.

"So I stepped back," he says. "Celestial had two hundred fifty people in Boulder and another company that acquired it might have bulldozed the whole thing and moved everyone to New York. But that would have taken away the uniqueness of Celestial that we were seeking."

By not instantly integrating everything, as Hain usually does whenever adding a new company to its stable, Celestial was encouraged to keep its focus. Accordingly, significant benefits from the deal immediately began to flow both ways. The whole firm, for instance, could now leverage Celestial's superior penetration in traditional grocery outlets to boost the exposure of the many smaller Hain products that were still predominantly distributed through health food stores. Additionally, Celestial's proven infrastructure and seasoned personnel could now be utilized by the larger company while packaging obligations for several Hain Celestial brands and various corporate computer and purchasing responsibilities could be shifted to Boulder. The new partner's key role was further underscored when Hain Celestial's new ten-person board of directors was configured to make way for three representatives from Boulder including Siegel; this, in turn, was indicative of the fact that Celestial officials now owned 38 percent of the parent company's stock.

While the tea maker's accounting functions were correspondingly moved to New York, the addition of several new company-wide duties and the decision to let Celestial be Celestial has meant that the Colorado facility was not downsized. Several top managers did exit as could be expected after the merger, however, and numerous changes aimed at streamlining operations and improving efficiencies were implemented. Among the first of these was a program to reduce the amount of tea inventory in the hands of distributors; another was the immediate end to production of money-losing thirty-count supplement packages in favor of a more profitable sixty-count size. New core products like Lemon Zinger Green Tea and Black Cherry Berry were also added to the mainstay line, as were catchy seasonal varieties such as Gingerbread Spice Holiday Herb Tea.

Simon's plan to acquire compatible under-performing companies with promise continues to bring newcomers to the Hain Celestial family, as evidenced by the late 2001 addition of Yves Veggie Cuisine (a leading line of meatless, low fat and cholesterol-free products in Canada that is now being expanded into the

U.S.) and the 2002 purchase of European companies Lima (a forty-six-year-old brand of natural/organic packaged foods with more than three hundred products) and Biomarché (whose fresh, organic fruits and vegetables mark a first for Hain Celestial). "Our goal is to build upon the success of our brands to satisfy demand for more healthful foods here and around the globe," the company noted in its Annual Report. And the strategy appears to be paying off: sales in 2001 increased more than 6 percent on a comparative basis over fiscal 2000, and then jumped 15 percent in 2002. For the future, Standard & Poor's has pegged the firm's growth rate for the next five years at 17 percent—compared to just 9 percent for its industry overall.

Things have changed a great deal at Hain in the ten years since Simon began assembling his vision of the biggest natural foods company in the world. They have changed even more at Celestial, over those ten years and the twenty that preceded it, as the firm bounced between management teams and private and public ownership more times than most high-profile success stories. But a success story it seems to be, flowering from the humblest of beginnings to become a major part of the goliath of its industry.

That said, observers couldn't help but wonder just how long Mo Siegel would stick around this time before he decided to pull back once again—a question that proved strangely prophetic when he retired for a third time in 2002.

"I've spent most of my life in this company," he said reflectively, once back in the familiar territory of his Boulder office after that Eastern trip for the Hain Celestial sales meeting just a short time earlier. "You never know."

Chapter Eight

Baking, Building and Benefiting

Company Name: Greyston Bakery
Primary business: Bakery
Type of Business: Private, for-profit part of the umbrella Greyston Foundation
Location: Yonkers, New York
Number of employees: 70
Founder: Bernie Glassman
President of the Bakery: Julius Walls
President of the Foundation: David Sweeney
Year founded: 1982
Web sites: www.greystonbakery.com
www.greyston.org

Mission

Greyston Bakery is a force for personal transformation and community economic renewal. We operate a profitable business, baking high quality gourmet products with a commitment to customer satisfaction. Greyston Bakery provides a supportive work-

place offering employment and opportunity for advancement. Our profits contribute to the community development work of the Greyston Foundation.

Greyston Foundation was created as a new model of community development and inspired by core values of the Buddhist tradition: commitment to a path of personal growth, development of wisdom and compassion, and celebration of the wholeness and interdependence of all life. To heal and enlighten our society by: empowering ourselves and others to lead self-sufficient and productive lives, and working with the rejected parts of society including the rejected parts in ourselves and creating and stewarding healthy institutions which in their very nature are catalysts for individual and community transformation.

More than two hundred fifty people were gathered on a brisk morning in March, 2002, along New York's Hudson River. Representatives of the city of Yonkers, along with bankers, contributors, employees and other supporters of Greyston Bakery, had assembled for the ceremonial groundbreaking of their new, state-of-the-art bakery. Maya Lin, who designed Washington, D.C.'s Vietnam Memorial, created the new facility—a twenty-three thousand-square-foot building that would allow Greyston to increase its workforce and production five-fold.

"Ground-breaking ceremonies are traditionally a day to honor the people who participate in the making of the deal," says Julius Walls, president of Greyston Bakery and chief operating officer of the Greyston Foundation. "Yet, I was there to credit those most responsible for this new building—the employees. It's only because of our staff that bankers, contributors and government agencies were willing to invest close to $10 million into this building. It would not happen if they didn't believe we could continue to perform."

With an atrium and a glass-enclosed mezzanine level allowing visitors to view the production floor, Greyston's new bakery will be far more distinctive than its prior home. Around the corner, where the original bakery had been located since its 1982 founding, the facility was anything but conspicuous. The unassuming building with a rust-colored steel door blended in with other structures in this non-descript industrial section. In fact, if it weren't for its small, hand-carved wooden sign hanging above the doorway, you could easily walk right by without noticing it all.

Once inside the door, however, you immediately knew you were in the right place. Invitingly rich aromas enveloped the front doorway. A pumpkin cheesecake rested on a hallway table. Before you were asked who you were and why you were there, the friendly receptionist invited you to sample a slice of the dessert. After two bites, you were encouraged to give your opinion. Is it too sweet? Would this work well for the holidays? Would a chocolate glaze be overkill?

Before you had been in the clean, efficient production area or up to the third-floor attic that housed cubbyhole-like offices, you were already part of the Greyston team. Everyone's thoughts counted here, and input was actively solicited. It became apparent that this attitude—making everyone involved with Greyston an important ingredient—permeated the company.

Greyston Bakery is a supplier of elaborate cakes and pastries to gourmet shops, department stores and some of New York's most celebrated restaurants. *Zagat Survey* describes Greyston as making "sinful desserts that support saintly causes." Brides flock from throughout the tri-state area to order one of Greyston's opulent wedding cakes. And though the facility was always relatively modest, it was capable of taking on huge jobs. Greyston recently produced a five-tier cake and ten smaller ones that were served to more than eighty-three hundred guests at Lincoln Center. Six pastry chefs assembled and decorated the cakes with ingredients that included two hundred twenty-five pounds of butter, ninety dozen eggs, and three hundred pounds of chocolate.

But the product that continually keeps the ovens warm and the production floor purring is brownies. Both ice cream and frozen yogurt companies buy Greyston's brownies to use in their products, including Ben & Jerry's, Cumberland Farms, Imagine Foods and Stonyfield Farm. In fact, Greyston's brownies are featured in three of Ben & Jerry's top ten sellers—Chocolate Fudge Brownie, Chocolate Fudge Brownie Yogurt and Two Twisted. Walls hopes to soon start selling the brownies in single-serving sizes, as well.

The current eight thousand-square-foot bakery, named for the solid rock formation quarried in this lower Hudson Valley area, operates twenty-four hours a day, six days a week, and employs seventy people who work in three shifts. Sales grew from less than $1 million in 1989 to almost $4 million in 2002. In addition to the excellence of the company's products (their cheesecake was rated New York City's best by the *Daily News*), Greyston Bakery, with its nonprofit parent, Greyston Foundation, is also rightfully acclaimed for its work to eliminate homelessness and poverty and to help those living with HIV in one of New York's most neglected areas, the southern portion of Westchester County.

The bakery is part of the Greyston Mandala, meaning circle of life, which is a network of for-profit and nonprofit organizations. Greyston Foundation raises funds from the government and various foundations for its network of nonprofit ventures. In addition, it earns money through rent payments, childcare payments and Medicaid reimbursements. These nonprofits include the Greyston Family Inn, which develops and manages renovated apartment buildings for formerly homeless and low-income working families. In the past ten years, the Greyston Foundation has developed $30 million of real estate for 176 units of permanent housing for families and single adults and has plans for another $15 million of projects. In May 2001, it completed a renovation of a downtown building with twenty-eight apartments, four storefronts and a five thousand square-foot ballroom. The building is the home to local artists, and the ballroom, once the site for presidential speeches by Theodore and Franklin Roosevelt, is now an arts center for dance, theatre, music and lectures.

Greyston's reach has gone to help the ailing as well. Greyston Health Services operates the Issan House, a thirty-five-unit housing facility for formerly homeless men and women living with HIV/AIDS. Greyston renovated a former Catholic monastery for this facility, which also includes the Maitri Center, a day health program that provides medical services, counseling and alternative treatment to HIV/AIDS victims. The combined facilities offer a full array of health, rehabilitative, counseling and complementary services to more than 150 people. It is Westchester County's only AIDS adult day health care program.

Greyston is a shining example of how for-profit and not-for-profit companies work together under the same roof to achieve its goals: making money while embracing a social mission. "The bakery was set up as a profitable business to help give it credibility within the Yonkers business community and to instill an entrepreneurial spirit into the entire foundation," said Charles Lief, former president of the Greyston Foundation. "All of our businesses make money, but the bakery is structured as a for-profit. Its profits flow up to the nonprofit parent. It's important to us that all of our programs are self-sufficient in order to ensure their long-term survival." Greyston runs all of its for-profit and nonprofit entities like a business, seeking partnerships as they grow.

Such an operation embodies the holistic approach of both Greyston's current management team and its founder, Bernie Glassman, to business and social work to employ chronically unemployed, house the formerly homeless and provide healthcare to those who most need it. "We provide a circle of activities—a job, a home, counseling, and support—that are a complete method of healing a family," said Glassman, who retired in 1997. Today, Greyston continues to set its foundation on its Buddhist principles while it embraces all of the faiths of its employees and its Yonkers, New York, community. These include the links between self and community, the importance of compassion, and realizing the inter-connectedness of all things.

A way to support

In 1982, as the recently appointed abbot (or leader) of New York's Zen community, Glassman moved his religious group ten miles north of New York City to neighboring Yonkers. In an effort by Glassman and his students to live self-sufficiently rather than depend only on contributions, the group investigated a variety of business opportunities. Earlier, Glassman had lived in Los Angeles, and worked as an aerospace engineer for McDonnell Douglas Aircraft. When he left his position to devote himself to the Zen community, he became involved with a variety of enterprises, including a medical clinic, a publishing house, and a construction company.

"When I came to New York, I was interested in pursuing a business that would be a vehicle for both growth and training, for both us and our community," he said. "Baking seemed ideal because it was labor-intensive." Glassman sent six followers to the successful Tassahara Bakery in San Francisco, famous in the area for its multi-grained, wholesome products. "They provided recipes, trained our people, and gave us great support," he says.

With $320,000 secured from grants and loans, Glassman founded the Greyston Bakery. But the product mix that worked in San Francisco was unsuccessful in New York. The bread-making business in the metro area was very cutthroat, and Greyston couldn't compete with well-established bakeries. In fact, with all of the competition, Greyston's foray into the bread-baking arena nearly bankrupted the burgeoning community.

Luckily, the bakery was also producing gourmet desserts, thanks to the owner of a local Italian bakery who offered his help. Glassman and his students learned the fine art of dessert making and the skill of cake decorating. With this, plus training from the Culinary Institute of America, Glassman and his followers were turning out delicacies like lemon and pecan tarts, chocolate mousse cakes and cheese cakes. Making the highest-quality products has always been the goal. "We use the best possible ingredients," says Greyston Bakery's Walls. "We never bake with premade mixes."

Greyston's reputation as a serious confectioner soon flourished with the gourmet desserts providing a better business opportunity. "Cakes and pastries can be sold to restaurants and specialty shops, directly and through distributors, so this was the better way to go for us," said Glassman.

Neighborhood support

Though Glassman initially founded the bakery to support the Zen community, it soon needed additional employees to help run the business. Because many of the students had volunteered their time and donated food to the local homeless shelters and soup kitchens, they were eager to reach out to the many unemployed people they served. "First, we needed additional good employees," Glassman said. "Second, we felt we could help."

Their original pool of employees consisted of totally inexperienced workers, so it was up to Greyston to teach them the craft of baking. "It was a challenge to think we could take people who had no skills, no job experience, and no affinity toward baking and train them to make gourmet desserts," said Glassman. "I know there were some skeptics, but I never doubted our ability to make it work." A decade later, Greyston still considers its most important role is to employ men and women that many would consider "chronically unemployable."

"We do not hire people to make brownies," says Walls. "Rather, we make brownies and cakes and tarts so that we can hire people." As such, the Greyston Bakery has an open-hiring practice. This idea stems from the view that everyone deserves an opportunity to get a job. "When we have an opening, we give it to the next person available to work that particular time slot," says Walls. There are no background checks and no skills assessment.

Whoever arrives on time gets a shot.

New hires come in and enter the apprentice program, where the initial pay is $5.50 per hour. As they train to become bakery production workers, superintendents evaluate such core areas as attendance, punctuality, attitude and productivity. For every positive evaluation, the apprentice receives a twenty-five-cent pay increase, until they reach $7.50 per hour. If the worker fails three evaluations, he or she is asked to leave Greyston, although they do have the opportunity to appeal. If successful, they join the company's "second chance" program, starting again at the base salary.

"Because we don't attempt to weed out any candidates, we do have a lot of turnover at the apprentice level," admits Walls. "Many people are just not ready to work as much as they would like to." Walls considers a person's potential much more important than his or her past experience. Mark, for instance, was living in a men's shelter and had previously gone through drug therapy to kick a ten-year crack cocaine addiction. When the youthful thirty-six-year-old interviewed for a position as a dough mixer, he didn't think he would get the job since he didn't have any prior experience. Yet, before he knew it, he was donning a baker's cap.

After a year of working on the night shift making brownies, Mark was promoted to a supervisor's position. "I've been here fourteen months, and this is the longest period I've ever held a steady job," he says. "I'm paying my own rent for the first time in my life, and I now have greater responsibility. I got it through a lot of hard work."

It's up to supervisors to identify good workers and then help them evolve within the company. "We develop people here," says Walls. "We give them an opportunity to advance as far as they possibly can."

Walls admits that some of the most successful employees today would never have been given the opportunity at most companies. Their prior situations would have made them far less desirable candidates for a job. "I have two supervisors that, knowing their situations, I initially thought would not succeed," he says. "But they have been successful here because we didn't pre-judge them. We let employees determine their success by their own actions."

Throughout the three-month apprentice program, employees learn for themselves what Greyston is all about and whether or not they want to continue working there. "We want it to be their call, and not ours," says Walls, who says many employees stay about one to two years. In that limited time, employees gain far more than a weekly paycheck. "In that time frame, they have developed a stable work history, which makes it possible to get a job elsewhere," says Walls. "Greyston has a reputation for turning out good and dependable workers, so other employers in the area are eager to hire Greyston workers," he says. These employees have an opportunity to go elsewhere and get other jobs built on the experience from Greyston. "We're well aware that most of our employees never longed to have a career in a bakery," says Walls. In fact, through the Foundation's services, employees are encouraged to analyze both professional and personal goals. "We have to figure out how we can support them," says Walls. "Given our mission, we consider it a success if someone is working here, or leaves here to work somewhere else. It's up to us to create opportunities for employees to pursue here. But it's not right for everyone, so we encourage people to do what is best for them."

Most of Greyston's current seventy employees moved up the ranks by starting in the apprentice program. And there are plenty of impressive success stories. Carmello, head foreman of the day shift and responsible for the intricate pastries, began as a dishwasher. Millie, a single mother of two, was formerly on welfare.

"It's great to see people getting somewhere," said Tom, Greyston's former production manager who now works in the Foundation's technology department. "We have ex-drug addicts and dealers who were in jail. We have people who were homeless and lots of people who never held a job for more than a couple of months. Often, this is their first paycheck. I see people taking responsibility for what's going on in the business and in their own lives."

And it's up to the supervisors to encourage the workers to take charge. "I want to instill in everyone that this is 'their own' bakery. I want to give the bakery away to these people. Sometimes they're not sure they can do this. But it's their ideas, energy and input that make it all happen. We are working to empower people," said Tom.

Moving forward

Over the years, Greyston has adopted more automated production techniques, systems that may be more efficient, but in certain cases requires less manpower—a potential problem given its goal to provide jobs. As a result, the bakery has had to balance its role to employ as many of its neighbors as it can, with the need to be an efficient and competitive production facility. "We have a guiding principle that the bakery will automate when it's fiscally appropriate in order to be competitive and to continue to build the skills of all of our employees," says Walls. Rather than hampering the production process, Greyston focuses on increasing employee levels through an improved sales and marketing effort. In fact, bakery sales have grown by more than 10 percent over each of the past three years.

Indeed, decisions to automate certain processes are made carefully. One recent move to automation occurred when the bakery purchased a semi-automated machine that cut the brownies, something workers previously did manually. "We always did it by hand," explains Walls, noting it was a time-consuming chore. "Now we have a machine that cuts and breaks the brownies apart. Yet, we haven't had to cut employees because of this. Rather, we have grown in sales."

Though just about every white-capped employee at Greyston is a success story, many employees do not work out. "I'd say one in five workers end up being successful," said Tom. Family, money, drug and alcohol problems all contribute to a hired employee's failure. "These people are facing extraordinary conditions. Unfortunately, for many, holding down a forty-hour-a-week job is sometimes too much."

Greyston used to be lenient regarding employee relations. Now, the company has adopted its open hiring practices and expects employees to act professionally and responsibly. "Employees must come to work on time and always be responsible. Obviously, alcohol and drugs are out of the question," said Tom. "It's hard to be firm sometimes, but we have to remember that we are running a business."

It's disappointing to Greyston managers when an employee does not work out. "What's hardest is when a person shows great promise. They have the aptitude, but because of the challenges in their lives, they can't hold jobs," said Tom.

Mark, the newly promoted supervisor, recalls his own attitude toward work before joining Greyston. "When I was on drugs and on the street, I used to look down on people with jobs like this," he says. "I used to think it was much cooler to hang out all day and the only jobs worth having were high paying. Soon I realized how wrong I was. I was strung out on drugs and hadn't worked in years. I got $42.50 every two weeks from welfare. Now I make twenty times that, and I'm proud to say I mix the brownie dough for Ben & Jerry's ice cream."

Wages for employees on the brownie production line start at $7 per hour, and the average now is $7.50. For skilled pastry makers, the average salary is more than $10 per hour. "Part of helping these people is getting them off of welfare and helping them be self sufficient," says Walls. According to the company's Guiding Principles:

> The bakery will empower its employees by compensating them fairly for their effort. While for some employees this salary may not constitute a "living wage," the bakery is committed to working with these individuals to improve their financial self-sufficiency. To this end, the bakery will

work with employees to increase their earning power by assisting them in improving their job readiness and baking skills. The bakery will encourage and support employees who seek outside vocational training, academic advancement, and professional non-bakery-related enrichment. The bakery will also support employees who seek greater self-sufficiency through employment elsewhere.

New challenges

For its first five years, the Greyston Bakery focused on baking fancy tarts and cakes. When Glassman met Ben Cohen of Ben & Jerry's ice cream at a business conference, the two men discussed their personal and professional lives. Soon a friendship blossomed. "Ours is an interesting relationship," said Glassman. "Ben is a business man reaching toward spirituality. And me, I am a spiritual person who is reaching toward business. We meet at the intersection."

This connection eventually resulted in a business deal. Ben & Jerry's asked the bakery to duplicate the recipe for the chewy brownie used in its brownie ice cream so that the ice cream maker wouldn't have to rely solely on their then-current supplier. If successful, they could win a contract worth more than $1 million in business a year.

For weeks, the bakers worked and experimented with all sorts of chocolate variations; finally, in 1989, they were awarded the contract. "It was great getting the business, but it almost did us in," said Glassman with a smile. Today, that contract is worth $4 million a year, or 70 percent of the bakery's business. Eventually, Walls would like to sell its brownies directly to consumers.

From baking to building

With the bakery up and running, the founders of the Greyston Bakery turned its focus to the greatest problem facing the neighborhood: homelessness. Westchester County, north of New York City and home to some of the wealthiest people in the state, also has the highest per capita rate of homelessness in the country: eighteen out of two hundred residents. More than half of the estimated forty-three hundred homeless are in southwest Yonkers, where Greyston Bakery is located. Many are single mothers with children.

"None of the $50 million our government spends to house the homeless goes into permanent housing," said Glassman. "We learned from our work at the shelters that most of the homeless families from this area were being placed in motels all over the county. When we saw the conditions they were living in, we were amazed. The rooms were dirty and roach infested. Then, on the weekends, the families would often be kicked out if the motel thought the rooms could be rented to someone else for a higher rate. Children would have to take the bus for hours to get to school. Often the mothers would keep them at the hotels, fearing they might be kicked out during the day. In our own small way," he says, "we wanted to tackle this issue."

Greyston Family Inn's first foray into housing was its Sixty-eight Warburton Avenue facility. The non-profit bought the apartment complex for $250,000 from grants and then secured a $2.8 million state grant.

Ten years later, Greyston now owns and manages eight renovated buildings housing eighty-nine families and thirty-five individuals. In the spring of 2002, it completed renovation of the Phillipsburgh Hall in downtown Yonkers. Artists and musicians who work in the hall's two thousand square feet of arts space and retail storefronts live in half of the building's twenty-eight units. Greyston also has recently bought four empty lots where it will develop properties for affordable home ownership as well as affordable rental units.

At the initial Warburton Building, which houses eighteen families and Greyston's child care center, visitors are greeted by Joan. She is a middle-aged former homeless woman who, for the prior decade, moved from shelter to shelter in New York City. Joan had learned about the Greyston permanent housing project when it appeared on a television program. She wrote a letter to Greyston and asked if there might be room for her as well. Joan lives in a studio apartment, and is anxious to show it off to visitors. The clean, though sparsely furnished studio is filled with her favorite mementos, including a statue of the Virgin Mary and a small vase of silk flowers. On her counter rests a portable typewriter next to a stack of neatly typed pages. Joan is a writer.

"This place is my haven," the native of Ireland says with a thick brogue. "I never thought I would be a person who would live on the streets, but circumstances came up that I just couldn't handle."

Next door to the studio apartment, the youth and infant-day-care center bustles with activity. It has recently been expanded to serve almost one hundred children in the community. Toys and furniture are scattered throughout the brightly lit rooms. When it was built, it was the only infant-care center in all of Westchester.

The two-bedroom apartments upstairs are also bright and clean. The official rent for the apartments ranges from $300 to $900 per month, though no tenant pays more than 30 percent of his or her gross monthly income.

They include Mary, a grandmother living with her ten-year-old grandson and who is now completing a high school equivalency program; Monica, a woman in her early twenties with a four-year-old son, who had been homeless for more than three years; and George, a single father to two young children. He had lost his job as a building superintendent two years before and soon found himself unemployed and homeless.

Though they don't keep a waiting list, there is far more need for affordable housing than Greyston has units available, so interest is strong. Those accepted are carefully chosen after inviting candidates into a training program where they participate in classes on subjects ranging from good parenting to personal finances. Before moving in, residents sign a contract that states they want to live self-sufficiently and are dedicated to self-improvement.

After they have moved in, the workshops continue. "We are all interested in living in a clean, safe home," says Joan. "We meet and discuss everything from how to prevent robberies to how to clean up any graffiti on the building to what to do if your neighbor has a radio on too loud. We all become one big family with our own separate opinions."

Residents and workers alike notice the improved behavior of the children. "Living here has transformed them," said Mitchell, a Greyston employee. "Many of them were emotionally troubled, coming from overcrowded environments with drugs and alcohol. The most common characteristic was inactivity and boredom. Their emotions ranged from being hyperactive to despondent. Now, they are best described as normal, happy children."

There are benefits for the adults as well. All tenants receive job training in conjunction with the bakery, the child-care center, and the builders. A job counselor is available to help with these and other employment opportunities.

Helping those with HIV

It's nearing the end of lunchtime at Greyston's Issan House and Robert and Tess invite David Rhone, Greyston Foundation's senior vice president for planning and his guest, to join them. Robert lives upstairs in one of the thirty-five units reserved for HIV-positive adults whereas Tess commutes from the Bronx every day. A white board details the events of the day: a community meeting, Latin support group, a session on holistic health, and art therapy. "Before I came here I was homeless, so this has been a great place for me," says Robert, who is HIV positive and also has diabetes.

The center, first the brainchild of Glassman, is home for thirty-five formerly homeless individuals and, according to Rhone, is Westchester County's only adult AIDS program. "This is all part of our holistic approach to community. We're not just a social service agency or a combination of a social service agency and a for-profit business," says Rhone. The idea is that a formerly homeless person can live in a Greyston property, and drop her child off at the day care center so that she can participate in the apprentice program at the bakery.

"It's very much an umbrella approach," says Rhone, noting that by offering a multiple of social and economic services, Greyston can illuminate a path for those it serves. "That is the important work we do here," he says.

Passing the torch

Charles Lief and David Rome knew Bernie Glassman through their shared Buddhist world. "I met Bernie in the 1970s. I appreciated how he combined social action with the spiritual core," says Lief.

Glassman recognized Lief and Rome's abilities as both spiritual followers and as businessmen. Lief, a lawyer and Rome, a publishing executive, first came to Greyston in 1992, working as consultants on a variety of projects. After one year, Glassman invited the duo to join Greyston full time. "Bernie was ready to move on, and to focus on peace projects in the international community," says Leif, who left the position in mid-2003. He and Glassman continue to be on the board and visit Greyston regularly. Walls considers Glassman to be his mentor and his inspiration. "We talk on the phone all the time. He's always there for everyone here whenever we need him," he says.

For Greyston's future, Walls says they plan to continue to improve its Yonkers neighborhood. "We will continue to grow by developing low income housing, with a greater focus on developing properties for affordable home ownership," he says.

With its childcare programs, Greyston plans to increase activities with school-aged children, providing after school programs for both grade school and high school students. "We're looking to develop an entrepreneurial program for the older children," says Walls. In addition, Walls and Rome hope Greyston, both the bakery and the Foundation, will continue to show that a business can contribute to a social mission by both making money and supporting its neighbors.

Chapter Nine

Still Rolling Along

Company Name: Sunrise Medical
Primary Business: Manufacturer/distributor of institutional and home health-care products
Type of Company: Private company
Headquarters: Carlsbad, California
Number of Employees: 4,000
Sunrise Founder: Richard H. Chandler
Quickie Designs Founder: Marilyn Hamilton
Chairman and CEO: Michael N. Hammes
Year Founded: 1983
Web site: http://www.sunrisemedical.com

Statement of Purpose

To improve people's lives by creating innovative, high quality products.

When Marilyn Hamilton arrived in Salt Lake City for the start of the 2002 Paralympic Winter Games, she relished the chance to finally sit back and enjoy the premier sporting event for the world's top disabled athletes. An accomplished athlete herself—with notable achievements on the snow and the tennis courts, both before and after she was paralyzed in a 1978 hang-gliding accident—Hamilton spent previous Paralympics totally enveloped in company business. But during these ten days in March she could visit with friends and associates and really get to watch the action, just like everyone else snatching up more than one hundred thousand live-event tickets and tuning into daily TV broadcasts around the globe.

That simply wasn't an option at the 1996 Paralympics in Atlanta. There, Hamilton spent virtually all waking moments representing her company, Sunrise Medical. As an official sponsor of the event, Sunrise made it the centerpiece of its first-ever global marketing push. Understandably, Hamilton and her colleagues never got to see much of it. They were too busy schmoozing and coordinating activities for hundreds of athletes and other customers who were there to support her business and its most well-known product: the lightweight, highly maneuverable Quickie wheelchairs that Hamilton herself was largely responsible for developing and popularizing.

There was an even bigger issue looming in Georgia in 1996, though, and it proved quite a distraction to those from Sunrise who should have been focusing on one of their firm's proudest moments. Virtually everyone was preoccupied with repercussions from an embarrassing scandal that erupted without warning several months earlier at another Sunrise subsidiary named Bio Clinic. Executives were dismissed, earnings were restated, employees were laid off, and an SEC probe was initiated. A strong performer on the New York Stock Exchange with a stellar reputation among customers, employees and the press since its founding a dozen years earlier, Sunrise was rocked to its core. Even more ominously, media accounts suggested that the company's long-time leadership position in several key areas—including wheelchairs from the flagship Quickie line—was wavering in the face of innovative new alternatives from competitors.

"That was a huge effort: $1 million in cash, another $5 million in our marketing program around the world. And it was all happening simultaneously with Bio Clinic," Hamilton, now fifty-three, recalls today. "I really credit Sunrise Medical with finding some sense of balance when we were going through that crisis, with not letting go of the opportunity and responsibility because it doesn't happen very often."

Most involved with Sunrise were nonetheless caught completely off guard by its problems and the accompanying negative publicity. More than a half-dozen years before "accounting scandal" was turned into a household phrase by Enron, leaders of this California-based company had to acknowledge that a seemingly high-flying unit in Ontario, Canada—maker of mattress pads and other foam medical products—had been misstating revenues and expenses for more than two years. And these figures weren't just misleading; actual discrepancies between fact and fiction were so great Sunrise had to restate earnings downward for the entire company by 16 percent for 1994 and 37 percent for 1995. Investors responded by dumping Sunrise stock, cutting its price in half and eliminating $340 million in shareholder value. The debacle also raised questions about the leadership style of charismatic Sunrise founder and CEO Richard H. Chandler, whose commitments to corporate decentralization and bonus-driven pay were seen by many as the primary culprits responsible for his firm's woes.

Until then, it seemed Chandler was on to something. Believing complete corporate independence and incentive-based policies could replace command-and-control, he combined a $25 million credit line, $4.6 million from venture capitalists, and cash of his own to acquire five U.S.-based medical businesses in early 1983. By that fall, his new Sunrise Medical Inc. also purchased its first European subsidiary and began trading on the NASDAQ stock exchange.

"We emerged fully grown as a $50 million public company with no operating history," he said a few years later. What he had was dreams of building a worldwide company that designed, manufactured, and marketed high-end medical products. He eventually purchased some two dozen more enterprises before consolidating them into product divisions—manual and electric wheelchairs, ambulatory and bath-safety aids, patient-room beds and furnishings, and specialty mattresses—that were manufactured in the U.S., U.K., Germany and Spain and distributed in eighty-five countries.

Hamilton's Quickie wheelchair business was among them.

An accomplished athlete and high school teacher at the time of her crash, Hamilton had completed rehabilitation therapy in record time and just as quickly grew frustrated with the cumbersome wheelchairs then available. She wanted to resume her active lifestyle, and that included a return to the ski slopes and tennis courts. But she quickly recognized that the heavy steel chairs of the late-1970s would not allow for that. In fact, they actually hindered her progress.

"I realized I needed more performance in a wheelchair, and one that would make me feel better," she recalls. "I felt okay, but people didn't allow me to feel okay in that steel dinosaur. They would pat me on the back and say, 'Can I help?' Or they looked the other way."

So Hamilton—whose office is adorned with pictures from her meetings with famous admirers like Barbara Bush, as well as a photo of her soaring through the air on a hang glider—asked two friends to build her a new kind of chair. They came up with one that weighed just twenty-six pounds, about half that of existing models. She packed it up and headed to the 1980 Handicapped Ski Championships in Winter Park, Colorado.

Hamilton's performance there, and the reaction to her new wheels by other disabled athletes, convinced her to go into business with her designer friends. Sales grew by 200 percent in one year as Hamilton tirelessly promoted her new product by competing in—and winning—event after event. Word spread, and new versions were introduced for non-athletes, children, and others who appreciated solid performance and lightweight convenience. Beside their distinctive design, a palette of striking colors (like candy red, blue opal and toxic green) also told observers that people using these sleek and sporty chairs were feeling good about themselves and their lives.

Turning adversity into triumph was a very motivating experience for Hamilton and her colleagues. It also set a foundation for their handling of the trying times surrounding those 1996 Atlanta Games, when the firm that eventually acquired Quickie—and now records some $600 million in annual sales—would need a motivational boost of its own.

Reinventing the wheel (chair)

Marilyn Hamilton was well acquainted with wheelchairs. Her uncle, Bill Hamilton, was thrown from a Model T while in high school and had been a quadriplegic since the 1920s. Gregarious and likable, he easily proved to those around him that people in wheelchairs could do anything that they set their minds to. Bill Hamilton, in fact, defied the odds from the start by making the most of the crude rehabilitative therapy and equipment available prior to World War II. His first wood-and-wicker wheelchair weighed ninety pounds, for example, and required attendants to push around. Still, he went to college and law school in it before turning the family fruit orchard into a successful business.

Like her uncle, Marilyn Hamilton is strong-willed and has an insatiable zest for life. She graduated from college with a degree in home economics, an art minor, and a secondary teaching credential. She taught high school in Australia for two years, and traveled extensively throughout the Far East before returning to her native California for another teaching assignment. She was in her fourth year at a West Coast high school when the crash on Tollhouse Mountain in the Sierra range forever altered her life.

"I found myself lying on the side of the mountain, at the age of twenty-nine, and wondering, 'Why me?'" she says now. But a little luck and something Hamilton calls her ABCs gave her the impetus to go on. "The 'A' is adjusting your attitude, like when someone comes to me with a problem and I just flip it to the solution. The 'B' is believing in yourself. And there are actually two 'Cs': challenging yourself to do things you never imagined and having the commitment to do what it takes," she explains.

"But there is also a 'D,'" she adds quickly. "You have to dream. And you have to continue to dream."

Bill was at Marilyn's side almost immediately after the accident to offer both reassurance and advice. When the school district that employed her proved reluctant to take her back, Bill offered Marilyn a job in the family fruit business. Marilyn accepted, and dove full-force into the corporate world while taking advantage of the operation's seasonal nature to travel the country and participate in athletic competitions.

Hamilton returned to the sporting world so quickly and so effectively because she refused to accept the limitations of the chrome-steel chair she was given upon her hospital release. Far too heavy for the tennis courts and much too clumsy to get her to the ski slopes, she asked two inventive friends—glider pilots Don Helman and Jim Okamoto—to build her an ultralight replacement from the same aluminum tubing they used to make hang gliders.

In a six-hundred-square-foot shed behind Helman's house, the two combined their knowledge of thermodynamics and engineering with seamless drawn aluminum developed by the aerospace industry. They visualized a revolutionary non-folding wheelchair that would be more mobile, more stable, more adjustable, and, ultimately, more competitive than anything on the market. Their creation, which they dubbed a Quickie, also looked more like a racing bicycle than a rolling hospital bed. It was sleek, sky blue, had comfortable nylon upholstery (instead of the standard vinyl or Naugahyde), and offered adjustments to enhance safety along with performance.

Hamilton bought the chair for $700 and took it on the road. After the ski championships in Colorado, she won the National Wheelchair Tennis Championships in singles and doubles both in 1982 and 1983. She also captured the National Disabled Ski Championships six times between 1981 to 1988, along with other ski and tennis titles. As she met with increased athletic success, other members of the disabled community—who had been modifying standard wheelchairs themselves to compete more effectively—began clamoring for Quickies. Hamilton teamed up with Helman and Okamoto in 1980 to form a company they initially called Motion Designs, and plowed the proceeds from each sale back into an effort that would change an industry.

"Everything was shoestring, garage mentality," says Hamilton. "We weren't taking salaries. We had no overhead. There was no cost."

The three did, however, sell Quickies as fast as they could produce them. Hamilton believes fifty chairs were sold the first year, maybe two hundred the second, but exact figures are unavailable because all early records eventually were lost. Whatever the number, rapidly escalating sales led the partners to move into larger facilities twice within four years. And they helped the trio convince a skeptical medical community that there was enormous potential in this unique new product.

"We filled a niche," Hamilton says. "When I look back, the success of the company came from finding a need and filling it, doing it better than anyone else, hiring great people, and having fun."

The need for products like Hamilton's was also expanding exponentially, as the number of wheelchair users in the U.S. alone rose from five hundred thousand in 1960 to nearly 1.25 million in 1980. Medical advances during those years, allowing more and more accident victims to survive catastrophic injuries, were largely responsible for the increase. Thousands of paraplegics and quadriplegics were subsequently released from rehabilitation centers and hospitals, and significant numbers wanted to pursue an active lifestyle like Hamilton. Many were also drawn to the Quickie's unique design, bright colors, and performance orientation.

To reach them and countless others who could benefit from the new wheelchairs, Hamilton also promoted them in entirely new ways. Existing manufacturers had long aimed their marketing efforts solely at medical personnel, and usually pictured empty chairs in hospital settings. Quickies were featured in modern promotional materials with real people competing in real wheelchair athletics. They were also the subject of intentionally provocative slogans like "Nothing beats a Quickie," and touted at staid medical trade shows in splashy silver, black and red booths.

Hamilton and her partners subsequently developed another model, the folding Quickie 2, which was aimed at the non-athletic market. Within six weeks of its release, three hundred of these easily maneuverable lightweight models were sold.

Quality remained the emphasis, and Quickie's blend of cutting-edge designs and advanced technology consistently produced innovative results. The pediatric Zippie and low-cost Breezy grabbed the allegiance of more new customers, while Quickie's progressive ideas and subsequent successes drew the attention of another young company named Sunrise Medical. In 1986, after three years of courting by Sunrise, Hamilton and Quickie agreed to become part of its fast-growing portfolio of rehabilitative and long-term medical businesses.

A new dawn

Dick Chandler always believed in success through teamwork. Many executives say such things, but Chandler—with a background in competitive sports as well as corporate America—walked the walk. With ideas developed at Princeton, the University of Chicago, and Belgium's University of Louvain, he organized volunteer fundraisers during his twenties to create a Chicago investment company for minority-owned enterprises.

His philosophies carried him to the executive ranks of several Fortune 500 firms during his thirties, culminating in the presidency of a nationwide chain of home health-care stores. After taking a year off to write a novel and travel with his family, he combined the things he believed in with the things he had learned and formed Sunrise Medical before his fortieth birthday.

In less than a decade Chandler acquired a collection of clear market-leaders like Quickie, which he purchased for subordinated notes, stock, and $21.3 million in cash. These helped him turn Sunrise into a $320 million company with thirty-two hundred employees around the world. It also allowed him to shift the firm from NASDAQ to the New York Stock Exchange, and fund community-minded spin-offs like the personal growth program for kids in wheelchairs called Winners on Wheels. Owing to Chandler's style, everything was operated independently but with powerful incentive programs designed to motivate the diverse assortment of individuals he had amassed into forming one committed team.

"I'm not comfortable with authority as a leadership tool," he said at the time. "True power comes from authenticity, which means demonstrating ethical values and a concern for people, not giving orders."

Chandler also believed "the best way to increase sales and profits is to do the right thing," and did all he could to show employees they were truly partners in a common enterprise. Everyone was on a first-name basis. There were no executive perks, such as reserved parking spaces. Each Sunrise entity was run autonomously. Liberal bonus and incentive plans were available at every level.

Most of the acquisitions blossomed under this arrangement. Hamilton, Sunrise's new senior vice president of marketing, certainly found this true for Quickie. The commitment to quality that was central to her operation was strongly encouraged on Chandler's watch, and staff responded by focusing on technical advancements geared to fit, comfort and adjustability. "For research we go to consumer electronic shows and bike shows," says Wayne, who joined Quickie's engineering team in 1983 and has been a paraplegic since age fifteen.

Like the other subsidiaries Quickie offered generous benefits and excellent working conditions under Sunrise, which cut turnover and attracted a diverse and passionate workforce. State-of-the-art production methods were introduced, and just-in-time manufacturing procedures freed floor space while improving quality and efficiency. As a result, sales grew nearly five-fold in the six years following the acquisition. Employees also received a tremendous psychological boost when Sunrise celebrated its tenth anniversary by announcing its sponsorship of the Atlanta Paralympics.

But everything changed in late 1995, when Sunrise suddenly announced it was putting several executives on paid leave pending an internal review into financial irregularities. "The net income and assets of the company may have been overstated for previously reported periods," the company warned in a statement. Information had surfaced through normal review procedures, Chandler added in an interview, which indicated there were inaccuracies in financial data submitted by Ontario's Bio Clinic.

Within three months the scope of the problem became apparent and Sunrise was forced to restate earnings to show that Bio Clinic actually lost money in 1995 rather than posting a profit. Bio Clinic's top official and three other employees left the company; two additional Sunrise executives also resigned. The federal Securities and Exchange Commission launched an investigation, and Sunrise laid off 250 (or 6 percent of its workforce). Its share price tumbled from $23.50 to $16.75.

The company revealed that Bio Clinic personnel had falsified revenue and expense reports for 1995, 1994, and perhaps prior years. They slipped erroneous figures systematically into regular reports in order to make their unit appear far more successful than it was, but never directly misappropriated any funds. Although Chandler refused to publicly venture a reason for the falsified financials, analysts speculated that bonuses tied to unit performance (which could amount to between 10 and 50 percent of an executive's salary) were likely behind the deception. The media, meanwhile, openly tied the culture that Chandler had so carefully crafted more directly to the fabrications. Such decentralized management and pay-for-performance arrangements, several publications declared, was known to have encouraged behavior of exactly this kind elsewhere.

The scandal was particularly embarrassing because Sunrise always prided itself on its institutionalized commitment to doing the right thing. It was especially difficult for them when phrases like "cooking the books" were tied to the firm just as disabled athletes from around the world were heading to Atlanta for the Games. Perhaps most disturbing, though, were allegations that the accounting fraud covered other problems. There were suggestions that Chandler's strategy of loosely linking his subsidiaries, for example, had in reality led to unnecessarily duplicative (and unjustifiably expensive) administrative structures. And that the current dip in fiscal performance was actually initiated by competitors who adapted more successfully to the changing health-care arena and offered superior products at better prices. Invacare, its closest rival in the global $3 billion home medical-equipment marketplace, was said to be prospering at Sunrise's expense by doing just that.

As Marilyn Hamilton and other company representatives were working twenty-four/seven to make the 1996 Paralympics a success, Sunrise was trying to regain its position. Chandler reorganized his U.S. sales force and European operations, consolidating their now-discredited independent structures into a more integrated one reminiscent of his main competitor. He also kept making acquisitions, adding industry-leaders like Jay Medical (manufacturer of wheelchair cushions) and DynaVox Systems (maker of augmentative communication devices). He opened new markets (Australia), reduced organizational complexity by reconfiguring all subsidiaries into three major operating groups (Home

Healthcare, Continuing Care, and Sunrise Medical Europe), and relocated the California corporate headquarters from Torrance to Carlsbad (in north San Diego County).

In early 1999 the SEC filed, and settled, a lawsuit against the former top Bio Clinic official it had been investigating for alleged accounting fraud and insider trading. Under the settlement the official neither admitted nor denied allegations that he had earned corporate bonuses after modifying fiscal reports over two years to the tune of at least $19.6 million by building up his books with nonexistent assets and fictitiously reduced liabilities. It also left publicly unaddressed the allegations that he exercised stock options despite knowledge that Sunrise's financials were materially incorrect. Without admitting or denying any wrongdoing, the company itself additionally consented to an SEC order that it violated laws relating to periodic reporting, books and records, and internal accounting-control.

And then, just after a $2.7 million loss was posted for the fourth-quarter of 1999 and the stock price fell to $6.75, a sad but determined team of Sunrise managers and board members asked founder Richard H. Chandler to retire.

Changing of the guard

Michael Hammes, at fifty-eight, was ready to tackle the challenge of Sunrise. For more than thirty years he had worked his way up through automotive and related businesses, attaining such positions as President of Ford of Mexico and Chairman and CEO of Guide Corporation (the former Delphi Automotive Division of GM). He also served as Chairman of Coleman Corporation and Vice Chairman of Black and Decker, where he was responsible for creating the DeWalt power tool line. When Chandler stepped down—noting in a written statement that the company now needed someone more skilled in operations and cost-containment—Hammes had been a member of the Sunrise board of directors for about a year.

In January 2000, he took over as its president and chief executive officer. His first task was to rid Sunrise of the diversions that were stymieing its forward progress.

"We really lost our way a bit in terms of focusing on the external world: the end-users, the dealers, the products," Hammes says. "Very good leadership was provided by Dick and by other people—I wasn't on the board at that point, so I can say that with a clear conscience—but rather than being the catalyst that moved us into the twenty-first century, those bad-news events let us flutter on down even further until we woke up."

Committed to Chandler's vision of building a company that truly served its customers, Hammes set about revitalizing Sunrise and returning it to the top of the healthcare pile. He began by assessing its true financial status and formulating a short-range plan for reinvestment and growth. One part involved slimming down and consolidating operations so all Sunrise units could listen more closely to their customers and communicate more effectively with each other. Another involved assembling a focused management team comprised of Sunrise veterans with "tribal knowledge" and outside specialists with critical skills.

But the most critical part involved a complete overhaul of Sunrise's financial foundation, for Hammes and his team had become convinced that a combination of low debt and low stock value made it an attractive target for unsolicited—and unwanted—takeover bids. Their solution was to once again make the company a closely held private firm. A group comprised of Hammes and more than two dozen other senior managers, supported by Vestar Capital Partners and Park Avenue Equity Partners, did just that in a $365 million transaction during December 2000. Long-time employees and newcomers alike were impressed by the way their new financial associates began forging a true partnership that thoroughly embraced their efforts. They also were pleased with the way their new partners seemed to truly share their socially responsible objectives.

With virtually a complete restructuring on the agenda, Hammes then began to consolidate support functions that were still handled separately within each division, including purchasing and finance. He also continued defining his top team by bringing in additional specialists like Allan Small, an international authority on engineering processes that deliver consistent product quality, and bringing back Sunrise veteran Sheila DeLany, an early Quickie employee who left after seventeen years and now was to handle North American customer service). Hammes further moved to optimize existing infrastructures, totally revamping the product development process to eliminate resource-eating duplication—a problem that appeared, say, when as many as five individual subsidiaries worked simultaneously but in isolation on new wheelchair designs.

"It goes back to what made Sunrise great, and what we had to change if we wanted to keep moving forward," says Hammes. "Dick Chandler really brought together some outstanding companies, and we at Sunrise let each stay by itself. You're not going to beat other people and provide a better product to the end-user if you're relying on individual groups of people all over the place."

The new approach—aimed at unifying sales and developmental efforts across core Sunrise brands, as well as across industries and countries—was implemented on a very fast track. Managers like Marilyn Hamilton, now vice president of global planning and strategic service, began spending eight of ten days on the road. Everyone was expected to operate full-throttle, which regularly meant delaying dinner for a late meeting or waking early on a Sunday for a 7:00 a.m. conference call.

Most employees proved passionately committed to the firm's goals and fully supported these efforts, says Raymond Huggenberger, the executive charged with consolidating European operations. Transforming processes and systems was another matter. "There were a lot of things that weren't getting done that needed to get done, everyday-type things that a company of this size should do," says Small, who has overseen engineering, quality, and operations worldwide for Sunrise since mid-

2001. "Systems needed to be put in place, data needed to be analyzed on a regular basis, just a lot of standard things that I would say needed to be done that we really weren't doing as good a job on as we needed to do."

Some people did leave amidst the overhaul, but the fresh approach also attracted some outstanding replacements. And the consolidation not only paved the way for technological advancements and cost savings, it identified opportunities for leveraging related products into original, integrated new offerings. Power wheelchairs from one unit could be combined with augmentative speech devices from another, for example, as well as with foam padding from a third. "That's how Sunrise is evolving from a very focused and very, very good rehab company into a broader-scope world company," says Hammes.

And the idea of doing the right thing, of contributing to programs that benefit customers and their communities, has certainly not been abandoned under the new ownership structure and strategic direction. In fact, thanks to a solid commitment from Hammes and active support from his financial partners, it might even be stronger now than before. A dinner scheduled to communicate the new Sunrise three-year plan to Vestar founding partner Dan O'Connell showed this clearly, according to Carey Winkel, another new team member, now senior vice president of global planning and marketing.

"He allowed us to present our strategies and actions and concluded that those were really great. But then he reminded us of why Vestar really chose to do an investment here: we are a company that has the ability to actually improve someone's life," Winkel recalls. "So he said, 'I didn't really see anything in your plan that talked about what you are doing to pay back to society. Where's your strategy? Where's your effort? Where's your action to drive back that community support?'

"We learned a lot about his character and about Vestar as our partners," she adds, "and certainly feel fortunate that the connection this company started on—which is to improve people's lives—can be very visible and in the forefront."

Giving something back

For the past two decades, David Kiley and Randy Snow have been part of the Quickie/Sunrise family. Accomplished athletes with the titles to prove it—Kiley has been MVP six times in the National Wheelchair Basketball Association finals, and Snow captured three medals at three Paralympics in three different sports—the pair have been as involved over the years as any of the eighty or so members of Team Quickie, a group of elite wheelchair athletes sponsored by the company. They have been funded and befriended and coaxed and celebrated. They have schmoozed with politicians and corporate honchos, and run their own basketball and tennis camps under the company banner. And they have each been rewarded with the ultimate sporting honor: Sunrise now offers the All Court Signature Chair bearing Kiley's name, and the Match Point Chair signed by Snow.

"Sunrise has been up, and Sunrise has been down," says Snow, now forty-two and a 2002 inductee in the inaugural class of the Wheelchair Sports, USA Hall of Fame. "Throughout it all, they've been my compass."

He and the forty-eight-year-old Kiley—a dedicated fly-fisherman as well as the first player to serve as commissioner, and then president, of the hoops league he so dominated—head the senior class of basketball, tennis, rugby, ski and racing pros who compete under the Team Quickie umbrella. They all know this is a business, and that they are helping to sell wheelchairs, but they also know what an impact events like the Paralympics and innovations like the Quickie have had on sports-minded members of the disabled community. "We were taking hospital-type chairs and hacking them up in the garage. Now, the athletes are jumping right into Cadillacs," Kiley says. And they're increasingly doing so in front of big crowds, in person and on TV.

Having been at this since well before Sunrise bought

Quickie, Kiley and Snow paved the way for the courts full of disabled athletes who are now competing at levels—and before audiences—never imagined in the past. The two have certainly realized personal gain, but in return they've brought a priceless authenticity and street credibility to the table that underscores how the benefits of programs like these truly flow both ways. Their direct input on design of their signature models, for example, led to breakthroughs like "center mass adjustment" that continually turn heads and demonstrate that Sunrise is serious about boosting Quickies back atop a wheelchair athlete's must-have list.

When her original two partners weren't sure that they could justify the commitment, Hamilton literally pushed the sports sponsorships into existence by the sheer force of her personality. She remains the effort's chief promoter, but is equally proud of the newer Lifestyle Ambassador program and a number of other ventures that Sunrise supports. That's because Hamilton and her colleagues understand all-too-well that disabled adults—even with technically superior products—still generally end up with less education, lower income, fewer job opportunities, and less social contact than their non-disabled peers. Knowing many of these problems stem directly from the experiences of disabled children, she and her associates set about developing one such program to help these youngsters ultimately share in the American dream.

The result was Winners on Wheels, or WOW, a not-for-profit organization founded in 1992 to "empower youth in wheelchairs to be all that they can be." Conceived by Hamilton and originally funded by Quickie/Sunrise with a $200,000 grant—a contribution that has since grown to more than $2 million—the effort created Scout-type chapters across the country where kids aged seven through twelve can regularly meet. Dozens of these chapters, called Circles, are now operating.

In the wake of WOW's success, several other programs for youngsters have been added to the Sunrise roster. These include the DeVilbiss Kids Club, which helps children deal with asthma; the Raggs Kids Club Band, which features five performing dog characters that convey motivational musical messages for those aged four through eight with disabilities; and the International Variety Club and Camp Kon-O-Kwee in Pittsburgh, which supplies mobility products and a summer activity center for kids with special needs.

The individuals chosen by Sunrise as Lifestyle Ambassadors, on the other hand, are intended as role models for people of all ages. Structured much like the sports program, this also is based on partnerships with extraordinary individuals who advance the overall cause of disabled people, receive assistance in realizing their own goals, and help the company drive and strengthen its brands. Among these impressive representatives is Cody Unser, daughter of racing champion Al Unser Jr., who was diagnosed with Transverse Myelitis in 1999 at age twelve and paralyzed from the chest down—and then founded the Cody Unser First Step Foundation, helped create a national TM research consortium based at Johns Hopkins Hospital, lobbied in Washington, met the president, and was profiled by *People* magazine, CBS's 48 Hours, and ESPN's Sports Center.

Sunrise additionally supports external non-profits like Wheels for the World, an ongoing program that engages prison inmates to refurbish old wheelchairs that are then sent to Third World countries. The company has also been active in Wheelchairs for Humanity, donating over 650 chairs to people with disabilities in Nicaragua, Indonesia, Mexico, El Salvador, Guatemala, Nigeria and Vietnam.

The deeply embedded corporate attitude behind such initiatives stems naturally from the work done at Sunrise, and is one of the real legacies left behind by founder Dick Chandler—along with a collection of great companies that he pulled together along the way. The current combination of new and old players on the management team definitely understands this, and how it fits into the overall goal of making the company more profitable so it can keep doing the right thing. And their efforts, while still in relatively early stages, seem to be paying off: EBITDA (or Earnings Before Interest, Taxes, Depreciation and Amortization) rose from $45 million in 1999 to $70 million in 2002. The company projects it will hit $85 million in 2003.

This resurgence—and the chance it affords Sunrise to continue making a difference in the communities it serves—keeps people like Marilyn Hamilton charged and on the go.

"Not many companies have this opportunity to really get out into the community and make a difference in people's lives," she says. "It's so exciting to see a child jump in a wheelchair for the first time and find freedom. The kid's eyes all of a sudden get bright, and they're able to start dreaming and doing things they never imagined."

Like hanging out on Saturday with their WOW Circle. Finding a wheelchair basketball team to join. Getting an education and a good job. Or watching worthy competitors win Paralympic medals in their own backyard.

Chapter Ten

Less is More

Company Name: Patagonia/Lost Arrow Corp.
Primary Business: Outdoor clothing manufacturer, distributor and retailer
Type of Company: Private corporation
Headquarters: Ventura, California
Number of Employees: 977
Founders: Yvon Chouinard, Malinda Chouinard, Tom Frost
CEO: Michael Crooke
Year Founded: 1972
Web site: www.patagonia.com

Mission Statement

To use business to inspire and implement solutions to the environmental crisis.

Throughout his life, Yvon Chouinard has always favored the road less traveled. As a member of America's pioneering rock-climbing fraternity in the 1950s, and a participant in its trailblazing entrepreneurial community in the 1970s, Chouinard understood that long-term triumph only comes when form truly follows function—a basic principle in the backcountry, and in the boardroom, that eluded many of his peers. So when the high-flying Patagonia outdoor gear-and-clothing company that ultimately sprang from his ability to balance on the edges of these two disparate environments threatened to implode from its own success in the early 1990s, he stepped back even more from traditional business thinking and completely redirected the very heart of his enterprise. At the same time he totally recommitted it to the waste-reducing, ethically grounded practices for which it had become legendary.

Ten years later—after trimming its workforce and product lines, downsizing its growth and development goals, reducing its manufacturing and operational impacts, boosting its environmental and social philanthropy, and solidifying its menu of progressive employee benefits—Chouinard has seen Patagonia enjoy the best period in its history. And while it's true that in the interim he also relinquished the reins of this company and its parent for the first time since founding them, he remains as involved as ever with their course of action and is still personally pushing the envelope in the business world and in the outdoors.

"The American Dream is to own your own business, grow it as quickly as you can until you cash out, and retire to the golf courses of Leisure World," Chouinard has written. To combat the disposable corporate culture that this represents he has pointedly developed Patagonia as an alternative: a highly focused niche company designed to function profitably over the long haul by living within its resources, caring for its people, and doing all it can to satisfy its customers. And Chouinard himself, now sixty-two, isn't selling out to any corporation or heading to any Leisure World.

"I still have the hundred-year plan and it still goes on for one hundred years from this point, not seventy," he says one afternoon during his firm's thirtieth year. He is at Patagonia's southern California headquarters this spring day, but preparing to leave on the type of extended excursion—to places like Argentina, Kenya, Belize, Hawaii, Nepal and Wyoming—that he still schedules throughout much of each year. On these getaways, Chouinard still climbs, sails, surfs, fly-fishes, kayaks and skis while advancing the distinct worldview and practical knowledge he has consistently relied upon to make Patagonia a company with a conscience and an undeniable success. "It is," he says with a hearty laugh when asked about this century plan, "just another ever-receding summit."

Climbing corporate ladders

Yvon Chouinard never planned to become a businessman. He envisioned himself as a craftsman, and his goal was turning out high quality goods that helped their owners perform more proficiently—and lasted forever while they did so. Although he certainly did become an accomplished businessman after launching his first company in the mid-1960s, Chouinard also succeeded notably on those other fronts. His products have played an integral role in countless expeditions, including the journeys of several space shuttles. And any longtime customer can point to pieces of cherished gear that look and function as well today as they did when they were purchased ten or even twenty years earlier.

Patagonia's solid position as the twenty-first century gets underway is testament to Chouinard's early vision for it as a business, and the often unconventional philosophies he instituted along the way to realize it. The company's products are now sold through some fourteen hundred outdoor speciality shops around the world. It also runs sixteen of its own stores in the U.S. (in California, Washington, Oregon, Hawaii, Colorado, Montana, Utah, Nevada, Georgia, New York, Maine, Massachusetts, and Washington, D.C.), three in Europe and eight in Japan. Its annual worldwide sales in 2002 totaled more than $220 million.

But it's the top-down emphasis on performance and quality—and of substance over style—that remains its foundation.

"My mandate is to produce the most functional products in the world, with the greatest technological improvements," explains Richard, a designer of alpine, mountaineer, marine and water-sports products. "My father worked for a company that manufactured steel parts in the Midwest," he continues. "It was a very classic company, very hierarchical, and the hourly wage earners were treated like dirt. It taught me how special it is here."

With its casually dressed young workforce and its open floor plan, the operation actually looks a lot like many other small and mid-sized corporations in California and up and down the West Coast. Beneath the surface, however, Patagonia's true essence becomes apparent. And like everything else in the company, the lens through which the viewer can see the business and its purpose is brought into focus with Yvon Chouinard.

Born to French-Canadian parents, Patagonia's driving force lived in the French-speaking town of Lisbon, Maine, until he was eight years old. An innate interest in the outdoors expanded considerably that year when his plumber-handyman father moved the family—Yvon, his mother, two sisters and a brother—to southern California. There, the omnipresent sunshine and nearby Hollywood Hills helped further cultivate the youngster's love of nature and the mountains, and by the time he reached his teens Chouinard was spending his spare time banding eagles and hawks for the U.S. Fish & Wildlife Service. Before graduation he summered in Jackson Hole, Wyoming, where he further reveled in all things outside and honed his burgeoning climbing talents in the spectacular Teton range.

Chouinard was an accomplished climber by the time he finished high school, and his passion for the activity overshadowed all else. He tried taking a few geography courses at a California community college after graduation, but left before earning a degree in order to better concentrate on his sport.

As Chouinard's commitment to climbing grew, so did his frustration with the inferior equipment available in the mid-1950s. He became especially dissatisfied with the quality of vital tools like pitons (steel spikes driven into cracks in the mountains) and carabiners (metal rings that served as links between the pitons and climbing ropes). Chouinard was certain he could improve them, and in 1957 bought a book on blacksmithing, pulled together $100 to buy an anvil and a coal-fired forge, and began making pitons in his family's Burbank backyard. He borrowed $800 from his parents about a year later to buy an aluminum forging dye, and started turning out carabiners. The work went well and he decided to produce as many as he could to sell to other climbers. He then traveled from climbing site to climbing site, peddling the gear to his many friends right from the trunk of his car.

Within five years, Chouinard Equipment Ltd. had become well-known in climbing circles for its innovative designs and first-rate products. Chouinard himself also was on his way, both in his business and in his development of a non-traditional approach to it. He fashioned his pitons, for example, out of aircraft-quality chrome-molybdenum steel rather than the malleable iron used by European competitors. Serious climbers appreciated the difference and were willing to pay up to four times the price for it. The market was small, however, and Chouinard was forced to support himself in other ways. One was to work part-time for his brother, Jeff, who was chief of security for Howard Hughes.

Chouinard also served two years in the army, and upon release in 1966 after a stint in Korea he moved to Ventura with fellow climber and longtime friend Tom Frost. There, the two rented a tin shack behind an abandoned slaughterhouse and began to redesign all of Chouinard's gear. They also assembled a one-page mimeographed "catalog" of their offerings and mailed it to everyone they knew. By 1970 this helped them capture some 80 percent of the domestic climbing market, and gross nearly $300,000. In 1972, Chouinard and Frost incorporated as Great Pacific Iron Works.

Around that time, Chouinard also decided to bolster his selection of hardware with a few soft goods. During a trip to

Scotland, he had discovered a regulation rugby shirt that he believed was perfect for rock climbing. He brought it home to duplicate and also made a pair of matching shorts, called Stand Up Shorts, on a machine that he had been using to sew leather patches onto climbing packs. When the new apparel was listed in his next catalog, it was snapped right up by his growing customer base.

Sparked by strong interest in its new clothing line, the company's total sales more than doubled to $1 million within a year, and in 1976 the partners spun off a new entity called Patagonia after the South American region that Chouinard liked so much to handle it. Frost, who always preferred climbing to business, decided to take his leave soon after. This left Chouinard and his wife, Malinda, as sole owners of everything that now fell under the banner of the Lost Arrow Corporation—the parent company they named for their first piton, dubbed the Lost Arrow, that Yvon had produced in his parents' backyard.

The climbing division continued to lead all of its industry's domestic-gear manufacturers in sales through the 1980s, but the nation's liability mania—in the form of accident-related lawsuits—eventually caught up. Chouinard's insurance premiums rose 1,000 percent in one year, and while he never lost a lawsuit resulting from faulty climbing gear, he and his friends feared that the threat of litigation clouded the future of what in 1987 had become a $67 million Patagonia line. Chouinard Equipment was sold to a group of employees that year, renamed Black Diamond Equipment Ltd., and moved to Utah. It continues as a respected name in the climbing industry, and is still employee-owned.

Clothes make the company

Yvon Chouinard can seem a bit reserved, even somewhat shy, when he is inside his company's Ventura headquarters. Wearing clothing from his lines that has seen more than a few seasons of rugged use, he looks like he'd be much more comfortable on a rocky outcropping or in the pounding surf. In reality, he would be, although over the years he's certainly managed to channel these and his other outdoor interests into an uncanny knack for pointing his business in the right direction.

"I'm the outside man," he offers. "My job is to be away from the office, getting ideas—on future lifestyle changes, where the world is going, how all this effects the company—and bringing them back." It is outside, in his real office, that Chouinard has long spent about half of each year. And it is there that he feels most at home, and does his best thinking about Patagonia's present and future.

While observers remain envious of his independent lifestyle and fans remain awed by his technical expertise—his 1978 book, *Climbing Ice*, is still a respected text on the essence of that hardcore sport—Chouinard complained years ago that he no longer gets the opportunity to undertake many real expeditions. That gripe should be put into perspective, however, considering the legendary excursions that have been launched over the decades by the man who once told *Forbes* magazine that his "number-one priority is to have free time."

Particularly illustrative is one outing that unfolded in the late 1980s, when Chouinard and three friends traveled to Chile. After being deposited by a fishing boat, the quartet proceeded to climb an as-yet-unclimbed peak in very bad weather. It only got worse during the after-dark descent, when the wind grew so strong the men had to crawl for four miles on their hands and knees to reach level ground. To return to their starting point they then had to embark on a seventy-mile kayak journey through rough seas, but were blown over by the continuing winds not long after they began. Chouinard and the others were all forced to bail out, and swim through cold water back to shore. There they built a fire for warmth before forging ahead once more in wind and water so rough the men had to hold tightly to each other until the strongest waves passed. "It turned out to be more than we bargained for," Chouinard later told the media. "It turned out to be an adventure."

Some would call Patagonia's adventures in the clothing trade an equally unnerving experience. The ride has certainly been just as intense.

It started off quickly with those Scottish rugby shirts and matching shorts, and built speed rapidly as other well-made and technically sound garments were added to the line. The real rush began in 1976, when the company introduced a collection of innovative lightweight jackets made from a new fast-drying synthetic material called pile. In no time, the cozy fleece-like garments became *de rigueur* in serious mountain getaways like Chouinard's old haunt of Jackson Hole. Word soon spread beyond the tightly knit outdoors community, too, and within three years pile accounted for half of all Patagonia's sales. It also set in motion a pattern that was to be repeated for decades.

To almost no one's surprise, the popularity of these jackets promptly spawned a series of knockoffs from various competitors—usually with fewer features and lower price tags. Chouinard, also surprising no one, had already been looking for something better. He found it in an even newer fabric called bunting, which featured a tighter weave than pile that improved its performance. After introducing a new bunting line the competition once again followed suit, leading Patagonia to develop an even softer and more comfortable material in conjunction with Malden Mills called Synchilla. This, too, was quickly picked up by other companies, which began selling their own cheaper variations as soon as they could crank them out.

Chouinard had emphatically made clear by his past actions that Patagonia would never compete on price, and would instead work ceaselessly to create superior products that left competitors in the dust. It had done so before with climbing gear and long johns—Patagonia eliminated its second-largest product line, polypropylene underwear, in favor of higher-tech Capilene once other companies from L.L. Bean to Kmart began pushing their own versions—and it was apparent it would do so in the future. Chouinard's loyal customers understand this and follow his lead. They still know that his company offers only the highest quality gear and remain willing to pay more to obtain it.

"Our products must be simple, functional and suitable to the task at hand. The function will dictate the form. If we've done our homework, if we have not compromised on the process, the aesthetics will follow. Functionally driven design is usually minimalist. Less is more," reads the official Patagonia philosophy. "We design so that you forget you're wearing the clothes or carrying your gear, and focus on the experience. This is our challenge and purpose.'"

To Chouinard, that sentiment still says it all.

"We never invented anything here," he says humbly. "When we made climbing equipment, we took existing products and made them better. Same with clothing. We have a commitment to make a better product." Price should never be part of the equation, Chouinard believes. If you can't afford the best available, "save your money until you can buy the one that will last the rest of your life."

Clearing new hurdles

The biggest challenge to the Patagonia philosophy came a decade ago, after the go-go 1980s and a national embrace of all things outdoors had combined to boost Chouinard's company to heights unimaginable only a few years earlier. By 1991, however, the downside to the fast ride was painfully obvious to everyone in Ventura. On the heels of record sales and increasing worldwide recognition, Patagonia found itself facing potentially disastrous personnel, production and financing problems. It was unable to adequately absorb, train, and devise internal systems for the hundreds of new workers demanded by the rapid growth. On-time product delivery was threatened. Banks refused to increase its credit line.

So how did one of the corporate world's most conscientious and successful young companies respond?

Some of the decisions proved relatively easy to implement: Patagonia immediately froze sales at existing levels, scaled back planned job additions, eliminated participation in consumer fairs and trade shows, and trimmed its overall product line by nearly 25 percent. Other moves were tougher: Chouinard removed the outside management team he installed in key positions just five years earlier—CEO, chief financial officer, chief operations officer, head of mail order, and director of personnel—admitting that his decision to bring in "so-called experts" who were unfamiliar with the organization's underlying beliefs in order to help it grow had been a mistake. And some actions were extraordinarily painful: In the summer, the company laid off one hundred twenty employees, or 20 percent of its workforce, from all levels including management.

Although some of these steps were difficult, the combination did put the company back on the path that brought it success in the first place. It also calmed those who feared it was getting too big for its britches. "To hit the sales goals we set, we would have had to move well beyond our core customers, beyond the specialty outdoor business," Chouinard explained in the layoff notice, which also announced that those affected would receive a severance package with four weeks' salary plus one additional weeks' pay for every year of service. "It was a case of mismanagement, and it was painful to affect so many people's lives," he said afterward. "I never want to be in that situation again."

Along with the cuts and freezes, Chouinard made another decision that probably held the most significance—both real and symbolic—to those who followed the organization: Patagonia, he declared, was going to expand its already generous "corporate tithing" program. While other firms might have vastly reduced or even eliminated such efforts in the face of similar corporate upheavals, Chouinard announced he was instead bolstering the charitable agenda that has now provided over $17 million to hundreds of grassroots environmental groups. Previously structured to fund these donations with 10 percent of the company's pre-tax profits, this so-called Earth Tax would henceforth equal one percent of total sales if there were no pre-tax profits to draw from.

To loyal employees and customers, that helped reaffirm everything the reorganization, the downsizing, and the restructuring had brought into question.

"Just because we don't make a profit doesn't mean we don't have a responsibility to give money away," Chouinard says when asked about the change.

Since 1985, Patagonia has donated money, products and expertise to such groups as Minnesotans for Responsible Planning, Appalachian Voices, Forest Watch, and Friends of the Payette. This is not surprising when one considers the commitment that Chouinard and his employees have made to the great outdoors. From the boss on down, these are people who regularly engage in the type of demanding activities for which their products are made. A diminishing outdoor experience, either through active encroachment by anti-conservation forces or passive neglect by uninterested conservators, would have a devastating impact on the workforce as well as company sales.

But there is far more to the way this company thinks, and operates. A perfect example was Chouinard's decision to put the brakes on its previously unchecked expansion after a 16 percent sales increase from 1990 to 1991 threatened to undermine its future.

"We don't want to exceed our resources," he says. "That is the one thing that rock climbing, whitewater kayaking, and some of the other risk sports tell you: Don't exceed your limits. If you do, you are dead."

It was, in fact, this potential transcendence of Patagonia's core principles—owing much, ironically, to its garments' increasing acceptance as a fashion statement by self-styled outdoor enthusiasts who rarely traveled further afield than their own backyards—that led the company to put its corporate foot down. Growth had been consistent but manageable throughout the pile-bunting-Synchilla wars and the polypropylene-Capilene conflicts, but as the 1990s opened the demands on employees and finances started to spiral out of control.

And since Chouinard has always absolutely abhorred conspicuous consumption, and worked continuously to convince consumers that their throwaway mentality is destroying much of what he and his friends hold dear, he had yet another good reason to slow everything down.

"We're not trying to get people to stop consuming; we're trying to get them to cut back and consume better," Chouinard explains. "But if I say we must confront these problems and also have a business that grows and grows, then I'm a hypocrite. If I don't put the halt to this company and stop growth, then I can't expect anyone else to do so, either."

Eyes of the beholder

A prominent passage on Patagonia's web site begins: "Everything we make pollutes. The production of clothing has a negative impact on the environment, period."

Strange words from any company in an era when businesses everywhere yearn for the green seal of approval. Stranger still—at least at first blush—from the pen of a firm that thinks long and hard about environmental implications in store lighting and catalog paper. But honesty is a virtue that Patagonia has never lacked. It first used a version of that unflattering assessment more than a decade ago, in the opening spread to the semi-annual print catalog that it distributes to more than four hundred thousand households. The popular and critically praised direct-mail piece is successor to Chouinard's original one-page mimeographed product listing, and the cornerstone of an astonishingly successful marketing program that employs only minimal traditional advertising. Like Chouinard, it also has never been shy about promoting issues close to Patagonia's heart and letting the chips fall where they may.

The company spiced up the thick book from the beginning with regular advocacy articles like "Save the Salmon" and "Mountains are Dying," and its companion web site picked up the beat as soon as it went online in 1996 with featured stories like a year-long series of essays "pertaining to the dangers of genetic engineering." Both also have addressed the comprehensive environmental review that Chouinard first ordered during that tumultuous 1991 season—and discussed how it has since led the company to utilize processed chlorine-free post-consumer recycled paper and soy-based inks in its catalogs and other print materials; change its sources of energy and its choices for building materials; eliminate chlorine bleach, polyvinyl chloride and other harmful industry staples; host an international conference on environmental impacts for every company involved in making Patagonia products; and even create a separate T-shirt company to build greater demand for organic cotton. (The firm says that its Beneficial T's operation is now North America's largest distributor of 100 percent organic cotton T-shirt blanks.) "We use all of our distribution channels to educate current and potential customers about the issues that affect all of us," says Jil Zilligen, vice president of environmental initiatives.

Zilligen's four-person department also oversees the company's novel internship program, which permits eligible employees to take up to two months of paid leave to work with a nonprofit group of their choice. The employees continue earning their paychecks and accruing benefits while assisting efforts like the Southern Utah Wilderness Alliance's crusade to save Canyon Country or Zanzibar's Chumbe Island Project for coral reef protection. Some of these volunteers even choose not to return to Patagonia, such as a retail employee named Tom who accepted a job as his nonprofit's new communications coordinator. But that's okay with Patagonia, too.

Employees, customers and residents of the communities in which the company operates are further offered an array of information on the environment and various human rights issues. This may take the form of an employee class on landfills and water treatment, or a traveling exhibit to show Californians the benefits of conserving old-growth forests. It might include appearances at public hearings, massive letter-writing campaigns, and impassioned newspaper Op-Ed pieces. There have even been singular consumer-directed ads, such as a controversial full-color spread on beach pollution in national magazines that featured a large photo of a littered waterfront and the word "SHIT" as a conspicuous magenta headline.

"We debated whether to use that word," says Paul, the company's environmental assessment director at the time, "but we wanted to wake people up."

And that, of course, has been one of Chouinard's main goals from the beginning. His early catalogs supported the move to so-called "clean climbing" well before it became popular, even though it spelled doom for his signature pitons and other early products that actually damaged the mountains when climbers physically wedged them into rocks.

In the mid-1980s, Chouinard expanded this thinking when he came to the realization that Patagonia could be more than a sporting goods company; it could, he decided, be used as a tool to change things he could not change on his own. The result was a company that became totally focused on the environment. Patagonia cut its own trash by 50 percent; it developed a special recycling program for plastic bags that cover its garments as they travel to the United States from overseas. It also helped form an active corporate conservancy group—the Outdoor Industry Conservation Alliance—which counts Patagonia's chief competitors among its members.

The company took perhaps its most far-reaching step in the mid-1990s, when it announced that it was permanently switching all of its cotton and cotton-blend clothing to organic cotton fabrics. Asserting that traditional cotton-growing methods pollute the soil, the water and the air, Chouinard immediately shifted all sixty-six affected items in his 1996 line to the alternatives he had been incorporating on an experimental basis for four seasons. Prices were hiked to accommodate these more expensive materials—the original Stand Up Shorts, for example, were raised from \$40 to \$45—but the company also trimmed its profit margin to keep costs as low as possible. "We're asking our customers to split the difference," Chouinard told *Women's Wear Daily*. "Pay a little extra now to save on the clean-up bill later."

By far, the most conspicuous and far-reaching aspect of Patagonia's activism has been its grant program. While touted only in subtle ways—small notices in sales material and on clothing hang tags are the primary public notice of its existence—this so-called Earth Tax now generates about twenty unsolicited requests each week for awards that usually range from $3,000-$8,000. Additional assistance, in the form of donated gear or in-kind help, also is offered regularly to these non-profit groups, Zilligen notes.

Not everyone, employee or customer, has always supported every one of these donations. Some of Patagonia's more controversial beneficiaries, like Planned Parenthood and the radical environmental group Earth First!, have led to hard feelings. Yet for Chouinard, it is more important that his company serve a greater good. "Maybe some of our employees don't agree with all of the groups we give money to," he says. "But most likely they back 90 percent of them. And that's more than most companies would do."

When it hears from customers upset by certain connections, Zilligen says the firm communicates with them—although not with a traditional apology. "We don't welcome the negative feedback, but the silver lining is we hope we have a hand in helping people think," she notes. "We are genuinely sorry to lose a customer but accept that it can happen. We know we can't change everybody's mind but at least we have gotten them to think about the issues."

A new era begins

By mid-morning the day is fully underway at the Great Pacific Child Development Center, Patagonia's on-site child-care facility. Like similar operations in big cities and small towns across the U.S., its rooms are filled with colorful toys and its walls are lined with bright artwork. Ninety kids from eight weeks of age through third grade are playing while a nutritional lunch is being prepared. One employee is taking a break from office duties to breast-feed her baby. Another is here because his child wouldn't stop crying. A few without youngsters of their own have come in to play with the children of others.

Opened in 1984—along with a cafeteria serving the kind of healthy food that Patagonia employees tend to prefer and a sand volleyball pit where they can burn off subsequent calories—it is exactly the type of center for young children that working parents everywhere long to find. Although open to non-employees if space is available, it is designed specifically to benefit the people who work at Patagonia as well as the company itself. "Benefits are here to make our employees more productive," says Chouinard. "Child care is here so that someone with a kid doesn't have to worry about what is going on in some child-care center. No one will have to quit work just because they have a young child."

They also will not have to quit simply because they find their schedule too confining. As befits a company founded by someone who always relished his freedom, Patagonia offers a liberal flex-time policy. If someone like Rosie, a five-year employee in the personnel department, wants to go out for a bike ride on a nice afternoon, she feels free to do so—but may then come back to the office to work as late as ten o'clock that night. Rosie's tan shows that she regularly takes Patagonia up on the opportunity.

Rosie's circumstances are also as unique, yet as common, as those of many of her co-workers. She met Chouinard while she was a climbing guide for the Outward Bound program in upstate New York and accompanied him back to Ventura when he offered her a job. "Patagonia was willing to take a chance with me," she says. "Since I was a guide and had never committed to any company, a lot of other employers would have wondered what was wrong with me. Patagonia took the risk."

Chouinard, though, has said he doesn't do these things simply because he feels an obligation to care for employees from cradle to grave. Rather, he does them because the benefits that accrue are mutual and they make good business sense. And it was for this very reason that he brought a number of respected industry veterans on board—including Michael Crooke—as the century turned.

After 1991, when Patagonia's well-publicized troubles led to crash-and-burn predictions from national magazines like *Inc.*, Chouinard realized he had to refocus on keeping with his hundred-year operational goal. The biggest change would be curbing the perpetual temptation to expand merely for expansion's sake, seeking instead a natural level of growth that allowed the company to progress steadily but within its means. The trick would be solidifying the business processes needed to do so, while also maintaining the firm's highly advanced combination of external philanthropy and internal support—and freeing it entirely from debt along the way. "I'm sick and tired of being under the thumb of the banks," Chouinard said at the time.

Crooke, who studied forestry before joining the Navy SEALs, had been a fan of Patagonia since getting his first bunting jacket. After stints as CEO of Pearl Izumi, a cycling and performance apparel company, and president of the Conservation Alliance, the industry environmental group Patagonia helped form, he felt he had the unique combination of outdoors savvy, social commitment and business acumen that the company needed. Chouinard agreed and named him chief executive of Lost Arrow, which in addition to Patagonia now oversees the child-care center and organic T-shirt business, a surfboard manufacturer, a paddling gear company, and a swim- and sportswear firm for young women athletes.

Concentrating on the consumer that Patagonia affectionately calls "the true dirt-bag"—the person who just lives for his sport—Crooke and Chouinard built upon its bedrock commitments to manufacturing quality, environmental responsibility, social obligation, and fiscal accountability to refashion a more highly focused company that will consistently grow by about 7 percent a year instead of the 15-30 percent rate that it flirted with a decade earlier. They also boosted charitable efforts by starting new initiatives like the Patagonia Land Trust, which under the direction of Kristine McDivitt Tompkins who worked her way up at the company from shipping clerk to CEO and is still a board member is striving to maintain wild lands in the South American region that inspired the firm's name. And despite a recession that brought widespread job reductions and other cutbacks elsewhere, Patagonia enjoyed its best operating profit ever in 2001 and laid off no one. "Plus, we're completely out of the banks," Crooke says. "We have no debt right now."

Not only have Patagonia's corporate fortunes turned around while it increases its activist positions, but traditional audiences appear to be more receptive to its unorthodox business message than at any time previously. Crooke had been taking it to colleges and universities long before the Enron debacle became public knowledge, and even once-skeptical audiences like those at Harvard now tend to concede its unconventional philosophy may be a solution for the future—and more schools want him to speak than he has time to visit. "There's way more demand than supply right now," Crooke says with a laugh. "Everybody's wondering what the new business paradigm for the twenty-first century will be."

For Chouinard, the direction remains clear. An ardent opponent of public corporations and their insatiable need for growth—"the greatest evil there is right now," he says—Patagonia's iconoclastic leader knows he has gotten as far as he has by recognizing his limits in business and the out-of-doors. But even as he approaches traditional retirement age, that doesn't mean he'll start taking the route that others choose.

"If we can take the radical end of it and show it's working for us," he says, "the more conservative companies will take that first step. And one day they'll become good businesses too."

Chapter Eleven

Uniting People and Ideas

Company Name: Tattered Cover Book Store
Primary Business: Retail bookseller
Type of Company: Private corporation
Headquarters: Denver, Colorado
Number of Employees: 320
Founder/CEO: Joyce Meskis
Year Founded: 1971
Web site: http://www.tatteredcover.com/

Mission Statement

The Tattered Cover Book Store is a retail business dedicated to the principle of freedom of expression. Its purpose is to bring people and books together in an ethical, profitable and socially conscious way.

The Tattered Cover maintains a delicately balanced relationship between financial and philosophical concerns. We all recognize that the store, in order to continue to exist so as to promote its philosophical goals, must have financial health as its primary consideration. At the same time we choose to do business in a way that encourages, as much as possible, what is positive in the human spirit, operating, as much as possible, in a manner of trust, believing this to be in the best interest of the business, the community and the society in which we live.

In April 2000, armed with a search warrant, five members of a U.S. drug enforcement task force strode across the hardwood ground floor of the Tattered Cover Book Store in Denver's historic Lower Downtown. The agents climbed a well-worn staircase at the rear of the refurbished pioneer-era warehouse, then purposely made their way to the entrance of an adjoining old building that houses Tattered Cover's corporate offices. At the front desk, they stood beside framed photos of past visitors ranging from Jimmy Carter to Yoko Ono and asked the receptionist to summon owner Joyce Meskis.

As she does with all who call, Meskis soon emerged to personally escort the quintet through a maze of corridors leading to her comfortable book-lined private office. Once inside, she invited everyone to sit on the same type of overstuffed armchairs and love seats that her store has used during the past quarter-century to help create its legendary customer-friendly ambiance.

Everyone who works at Tattered Cover remembers that day. It had been anticipated since DEA agents raided a Denver-area home one month earlier, finding a methamphetamine lab along with a pair of drug-making manuals and evidence that something in the house may have been purchased by mail from the bookstore. Still, those in offices near their boss grew apprehensive as they watched the intimidating group of outsiders sweep past. Their confidence and conviction returned, though, as they also noticed Meskis maintaining her customary calm during what certainly was one of the most disconcerting moments in her sixty years. She even offered to get the agents something to drink, just as she would any visitor seated on her comfortable Grandma's attic-style furniture.

"Joyce stayed on such an even keel," recalls Barb Bush, the company's general manager for finance.

Like everyone at Tattered Cover, Bush has always taken her cues directly from Meskis. She was some twenty years into two careers—one as a lab technician at a local hospital, another as a CPA at an accounting firm and a cable company—before realizing in 1989 that a change was in order. "I was a very square peg in a very round hole," says the Kansas City native, "and decided to open my own bookstore. I was just about to sign the franchise agreement when I thought, 'Gee, maybe I ought to work in a bookstore for five minutes first.'" She accepted a job at the Tattered Cover as a holiday temp, making just $4 an hour. "Something drew me here," she recalls.

The holidays came and went, but Bush liked the idea of working for Meskis more than the idea of competing against her. After one stint helping with personnel and training and another in the controller's office, she assumed the general manager's slot in 1995 and took over all matters financial. "I loved Joyce's philosophy and approach," she says. "And my husband said I never looked happier."

Bush is among those who vividly recall the arrival of the drug agents, chuckling now over the incongruity of their business-suit formality in the fiercely casual atmosphere of the bookstore. Their very presence, though, was unsettling. Bush does not liken what she does to working for a firm that sells commodities such as sporting goods or services such as eye care. She instead considers herself a "bookseller," a direct descendent of the tradition- and principle-bound literary professionals who for centuries have worked to bring people and ideas together while protecting basic liberties like privacy and free speech. "I feel like I'm making a contribution to my community," she says of her job.

It really didn't surprise her or other staffers, therefore, when the low-key owner/CEO of this sprawling operation—which now serves up lattes and pastries at two coffee bars and fancy cuisine at a tony restaurant, along with the usual Stephen King novels, investment primers, travel guides, bibles, children's books and, yes, even a manual or two that some find objectionable—drew her line in the sand. They applauded when Meskis told agents she would not turn over any purchase records. And they rejoiced when scores of outsiders joined to support the ensuing legal struggle.

"It goes with the territory," Meskis says matter-of-factly more than a year after the Drug Enforcement Administration visit. While awaiting a Colorado Supreme Court decision on whether she must ultimately release the records, she recalls bygone days when books were routinely "banned in Boston," and more recent times after Salman Rushdie drew death threats for publishing *The Satanic Verses*. She says such incidents convinced her to join her industry's anti-censorship efforts, while striving to ensure her store never shied away from controversy because of personal opinion or commercial implication. By way of example, she cites book signings by Larry Flynt, Newt Gingrich and Hillary Clinton. All attracted far-flung media coverage, frenzied local protesters, and vows by some to never shop at Tattered Cover again. "We sell books that, on a personal level, I'd prefer would never have been published," she concedes. "But it's important to have them. It's what we're about: to give access to ideas. In the debate that follows, we hope the good ones lift and the bad ones fall. How else will that happen?"

This attitude has long helped Tattered Cover exert an influence that far outstrips its geographic base. Denver is relatively modest in size, with a metropolitan area ranked around twentieth in the nation. Nonetheless, the city is viewed as one of America's top bookselling markets and the store is considered one of its top booksellers. While Meskis declines to share her private corporation's internal numbers, the *Industry Standard* magazine estimated annual sales at $40 million while the sales-per-square-foot formula applied to large bookselling superstore chains pegs the figure at more than $22 million. Either way, such accomplishment in this challenging field is considered remarkable.

When Meskis bought the original store, a 950-square-foot hole-in-the-wall in a slowly awakening neighborhood called Cherry Creek, books were primarily sold by similar independents or in department stores. Combining a staggeringly deep selection of titles, an attentive staff that is impressively knowledgeable yet intentionally accessible, and a cozy atmosphere which encourages browsing, she caught the attention of a growing local population that was highly educated, exceedingly loyal, and flush with disposable income. She constantly expanded both the size of her store and the concepts on which it was founded, and consistently attracted a workforce as sharp and committed as her customers. Along the way she also opened three dining spots in response to increasingly difficult business conditions, while expanding her already eye-popping selection to more than eight hundred thousand books (representing some one hundred fifty thousand different titles) and dozens of related products in two distinct locations: a four-story former department store, ironically enough, in the now-thriving Cherry Creek shopping district, and the three-story one-time warehouse in the up-and-coming historic LoDo neighborhood downtown. Many ideas she pioneered have also been embraced by other independent bookstores, along with the burgeoning big-box chains that now comprise her most serious competition.

Characteristically, the soft-spoken Meskis embraces such challenges and opportunities while downplaying the pivotal role in which she often finds herself. "All I really want to do," she says with quiet determination, "is sell books."

In the beginning

In the mid-1970s Denver was a sleepy cow town. Isolated by geography and history, it was situated where plain meets mountain and on the cusp of pending civic change. Furnished two-bedroom houses in nice neighborhoods could still be rented for $200 a month, or bought for under $50,000. There was plenty of free parking downtown, even if there rarely was any good reason to go there. Skyscrapers were any buildings that reached ten stories, and only one part of Denver's long-neglected historic core had been refurbished—Larimer Square—making the city's original main street its lone bright spot amidst a sea of dilapidation and disregard. Even the beloved pro football team remained the on-field joke it had been through years in the American Football League, while the basketball franchise was still transitioning from the small-potatoes ABA to the big-time NBA.

People elsewhere, though, began noticing the possible benefits of this slower-paced lifestyle in such close proximity to the glorious Rocky Mountains. Accordingly, as the middle of the decade approached, the latest in a long line of eager immigrants to the Mile High City began arriving in force with their own hopes and opinions and expectations. Resultant changes occurred seemingly overnight: More and better restaurant and retail choices sprang up everywhere; bigger and bigger stars added Denver performances to their schedules; improvements to public facilities from libraries to airports were put on the drawing board. Major changes arrived downtown when blocks of nineteenth century commercial properties were given blanket historic protections and the buildings around them shot up five times higher than any ever had before. Parking, of course, became more difficult to find and housing costs rose steadily. At least the local orange-clad football squad improved significantly, although the jury remained out on the basketball team.

A young Joyce Meskis was among the burgeoning crowd of transplants who were transforming Denver. The daughter of a salesman and a nurse, she was raised on Chicago's south side before attending Purdue University with the goal of teaching mathematics at a university. To pay tuition there and in graduate school at the University of Denver—where she by now was studying to teach English—Meskis worked regularly in bookstores and libraries. Married at the time and with two young daughters, she has told people that she awoke one day and realized those literary institutions were the ones that really captured her heart. When her marriage ended and she and her husband divided their possessions, Meskis pursued her dream and opened a one thousand-square-foot bookstore in the tiny rural town of Parker.

Alas, the idea wasn't so great. Even though Parker was barely twenty minutes from Denver, the boom in the city was slow to reach the surrounding countryside. Meskis experimented with some of the ideas that would later become her trademark, but business never materialized and in 1973 she was forced to bail out. Casting about for other opportunities, she found the Tattered Cover for sale and purchased it the next year with the help of loans from friends. She hired two employees, established the atmosphere she wanted as best she could in the cramped space she had, and threw open the split Dutch doors that would soon become one of the most popular shopping portals along East Second Avenue. She also put an old wing chair with a reading light beside it in her storefront window, signaling the environment she hoped to create. "That was the biggest piece of furniture we could get in the place," she says now with a laugh.

Matt Miller had moved to Denver from Massachusetts one year earlier. Like many, the twenty-something director of a child-care center quickly became a Tattered Cover customer and fan. Also, like more than a few, he took a part-time job on the sales floor one summer and just never left. Hired as the store's tenth employee in 1977, Miller has since been its children's book buyer, mass market paperback buyer, remainder buyer, and store manager. He ultimately earned a master's degree in organizational management and for the past half-dozen years has been the general manager for buying. His responsibilities include supervising thirty-four individuals who recommend initial purchases and reorders in specific categories like those in which he started.

"Our basic values haven't changed in all that time," he says now, coming in on an off day to discuss the bookstore and the book business. At fifty-one he has been at Tattered Cover nearly half his years, and is one of a surprisingly large block of "lifers" who have worked at the store for two decades or more. But even while undergoing some very dramatic events—relocations, computerizations, diversifications—he believes the principles Meskis instilled at the beginning are the same ones guiding everything today. "We're still treating customers and each other the same as we always did, still operating from a position of trust," he says. "We may be using some different procedures, but our essence will remain the same as long as our core values don't change."

From 1975 to 1983 the original store expanded seven times into adjoining space, mirroring the steady growth in surrounding Cherry Creek. Meskis developed a bond with employees by making Tattered Cover a great place to work and offering all the benefits she could to counter the low wages necessitated by the business's tight margins. She built a relationship with the community by trusting it (IDs have never been required with personal checks) and assembling an enormous selection of books on an astounding variety of topics. She initiated a number of appealing services that were unique at the time, like special ordering any book in print for no extra charge. And Meskis reached out to the community by scheduling story times for children, creating fundraising opportunities for nonprofits, working with schools, and supporting programs that promote literacy. One, the Children's Holiday Book Drive, now provides scores of new and "gently used" books each year for young patients at clinics operated by Denver's Children's Hospital and Neighborhood Health Program.

Additionally, Meskis was literally handed the outreach program for which her store is now justly renowned: author appearances. These days, Tattered Cover hosts an astounding six hundred or so each year as first-time writers and Pulitzer Prize-winners alike make their pilgrimage to this literary mecca. Back in the 1970s, though, most publishers ignored everything between Chicago and San Francisco, and even Meskis felt there were better ways to promote books. But all that changed one day when she took a call from a sales rep who mentioned that a certain photographer would be passing through town on his way to New Mexico to visit good friend Georgia O'Keeffe.

"Did we think the Tattered Cover would like to have Ansel Adams come in for a signing?" she says now, repeating the dead-panned inquiry that helped her make a new mark in Denver book-selling. "I said 'Yes!' but I was scared to death; I had heard stories about how curmudgeonly and meticulous he could be. Well, he came and he was just a peach, and the line was out the door. The magic of the moment was so incredible that I said, 'You know, maybe we can try this a little bit here and a little bit there.'" Meskis and her team began pushing publishers to send their top authors to Denver, and were rewarded when giants like Tom Wolfe came to present their latest works—as well as when local authors stepped up to the podium to read to a few friends.

Such efforts spurred demand her increasingly tight quarters simply could not meet, and so in January 1983 Meskis leased a second location in a spacious, modern, two-story building that was just a block to the east on the opposite side of Second Avenue. Incredibly, when customers heard about it, they volunteered to help move everything that was going. Both sites were then operated as a single entity—"one store with the misfortune of being divided by a street," Meskis says—with the original handling bargain books, non-book items and most office functions, while the new one housed receiving, all other retail operations, and plenty of the cushy furniture that Meskis never before could squeeze in. The store's reputation and business soared, and all-too-quickly sparked the need for the biggest relocation of all.

The middle years

The move in November 1986 to what became Tattered Cover's flagship store is the second act in one of the business world's truly great customer-relation stories. Denver was undergoing yet another wave of growth and development in the mid-1980s, and Cherry Creek was blossoming from construction of what would become the swankest shopping mall in the Rocky Mountain

West. More customers than ever would soon be streaming into the neighborhood. Yet the bookstore was constrained by the cramped eighteen thousand square feet of retail space that Meskis had straddling the street.

The solution turned out to be a one-time department store more than twice that size for lease just a hundred steps away on East First Avenue. It offered not only room to immediately expand the store's products and amenities in one place, but its freestanding four-story structure sat on one of the city's most visible spots: along a major thoroughfare and directly across from the coming mall's new sites for Neiman Marcus, Saks Fifth Avenue, and other high-profile retailers. Moving, though, would not be easy.

"The first time," Meskis recalls, "I contacted a bookstore in St. Paul that I heard the customers had helped move. They said, 'Just put up a sign-up sheet and see what happens.' So we did and people signed up very willingly. Then, not even four years later, it was time to move again. I said I couldn't be so presumptuous as to put up the sign-up sheet again; we'll figure out another way to do it. But people started asking and wanting to be part of it." Loyal customers arrived in droves a second time, and along with the staff—now numbering about sixty—they moved everything from the old stores to the new one over a single weekend, necessitating closure only on Sunday. Even so, Meskis adds, "we kept the newsstand open so people could get their *New York Times*."

The new location offered three ten thousand-square-foot floors for retail and a basement of the same size for administration. (A restaurant on the top remained occupied by an outside entrepreneur.) To position further for anticipated growth, all processes related to inventory had been computerized three months earlier—on a date still indelibly etched in Meskis's mind—when the owner finally located a system both affordable and reliable enough to handle the tens of thousands of distinct items that a bookstore sells. "It gave us the opportunity to make better decisions," she says, allowing them to replace the "billions and billions and billions of inventory control cards that we shuffled and filed and un-filed" with an instant and more reliable electronic window into the status of any product that any customer might want at any time.

Heather Duncan, who arrived almost exactly three years after the big move, quickly learned what such customer orientation is like in a store busy most of the ninety hours a week it is open. Among the ten or so temporaries hired each year to help out during the Christmas season—a period that accounts for a full quarter of a bookstore's annual sales—Duncan had recently earned a bachelor's degree in International Business from the University of Colorado. Her sister worked at the store, and the Denver-area native says, "It was one of my favorite places." To earn some holiday cash while casting about for a job in her field, she started at the bookstore's counter. When the new year arrived, she decided to stay on.

Duncan worked first in the basement, where she processed vendor orders with the low-tech index card system the store still used. She then went outside as its sales representative, developing corporate customers through events such as business-author luncheons. In 1995 she left to take a higher-paying job with a local publisher, but after a few months returned as Tattered Cover's director of marketing and community relations. She holds that position today and, with a staff of eight, oversees all advertising, publicity, promotion and community activities. She seems to sincerely love her job, the fact that her colleagues are close enough to socialize after work, and the chance she gets to read everything and then meet the authors she enjoys. But the best thing, for her, is becoming a bookseller. "Working with Joyce offers a great sense of doing something that's important," she explains. "Being here makes me feel like I'm doing my part for the world."

Duncan and others from top to bottom will readily admit, on the other hand, that nobody works at Tattered Cover for the money. Regardless of background or experience, newcomers start on the sales floor at just $6 an hour. Non-salary perquisites, though, are a somewhat different story.

"From the beginning," Meskis says, "we always had what benefits we could." At first they were decidedly modest: scheduling flexibility within the constraints of an operation open nights and weekends, the opportunity to buy books at cost, life and disability insurance, standard vacation time, the usual sick leave. In a move designed as much to please employees as to keep them on top of the store's wares, she allowed everyone to borrow anything on the shelves at any time as long as it was returned in pristine condition. Also, for a while, she even permitted employees to give themselves cash advances from the register between paychecks. And, she notes, "as soon as we could we offered a health package with premiums paid completely by the bookstore."

About the same time she moved to the unified Cherry Creek location, Meskis also heard about companies crafting their own self-insured health care plans. Tattered Cover was then of a size that made it feasible; her costs under the current system were increasingly onerous, and she wasn't too happy anyway with the stance these standard policies took toward touchy items like mental health coverage and acceptance of domestic partners.

"These were things that were really important to us, so we pushed to put a package together that included them," she says. "Much of what we did is now being done as a matter of course, but it wasn't then." As marketplace pressures increased in recent years, Meskis has kept this program intact but now requires employees to pay a portion of their premiums. To help compensate she's added other benefits like a 401(k), dental and eye care insurance, and free monthly passes for the region's mass transit system.

As the store and its reputation grew, so did the role Meskis played in the book world and her community. She became president of the American Booksellers Association in 1990, and began urging her peers to upgrade their operations as she had. That same year she also joined with local restaurateur John

Hickenlooper, the pioneer responsible for first pumping life into Denver's Lower Downtown and who was elected mayor of Denver in June 2003, and assembled the largest mixed-use commercial project proposed in decades for the city's historic core. In a quiet corner of LoDo that had yet to see redevelopment, the $18 million project within several adjoining old warehouses would eventually include more than ninety apartments—most reserved for low-income residents—a restaurant, and a branch of Tattered Cover. To reinforce her commitment to the area, Meskis even moved into a loft two blocks away in the first warehouse that Hickenlooper had refurbished into a combination brew pub-pool hall-residence. "I live right above pool table fourteen," she says. "And I've got the best alley view in Denver."

Just a few months after the LoDo project began Meskis was able to shift the store's shipping and receiving operations, as well as most of its administrative duties, into the new complex. All retail attention remained focused on Cherry Creek, however, and the removal of back-shop functions allowed the basement to be opened almost immediately for additional shelf space. This consequently provided more room for author appearances, which boomed through the mid-1990s with visits by an eclectic assortment of literary celebrities that included John Irving, Martha Stewart, Clive Cussler, Miss Manners, George Plimpton, Jimmy Carter and Yoko Ono, who actually asked the former president to sign a book for her when they appeared in the store on the same day. Meskis also remained just as attentive to the book launches of Colorado authors, and even hosted parties in the still raw LoDo space for all locals published during the preceding year.

Downtown denizens awaiting the unveiling of a new Tattered Cover in the renovated warehouses were finally rewarded in October 1994, when a small temporary version of what was to come opened on the ground floor of the spacious brick-and-hardwood C.S. Morey Mercantile Building. Featuring a few tidy book departments, an expansive newsstand and a pleasant cafe, it clearly marked the arrival of a distinctly new chapter for the area as well as for Meskis and her staffers.

LoDo and beyond

Most mornings from 9:00 till most evenings at 11:00, the two massive Tattered Covers—which today total eighty-five thousand square feet of retail, dining and administrative space—are perfect representations of the neighborhoods they serve. Visit LoDo on any afternoon and you'll likely see a few young business people browsing the second-floor architecture section, or an older couple enjoying a coffee table book in the bargain area, and small clusters of college students and loft-dwellers downstairs amidst the art magazines, out-of-town newspapers and newest non-fiction. On a similar morning in Cherry Creek you might see young women with strollers packing the giant kids' department, a teenaged boy and girl whispering to each other on the pew in the second-floor religion section, and a well-dressed middle-aged woman in travel on the third floor talking about an upcoming trip with an employee she obviously knows quite well. At both locations, streams of customers and staffers of all ages and persuasions will be walking and talking and looking and reading. And at all hours of the day and evening, long lines will usually be snaking from most of the cash registers near each door.

Tattered Cover has certainly grown up a lot over the past three decades, and many of the changes parallel those experienced by Denver and the book business. Sleepy LoDo became home to new Major League Baseball and National Hockey League franchises, for instance, followed by block upon block of trendy nightspots, hip restaurants and high-ticket residential buildings. Cherry Creek matured into one of the most popular addresses in Denver, with the combined mall and shopping district developing as the state's top single tourist draw. At the same time, the art of book retailing had to be completely rethought as department stores abandoned the business and mammoth discounters like K-Mart and Target—along with niche retailers selling everything from sporting goods to cookware—moved in. E-commerce had its fits and starts, but undisputed online leader Amazon.com continued moving truckloads of heavily discounted books to former independent book store customers. And the biggest threat of all emerged with the appearance of superstore chains such as Barnes & Noble and Borders, which successfully merged the comfortable-furniture-and-coffee-bar concept perfected by Meskis with the mass retailing practices pioneered by Wal-Mart and spread the big-box result across America.

"Competitively, it is very different," Meskis muses. "But if you go back and read the history of bookselling in America, it's always in a state of unbelievable disquiet. The good news, though, is that books are everywhere."

Still, selling books remains a unique challenge. All retailers must deal with specific publishers for specific authors—there's no going elsewhere for better deals on the latest John Grisham novel—and items themselves carry imprinted price tags for all to see. Try finding the cost emblazoned directly on a music CD or most other consumer products. With increased competition, and the zealous way these new outlets initially discounted bestsellers, the pressure on independents became intense. Some matched the cuts, but few could sustain them without the heavy volume and economies of scale enjoyed by the nationwide giants. Others, like the Tattered Cover, simply refused to lower prices, and instead built upon their existing strengths. They played up their knowledgeable, well-trained, helpful staffs. They emphasized their deep and wide selections, personal touches, community involvements, and local roots. Smaller stores and those without well-developed customer bases often couldn't turn the tide and many closed. Tattered Cover—which has at least thirteen Barnes & Nobles and four Borders within a twenty-minute drive—lost business but held steady. Ultimately, many independents started initiating creative offensive strategies of their own to battle the competition.

One, aimed directly at customers' stomachs, initially appeared in Denver when Meskis opened a cafe in the first stirrings of the LoDo store in early fall of 1994. It was expanded around Thanksgiving when a similar coffee shop was opened in the Cherry Creek Tattered Cover. But the big step came the following February when Meskis unveiled the Fourth Story Restaurant & Bar on the fourth floor of the flagship building in space previously leased by other eateries.

"We have food for thought, and good food for the body," Meskis told *Nation's Restaurant News* for an article about such bookstore/restaurant combos opening around the country. A true extension of her original enterprise, the Fourth Story is furnished with overstuffed chairs and its walls are lined with bursting bookshelves. Its menu features local ingredients and is changed seasonally. Special events include Sunday brunch and wine tasting seminars. Tea is served in the lounge every afternoon, and Monday nights are reserved for live jazz and martini specials. Not surprisingly, customers of the restaurant and customers of the book store tended from the start to be one and the same.

Various strategies designed to directly aid retailing efforts were also advanced by the bookselling industry's independent contingent itself—a group that, as its name implies, never really has been known for such cooperative efforts. Adversity changed that, however, and an initial internal response was the creation of a consortium to help geographically dispersed members better network with each other. A more effective external venture appeared somewhat later in the form of the American Booksellers Association's Book Sense program, which markets participating independents as a group and provides them with helpful tools they can build upon to a degree they feel comfortable. One is an easily customized web site that allows even the smallest store to combine a polished online presence and secure transaction system with a product database drawn from all twelve hundred stores in the program. Another is a gift certificate that can be bought in any location and used in any other. A third is a bimonthly flyer with recommendations in various categories from independents around the nation, mirroring the respected verbal suggestions that independents have been giving individual customers for years.

Tattered Cover expanded fully into LoDo in the midst of this, shelving about three hundred thousand volumes on three renovated floors in 1996 while an expanded computer system was installed to fully link all functions in its two locales. The moves helped the book store serve customers more effectively and keep closer track of all key business operations. But what the staff and public most marveled at when the new store opened was the vast space on its second floor developed specifically for author appearances. Seating over two hundred fifty, it is lined with photographs of the building in its 1880s heyday, as well as black-and-white portraits of many who have come to read and sign there. More than a few, like *Girl With the Pearl Earring* author Tracy Chevalier, proudly tell the crowd how excited they are to be in this paradise for readers and writers. Others announce it to the world. "I am coming to my favorite bookstore in America," former President Jimmy Carter told the *Denver Post* as he was headed to the store in December 2001 for his fourth visit since 1988.

"It's a chance for authors to meet their fans, and for fans to meet the authors they like," event coordinator Charles Stillwagon says of these appearances, which can draw a couple of dozen for a local writer or a couple of thousand for a Jimmy Carter, a Colin Powell, or a John Glenn. "We even have regulars who come to events all the time, no matter who is featured."

Stillwagon now works with a half-dozen other staffers to pull off the heavy volume of appearances scheduled throughout each year, dealing along the way with publishers, literary escorts, and some two hundred media representatives, as well as the authors. But the Pittsburgh native was waiting tables elsewhere six years ago when he drove to the store with a friend who was seeking work. Stillwagon liked what he saw, took a job himself at Cherry Creek, and relocated to LoDo when it opened. He worked the counter, the coffee bar, the reservation desk, and with non-book items before accepting his current position.

"I don't know if I'll be a bookseller for life," he says, "but I do think I'll remain connected to this industry. I lucked into it, but now I'm comfortable with the store, the community, and the web of booksellers I come in contact with from across the country."

All is not sweetness and light, of course. The book business has always been difficult and it was particularly weak even before the attacks of September 11th and the subsequent national recession. Locally, economic conditions in early 2003 grew so bad that Meskis was forced to cut twenty-seven jobs—nearly 10 percent of her workforce. Still, she reinforced her commitment to the community even in the face of such adversity. A few months after the layoffs, the store announced a new initiative called Tattered Cover Gives Back. Under it, customers are encouraged to select a local nonprofit, like the Colorado AIDS Project or Denver Public Library, and then each time they make a purchase the store will donate 1 percent of the total sale to it. And not only is the program free to customers, but they receive a coupon good for 10 percent off their next purchase when they join.

But even while such business and social issues continue to vie for her attention with everyday gripes about everything from the movement of a favorite chair to slow service at the Fourth Story, angry complaints about certain books or certain speakers or certain positions that the store decides to take continue to show why the book business is different from most others. A prime example was the DEA search warrant and subsequent public fallout. "Many people I have spoken with are angered over Joyce Meskis's refusal to hand over the meth lab suspect's purchasing records to the police," one man from the suburbs wrote about the case in a letter to a Denver newspaper, "and I have vowed never to shop there again."

The position of Meskis and her store in that high-profile case was ultimately upheld. However, it took almost two years to the day after those drug enforcement agents strode into the LoDo store with their search warrant for the decision to come down. In a unanimous fifty-three-page decision, the Colorado Supreme

Court said it would not force the Tattered Cover to turn over the records in question. "Bookstores are places where a citizen can explore ideas, receive information, and discover the myriad perspectives on every topic imaginable," Justice Michael Bender opined. "When a person buys a book at a bookstore, he engages in activity protected by the First Amendment because he is exercising his right to read and receive ideas and information."

Meskis, who first learned of the decision from the court's web site, celebrated briefly in her low-key way before holding a press conference to discuss it. Then, she immediately went back to focusing on the same long-term goals she has had since buying the store in 1974. "I get tired, but I'm older now," she laughs. "Still, there is just nothing like going out on the sales floor and seeing a happy kid running through the children's section, or hearing somebody say, 'Oh wow! You've got the book!' and knowing you've played some small role to make that happen."

And the infamous book that brought down the agents as well as the wrath of certain Denver-area consumers? In April 2003, almost exactly one year after the store's landmark First Amendment victory, it was revealed in a documentary film about the case that the controversial purchase in question was actually a paperback called *A Guide to Remembering Japanese Characters*—a book on calligraphy, not a how-to on producing methamphetamine.

Chapter Twelve

In Their Own League

Company Name: Kansas City Chiefs
Primary Business: Professional football team
Type of Company: Private corporation
Headquarters: Kansas City, Missouri
Number of employees: 210
Founder: Lamar Hunt
CEO: Carl Peterson
Year Founded: 1960
Web site: http://www.kcchiefs.com

When the Kansas City Chiefs hosted the New York Giants on September 23, 2001, the organization wanted to do something momentous. After all, only two weeks had passed since the terrorist attacks on the World Trade Center paralyzed the country. Security was at an all-time high at Arrowhead Stadium as the almost eighty thousand fans, dressed in their customary all-red attire, came to cheer on their beloved Chiefs that sun-filled autumn day.

But the day's football game was not on the forefront of everyone's minds. Rather, it was the thousands of men, women and children who lost their lives on September 11th. As much as the Chiefs' faithful had come to watch a football game, they also were there to show solidarity and support for the visiting New York team and its wounded hometown.

Lamar Hunt, founder and owner of the Chiefs, was on a business trip in Columbus, Ohio, on September 11. Like thousands of stranded travelers throughout the country, he rented a car and drove home. For him, it was a one thousand mile trek back to Dallas, Texas. During the long drive he came up with the idea to collect donations when the Giants came to Kansas City the following week. Hunt further pledged that the Chiefs' organization, including the players, coaches, staff and his family, would match any donations collected from fans.

Throughout the first half of the game, hundreds of Kansas City firefighters and their families moved throughout the stadium, passing traditional firemen's boots row-by-row. Fans dug deeply into their pockets, filling the boots with bills, checks and coins. The money collected was to go to charities assisting the families of the New York City police and fire departments, emergency medical technicians and the Port Authority.

In the team's back offices, staff members carefully counted the bills and coins. By the end of the game, the stadium announcer broadcasted that an estimated $225,000 had been collected. With the matching donations by the organization, the Chiefs would be sending a check to New York for more than $450,000. The crowd roared so loudly at the news that it was reportedly heard ten miles away in downtown Kansas City.

Arrowhead Stadium was the only venue among the NFL's fourteen teams hosting games that Sunday to organize such a collection. In addition, it's believed to be the largest single-day outpouring of aid by a group of fans and a pro sports team. "The Chiefs family has never been more proud of the Kansas City community and of our fans than we were on Sunday," said Carl

Peterson, the Chiefs CEO and general manager, a few days later. "The fans were terrific."

The Giants, who would go on to win the game, were visibly touched. Their general manager, owner and coaches personally thanked the Chiefs and the Kansas City community for supporting a cause halfway across the country. And later that week, the Giants took the unprecedented step of placing a full-page ad in the *Kansas City Star* to publicly thank the Chiefs and the Kansas City community.

While the support of fans and the organization was particularly keen that September Sunday, it certainly was not unprecedented. In fact, the Chiefs and their fans have a rich history of mutual admiration and support. "In all my years in football, I've never seen an organization more committed to its fans, or fans more committed to an organization," says Dick Vermeil, head coach of the Chiefs. Vermeil has a good basis for comparison, having led teams to the Super Bowl in both St. Louis and Philadelphia, and as a previous coach at ten organizations. When asked why Kansas City is a step above other teams, Vermeil doesn't hesitate. "It all starts with Lamar," he answers.

The perfect owner

In an age when some NFL owners seem to run the team both on the field and off, Lamar Hunt, with his altruistic, behind-the-scenes ways, is an anomaly. Though he's the multimillionaire son of famed Texas oilman H.L. Hunt, colleagues and friends describe him as thrifty, simple, thoughtful and unpretentious. Both Peterson and Vermeil call Hunt "the perfect owner." Though he lives in Dallas, he and his family are regulars in Kansas City. Now in his early seventies, Hunt is also co-founder of the American Football League, the North American Soccer League, is a 12 percent owner of the Chicago Bulls, and is owner-operator of two Major League Soccer franchises, in Columbus, Ohio, and Kansas City. In addition, he has mining, real estate and entertainment companies in Kansas City.

Yet, it's the Chiefs that he considers his own crown jewel. "In my realm of thinking, the Chiefs organization is the most important entity in my sphere. I spend a lot of time dreaming up ideas to make coming to a Chiefs game a great experience," says Hunt from his two-story apartment overlooking the fifty-yard line inside Arrowhead Stadium. While other team owners fret over draft picks and weekly rosters, Hunt crafts ways to improve the stadium's ambience. This includes inviting high school pep bands to come play in the parking lots before the games, where throngs of fans gather for what is considered the NFL's most elaborate tailgate parties. "Having some live music out there will add to the entertainment aspect of coming to the games," he says. His efforts also include enhancing the area surrounding the stadium.

On a spring afternoon, Hunt takes a visitor in his rented car on a tour around the perimeter of Arrowhead Stadium, undoubtedly one of the most captivating arenas in all of sports. Surrounded on three sides by rolling hills and trees, it's next door to Kauffman Stadium, home of the Kansas City Royals. But now, Hunt wants to show his guest some of the dozens of trees he and his wife, Norma, have had planted over the past several years.

First, there was the Millennium gift of dozens of blue spruce trees placed at the entrances to the parking lots. Then there were the additional ash trees planted on the border, so that the entire circle around the stadium would be tree-lined. Most recently, Hunt planted a grove of more than forty redwood trees to celebrate the team's fortieth anniversary in Kansas City in 2002. As is often the case with this soft-spoken owner, history played a large part in the project. Hunt selected redwoods because of something the opposing quarterback said after the Chiefs won 23-7 in 1969's Super Bowl IV: "The Chiefs defensive line...looked like a redwood forest. They just seemed to block things out." The grove includes a picnic area that Hunt hopes will serve as a green and lasting legacy in the decades ahead.

Hunt admits his preoccupation with landscaping strikes some of the staff as "a bit hair-brained. I don't think our public relations department here ever thought they would have to write press releases about planting trees," he says with a laugh. But, as Hunt has learned, it's the little efforts that add up to great results.

Their own league

In December 1958, then twenty-six-year-old Lamar Hunt watched an edge-of-the-seat NFL Championship match between the New York Giants and the Baltimore Colts, with the Colts winning during the extra period 23-17. Hunt, a former third-string end from Southern Methodist University, was already a huge pro football fan, and had been yearning to get involved. The excitement of that championship convinced him. He first approached the National Football League about adding an expansion team in his Dallas hometown. When they said no, he tried to buy an existing team that he could move to Dallas.

It was during this time that he learned of other men around the country who were also attempting to bring teams to their hometowns of Los Angeles, Buffalo, Boston, Houston and Denver, among others. It dawned on Hunt that this group should just go ahead and create a second football league, which he wanted to call the American Football League. "There was both an American and a National League in baseball, so why not football?" he said. After many discussions among the seven other interested parties, each contributed $25,000 to get the AFL off the ground. Later that fall, however, the NFL approached Hunt; officials said it would be expanding into the Dallas market, after all, and wanted to offer him the franchise. But at that point, Hunt had already invested money, time and energy into his new league. More importantly, he felt an obligation to the other new owners and partners in the start-up operation. He declined the NFL's offer and began to concentrate on his new endeavor.

In 1960, his team, the Dallas Texans, played its first season in the AFL, with mixed results. Football fans didn't initially embrace the new AFL teams, with an average of just sixteen thousand attending each weekly game. Things were even more dismal in Dallas, where the Cowboys and the Texans shared a stadium, played alternate Sundays, and vied for a finite number of fans. Each team drew only ten thousand fans each weekend. Although the Texans won the AFL title their second season, the team still couldn't make a profit. Within three years, it lost $2.5 million.

In late 1962, Kansas City Mayor H. Roe Bartle, nicknamed "the Chief," urged Hunt to move his team to this burgeoning Midwestern city. Bartle, a gregarious man weighing more than three hundred pounds, promised Hunt that there would be welcoming fans and a supportive business and government community. To further entice Hunt, Bartle guaranteed the team fifteen thousand season ticket holders in its first season. In May of 1963, Hunt announced that he was moving the team and renaming it the Kansas City Chiefs, in honor of the persuasive mayor.

The Chiefs did well in their new home and within a few years Hunt, along with Cowboys general manager Tex Schramm, worked out a deal that would help make pro football America's favorite sport: the 1966 merger between the AFL and NFL. The new conferences agreed to play each other in a season-ending Super Bowl, a term Hunt came up with after seeing his son play with a "super ball." These key contributions to the development of football are now acknowledged each year at the annual AFC Championship Game with the winner being awarded the Lamar Hunt Trophy.

Setting the tone

The Chiefs had memorable moments in their new hometown, including winning Super Bowl IV following the 1969 season. When they first moved to Kansas City, the Chiefs played in forty-nine thousand-seat Municipal Stadium. In 1972, they moved to their current home, Arrowhead Stadium, which seats more than seventy-eight thousand.

Throughout the 1970s and 1980s, however, the team struggled. It only made the playoffs two times, in 1971 and 1986—the latter followed by hugely disappointing four-win seasons in 1987 and 1988. The results were game days with the stadium about one-quarter full and a fan base that was lackluster, at best. Things changed, however, once Lamar Hunt hired Carl Peterson as President, General Manager and CEO.

Since joining the Chiefs in 1988, Peterson is credited with elevating the outfit into what NFL Commissioner Paul Tagliabue considers "a model NFL organization and one of sports' most respected entities." In fact, the Chiefs often host staffs of other teams, particularly NFL newcomers, who want to see how they've done so much, so well.

When Peterson joined the Chiefs he found a struggling franchise both on the field and off. "When I first came, the Chiefs had only one winning season in seventeen years," he says. "There were only twenty-five thousand season ticket holders, and thirty-three thousand paid attendees in a stadium that holds almost eighty thousand. It looked awful on game days with so many empty rows. But I knew it was a great football market with a great facility. All the right ingredients were here."

Peterson first hired Marty Schottenheimer as head coach. Over the next ten years Schottenheimer would lead the team to unprecedented regular season records followed by heartbreaking playoff losses. During his tenure, the team posted more regular season wins than any other team the AFC had in that time frame. The team made it to the playoffs seven times, with three AFC West titles and one AFC Championship appearance. Yet, the coveted AFC Championship crown and a chance for the Super Bowl eluded them.

Peterson, meanwhile, was rewriting the way a pro football team should be run. With a PhD in education from UCLA followed by years of coaching and scouting at both the collegiate and professional levels, he first started a number of programs to enhance the Chiefs' image. Though the team was finally on a successful streak on the field, Peterson was determined to build a faithful fan-base around the Chiefs that would support the team even if they didn't always win. "Many of my peers in the NFL have the archaic view that, 'if you win, they will come; if you don't, they won't,'" he says. Peterson adopted a far broader approach, considering professional football as a sports entertainment business.

When he first joined the Chiefs, Peterson worked to provide more interaction between the players and the community. Noting that players wear helmets, pads and are relatively far away from the fans at the stadium, Peterson started organizing regular visiting caravans to introduce the players on the team to the people who came to the games and watched them on televisions. Players went out to public events including Rotary meetings, school functions, parades and picnics to meet personally with fans—not just in Missouri, but also in Kansas, Nebraska and Iowa. "We did this the first couple of years with players, coaches and cheerleaders," he says. Besides building relationships, the gesture also helped sell tickets. Peterson illustrates this with a story about Christian Okoye. "Christian was a six-foot four-inch, two hundred sixty-pound running back from Nigeria. His nickname was the 'Nigerian Nightmare' and he spoke with a clipped English accent. On one of the caravans, Okoye was chatting with a little boy and signing an autograph. When the little boy's father arrived, Okoye looked him straight in the eye and said, 'and you, you are going to buy season tickets, right?' The father bought them on the spot."

A ticket to success

Thanks to these Midwestern caravans, not to mention their improved win-loss record, the Chiefs increased their season ticket base from twenty-five thousand to seventy-one thousand in just three years. But other factors were involved as well.

Every sports franchise knows the importance of its season ticket holders. They also know that getting them is one thing and keeping them is another. One of the ways the Chiefs organization encourages these sales is through its unique "Red Coaters" program. All of the 150 dues-paying members of this organization are season ticket holders. They take to the phones several times a year to encourage other fans to first sign on, and then to renew. Participants earn their esteemed red coat—not to mention signed balls and trips to away games—once they reach a certain level for selling tickets, renewing tickets, and other activities, including helping out at charity events and serving on the board. One of the greatest honors for Red Coaters is that they're invited to line up on the field in their red sports jackets and welcome the players as they enter the stadium on game days.

The Chiefs organization further works with its most loyal fans by keeping prices relatively affordable. In spite of the huge demand for season tickets and continually sold-out games, the Chiefs maintain their prices in the median range of all NFL season tickets. In addition, the management takes a one-on-one approach with these key "customers." If better seats become available, they first are offered to veteran season ticket holders. Any of them who send Peterson a letter, fax, email or call him on the phone can count on a personal response.

Fans wanting to buy single day tickets are not forgotten, either. Thousands of seats are kept out of the season ticket pool so they will be available for every game. The first priority for these unsold tickets goes to residents in Jackson County, Missouri, which owns the publicly funded stadium.

Making sure the fans have a great time on game day is the next priority. "Even when we lose at home, we want every fan leaving the stadium feeling that they had a great day and they can't wait to return," says Peterson. He notes that about half of all attendees are women, and that lots of families come together as well. Take tailgate parties, for instance. Having scouted dozens of American colleges over the years, Peterson figured out something early on: Midwesterners love their pre-game parking lot parties. Indeed, when the Kansas City Royals management banned tailgates before baseball games in order to sell more food inside the stadium, the Chiefs encouraged their fans to increase their tailgate parties. They now hold contests at every home game with Lamar Hunt acting as judge to find the most unique tailgate parties. "People bring out their candelabras and their china. It's priceless," says Peterson. When the Chiefs got to the point of selling out their games, fans without tickets started driving out to the parking lots to enjoy the tailgate parties and then watch the game on battery-operated televisions. The Chiefs further enhance their pre-game ambience and activities—not to mention their bottom line—by selling dozens of VIP tents to area corporations and groups.

Heroes among heroes

It's a dismal April morning in Kansas City as sheets of rain dampen the entire city. Inside the Children's Museum, however, it's bright and lively. A group of four- and five-year olds from a local Head Start program are sitting at tables making brightly colored flowers out of coffee filters. The big guy both directing and encouraging them is John Tait, a three hundred-pound tackle for the Chiefs. After finishing the art project, Tait leads them to the museum's indoor play area. The kids take turns going down a slide so the friendly blond guy can catch them at the bottom. The kids squeal in delight. They may not be old enough to know that their playmate is a starting offensive player in the NFL, but they do know he is good at art and a lot of fun to play with. They relish the attention.

Five-year veteran Tait is a regular visitor at both the Children's Museum, where he serves as an ambassador, and at the downtown Kemper Museum of Contemporary Art, where he is a volunteer docent. An art aficionado who likes to dabble in oils, Tait, through his own charity work and the non-profit foundation he has developed, is committed to introducing the joys of art to as many children as he can. "It's a shame that so many school systems drop art when budgets get tight," he says. "My parents always encouraged me as a kid to pursue my interest in art, and I want to do the same for others."

Tait is one of several current Chiefs players who have developed their own non-profit foundations through the Greater Kansas City Community Foundation. Other players, including Will Shields (Will to Succeed), Trent Green (Trent Green Family Foundation) and Tony Gonzalez (Tony Gonzalez Foundation) all raise money for causes close to their hearts. John Tait's foundation focuses on children and the arts. Will Shields' foundation supports abused and neglected women and children though direct assistance as well as literacy and educational aid. Tony Gonzalez's foundation works hand-in-hand with a Kansas City program, Shadow Buddies Foundation, that helps children understand more about disabilities. The goal of this program is to teach classmates and friends of children with disabilities about them so that that they can overcome any fears. As these organizations show, none are just fund-raising vehicles. The players become actively involved as participants, as well. "Everybody should give back to the community. When you do, you get that adrenaline in your heart, like you do on the football field. Everybody should try it. There's nothing like it," says Gonzalez.

And if you are on the Kansas City Chiefs, you will be involved in the community. Almost ten years ago, Peterson took the unprecedented step of placing an addendum in players' contracts that requires them to be available for a minimum of five charity events each year. The Chiefs were the first pro football team to make this a requirement, but the practice is common with many in the NFL today. "At first, a number of agents said 'no.' But I found that when I was handing players their signing bonus check, I would mention that all the other players do it, and they happily agreed," says Peterson. To him, it's imperative that Chiefs players live in the community and support its causes. And the impact of this principle continues to be strong. In 2002, the Chiefs, through charitable events and player foundations, raised almost $2 million. Since 1998 they've raised more than $8 million. Much of the money raised comes from the team's own Chiefs Children's Fund, which raised more than $685,500 during

2000, primarily through proceeds from a pre-season game. Since 1983, the Chiefs have raised and donated more than $4.5 million through its Children's Fund. "I feel fortunate to be in a city with a team that is so civic-minded," says Kay Barnes, mayor of Kansas City. "What most impresses me is how often players are out and about, involved with so many organizations. It's great for the fans."

In 2003, another Chiefs' player joined his many teammates in launching a foundation. Priest Holmes, the NFL's top running back, launched a combined foundation and company called Team Priest. Holmes' impact on the field has been making headlines for the past three years, primarily for being the NFL's most improbable star. As an undrafted free agent out of the University of Texas, the five-foot nine-inch Holmes was considered too small to play in the NFL. In 1997 the Baltimore Ravens signed Holmes as a free agent, and in his second year he rushed for more than one thousand yards and contributed to that team's 2001 Super Bowl victory. But the Ravens didn't keep Holmes, and when coach Dick Vermeil took over the Chiefs in 2001 he signed the "comeback kid" to be the team's running back. In his first year with Kansas City, Holmes rushed for more than fifteen hundred yards. During the 2002 season, Holmes rushed for sixteen hundred yards and had twenty-four touchdowns, becoming a favorite of Chiefs fans and fantasy football players worldwide.

Yet, after years of contributing to others' foundations, Holmes waited until 2003 to form his own philanthropic group. "In years past, I always 'piggy backed' on my teammates' organizations and did not have one of my own," says Holmes. "With Team Priest, I can give back in a way that is truly making an impact."

Holmes tapped an old neighborhood buddy—successful Houston businessman Christopher Bush—to run the foundation. Bush says Holmes' inherent competitiveness propels him to create a foundation that is different. First, he notes, there's the www.teampriest.com web site. Launched in July 2003, the site had a remarkable nine million "hits" in its first fourth months. "Priest can be a bit stand-offish, so his web site serves as a way he can interact with fans directly, versus via the media," says Bush.

For instance, in a daily diary written during the team's pre-season training camp, Holmes wrote honestly about the ups and downs of professional football—such as the ants that infiltrated his dorm room, the rigors of the workouts, and his occasional irritability around teammates. "Yes, the on-line diary showed his moodiness, for sure," says Bush. "But, that's Priest."

Team Priest is also interacting with fans through the Priest Mobile, a painted van that Holmes himself drives to and from games and to personal appearances. Both Holmes and Bush are working to make Team Priest a profit-making company as well as a foundation. One of its first profit-making ventures is to sell a variety of "Team Priest" logo items via its web site. "The profit and non-profit sectors will work together in a variety of ways," says Holmes. "A certain percentage of all proceeds generated by the company will go to the foundation. That is one of the goals we set out when we first had the vision of Team Priest. We do not want to be a foundation with our 'hand out,' but to have a viable source of income so we could continue our efforts in the community without depending on grants or donations."

Team Priest's activities include a chess club called Team Priest Checkmates held at the Lincoln Prep Middle School in Kansas City. Holmes, an avid chess player who learned the game from his stepfather, often equates the prowess needed to succeed at chess with the strategy one needs to excel on the football field. "The chess club is for kids that want to learn the strategy, patience and planning it takes to be successful in life," says Holmes, who notes that chess can expand a child's mind to "think beyond the next step." The star running back is proud that many of the kids who participate in his chess program tend to improve their overall grades. Another initial program initiated by Team Priest was to provide student-athletes in the Kansas City school district who participate on the football, basketball, wrestling or soccer teams with specially fitted mouth guards for the 2003 athletic season. "Most public school kids are issued inadequate mouth guards. Good mouth guards can help prevent concussions, so this was a straightforward way to make a difference," says Holmes. Team Priest partnered with the Chili's Restaurant chain to finance the mouth guard program.

A player remembered

As beloved as the 2003 Chiefs squad is, the player whom, undoubtedly, contributed the most both on and off the field was the team's much-adored Derrick Thomas. A first round draft pick in 1989, Thomas became an instant star and was chosen to play in the Pro Bowl in each of his first nine seasons in the league. Yet, it was his accomplishments off the field that won the hearts of so many fans. Very early in his Kansas City career, he began an inner-city reading program and a nonprofit foundation called the Third and Long Foundation. Thomas visited public libraries throughout the Kansas City community on Saturday mornings and read to children, often bringing other players along. President George H.W. Bush named Thomas to his "Thousand Points of Light" program; he received the Bryon "Whizzer" White humanitarian award from the NFL Players Association, named for the recently deceased Supreme Court judge, and he was awarded the NFL's Man of the Year award, the most prestigious honor in professional football.

All of these accomplishments abruptly ended in February 2000 when Thomas died at age thirty-two following complications from an automobile accident. News of his death sent a shock wave through the Midwestern community that revered him for his work both on and off the field. Tens of thousands of fans paid their respects at Arrowhead Stadium. It was also a huge loss for the organization. "Derrick had the great ability to touch everyone he came across," remembers Peterson, who says Thomas never refused to sign an autograph for a fan. "Even after a tough loss, or a difficult time, he always complied, and with a smile." One example of his warm heart was the time Thomas read about a little boy in Oklahoma with AIDS who was being shunned by his schoolmates. Thomas went to visit the boy, and the two went to the school grounds to play basketball, demonstrating that there was nothing to fear. "Helping others was a constant for him, and he was beloved by everyone involved with this organization," says Peterson.

A day of thanks

A beautiful, mid-April day was declared *Thank You Kansas City!* day by the Kansas City Chiefs. Vans full of current and former players—as well as Coach Vermeil, his wife, Carol, Carl Peterson, Lamar Hunt, and a group of cheerleaders—fanned out to points throughout the metro area, unannounced. The goal was to hand out stickers and to thank fans for supporting them for forty years in Kansas City. Quarterback Trent Green, Will Shields and John Tait joined Coach Vermeil in the city's plaza and downtown areas, walking into restaurants to shake hands and sign autographs. Peterson and Priest Holmes visited the employee cafeterias of both the Yellow Freight and Sprint Headquarters. And team founder Hunt joined players including Tony Richardson and Eddie Kennison as they visited the General Motors Fairfax Automotive Assembly plant in Kansas City, Kansas.

At the plant, workers along the modern-day conveyer belts where Grand Prix autos were in different stages of assembly came out to greet the players. More than three thousand people work each shift at this plant. On Fridays during the football season, it's a sea of red, with employees wearing the color of their favorite team, a unique and common practice at workplaces throughout the Kansas City area. As happy as they are to meet players, the person causing the greatest stir is the founder, the guy everyone refers to affectionately as "Lamar." Hearing that a worker has been a season ticket holder for almost thirty years,

Hunt shakes his hand warmly, thanking him for his support.

Later that night, Chiefs management extends its heartfelt thanks to 155 staff members for their devotion to their jobs and the team. "The public sees the players and the coaches. They don't realize that we are running a $175 million per year business with more than 150 employees, not including the players," says Peterson. As dinner was ending, Peterson took to the podium to laud his administrative team, noting some important milestones. The previous season, the franchise renewed more than 98 percent of its season tickets and continued its consecutive game sell-outs at ninety-two. The Chiefs also marked their tenth consecutive year of total paid attendance exceeding seven hundred seventy thousand. More than seven million people logged on to the team's web site from more than 120 countries, with more than fifty thousand checking in each day during the season.

Peterson then went on to thank everyone in the room, from coaches to operations to support staff. "We have people here who are not concerned with how much time they have to put in, people who are not concerned with who gets the credit, but people who always say, 'we can do this,'" he said. Chiefs employees who had worked at the company five, ten, fifteen, twenty, twenty-five and even thirty years, were recognized and applauded, including Ann Roach, a thirty-year veteran secretary who has worked for each of the team's nine head coaches, and Brenda Sniezek, who is responsible for the Chiefs eminent community relations program.

A winning touch

With all the handshaking, autograph-writing, and overall congratulations that April day and evening, it would be easy to think that the Chiefs had won just won the Super Bowl. But, in reality, the Chiefs had just experienced a disappointing losing season. The head coach, Dick Vermeil, had recently been brought in to improve the Chiefs' standing.

"There are two factions in the NFL," he says from his red-carpeted office in Arrowhead. "There are people in the fo business and people in the winning football business." Af a one-year hiatus after winning the Super Bowl in St. Louis following the 1999 season, Peterson lured Vermeil to work his coaching magic in Kansas City. The two had worked together, on and off, over much of the past three decades. As coaches at UCLA, their team upset Ohio State to win the Rose Bowl in 1975. Later, they were credited with resurrecting the long-dormant Philadelphia Eagles starting in the late 1970s. "The only reason I came here was because of Carl Peterson," says Vermeil. "We've had good working and personal relationships, and there's a huge trust level between us."

Taking over a football team is a huge challenge. When he arrived for the 2001 season, Vermeil realized the potential. "The Chiefs had a great thing going here, and then things slipped over several years. Sometimes it's hard to get a team back on track," he says.

Trust, he says, is the most important component on any given team. Motivating players to achieve their best is second. Vermeil pulls down some well-read business handbooks by Price Pritchett and Ron Pound, with titles like *The Leadership Engine*, *The Stress of Organizational Change* and *Teamwork.* With the dog-eared corners and the many highlighted passages, it is obvious that Vermeil has long pored over them for ideas that can be translated to his football teams. "It's all about motivation. They seem to write down all of the ideas I think about," he says. "From these, I put together my own motivational books for my players."

Vermeil says there is a definite parallel between running a football team and running a business. "It's all about dealing with people. If you can't lead, or set a direction, or handle pressure, then you won't succeed." After two seasons of failing to make it to the playoffs, Vermeil felt very strong about his team going into 2003. "The chemistry is great with this team," says Vermeil early into that season. "The players have already bought into what we are doing. The expectations, morale and confidence levels have set a stage for a good season."

After two come-from-behind victories early in 2003, Vermeil told reporters that "there's something special about these Chiefs. They're not the best team in football simply because they have the most talent—in fact, there are probably two or three teams out there with more overall skill. They're the league's top team because they believe they're not supposed to lose."

Much of this belief comes from the veteran coach whose legendary commitment to and faith in both players and fellow coaches transcends the football field. "The philosophy of not mixing business with pleasure is baloney," he says. "The better I know someone, the better I can help him achieve his best. He trusts me more and sees me as a person who wants him to excel. The more he trusts my advice, the more he listens."

It's widely known that players under Vermeil love playing for him. "I can say that I am a Chief because of Coach Vermeil," says Holmes. "He called me personally and asked me to be part of his team and his vision. His impact on me as a player is personal as well. I feel personally responsible on the field to not disappoint him."

Part of the close relationship between the coach and the players derives from activities off the field. For instance, Vermeil and his wife, Carol, host dinners for the players at their home. Players may expect a catered meal, but it's their head coach barbecuing at the grill and Carol orchestrating the preparation of side dishes, with plenty of players and their wives pitching in to help.

Having players in their home is nothing new to the Vermeils. "It started when I was coaching high school kids, and Carol would make victory cakes and we'd have the team to our house," says Vermeil. "As I went on to coach at the university level and, eventually, professional level, it's something we do each year." It's also a gesture that is meaningful to players. Star punt returner Dante Hall said that he had never been invited to a head coach's house for dinner before playing for this one.

Vermeil admits that becoming personally involved with players can make it more difficult when he has to cut someone from the team. "Some of my best friends are players I've cut, some of them two or three times. But I always talk about the tough decisions, and that what I do is always the best for the team and the organization."

As the team moves forward, Vermeil's goal is to lead the Chiefs to an AFC Championship. Then, finally, the Chiefs can bring home the trophy that bears Lamar Hunt's name—and get a chance to win the Super Bowl. For the team's community of fans, employees, management and founders, however, success comes on many levels. A trophy would merely be the icing on what is already a multi-layered cake.

Chapter Thirteen

Thirteen Lessons of Conscientious Leadership

One of the best things about examining today's companies with a conscience—for the very first time, or a decade after originally getting to know them—is the opportunity it affords to meet with the leaders behind the well-known and not-so-well-known company names. From visionary founders like Yvon Chouinard of Patagonia to second-generation shepherds like Yves Couette of Ben & Jerry's Homemade, these are the people directly responsible for their organizations' notable commitment to the community as well as the bottom line. They often combine a social worker's sympathies with an M.B.A.'s business savvy. They usually are interesting to, and interested in, all of those around them. And their actions consistently make them worthy role models for a twenty-first century corporate world that increasingly values more than just profits.

As evidenced by the previous pages, these individuals have also put together a variety of businesses that operate in a variety of ways. There are, however, a great many common threads that run through them. Some of the most significant are detailed below. Businesses large and small that are thinking about joining these ranks would do well to take heed.

1. *All of these companies with a conscience were initially created, and still continue to be run, by hands-on risk-takers who personally established their firms' unique tone and specific direction.*

Without exception, every one of the organizations profiled in this book was the brainchild of one person or a few closely aligned individuals who purposefully set the moral and corporate course that it follows to this day. Also without exception, these founders—and, in most cases, the leaders who have since come to replace them—truly understood how their business practices, personnel policies, relationships with customers, and actions in the community all have an indisputable impact on each other. These are people, in other words, who had a total vision and were eager to personally work to see it realized.

Accordingly, their companies were run from the start by leaders who have never been afraid to roll up their sleeves and toil on the shop floor. It was not uncommon over the years to see Ben & Jerry's Jerry Greenfield filling ice cream pint containers on the production line, for instance, or Joyce Meskis of the Tattered Cover Book Store wrapping Christmas packages. Those at the top consequently learned their businesses from the ground up, and their employees knew to listen to them when they offered suggestions and shared advice.

2. *Like all successful businesses, these companies stick to the basics and produce only top-quality goods or services once they have identified the right niche.*

The leaders of every one of these firms subscribes to the same school of thought: Their commitment to corporate responsibility would have no impact if they were not also running a successful business, and they would not be running a successful business if they did not have something that the public was willing to buy.

Such consumer demand usually starts with an uncompromising dedication to quality, and this focus is obvious here. All of these companies began by identifying a specific market area that was going unserved, and then serving it in a first-rate manner. Marilyn Hamilton, for example, couldn't play tennis with existing wheelchairs so she went out and had the superior Quickie product designed. Likewise, Margot Fraser couldn't find comfortable sandals so she began importing better Birkenstock models herself from overseas.

3. *These companies have developed a public image that emphasizes this commitment to quality, and they often use non-traditional means to promote it and to speak directly to their customers on this and other matters.*

Unlike businesses that realize their environmental and social duties late in life, and then spend $2 million to tell the public that they spent $1 million on some worthy cause, true companies with a conscience go about their twin pursuits of social responsibility and corporate excellence in relative quiet. Rather than toot their own horns, though, several of those who do advertise regularly (like Stonyfield, Patagonia and Ben & Jerry's) consistently use their time and money to promote their philosophies along with their products. And even those who lean toward more traditional marketing campaigns (such as Shorebank, Tattered Cover and Quickie) tend to produce advertising that unambiguously underscores the need for the very principles that set them apart.

A very personal involvement in promotional efforts also is common here. Some firms (Quickie, Ben & Jerry's, Kansas City Chiefs) consistently use their brand identity to support activities that help the causes and people they have targeted for assistance. A few (Stonyfield, Ben & Jerry's, Celestial) make an additional statement with their packaging. Most use the web to educate their communities on the issues that are closest to their hearts. And all rely on word-of-mouth testimonials that loyal supporters are happy to give to friends and acquaintances.

4. *These are companies that firmly believe in—and practice—the dual principles of self-management and decentralization.*

Nowhere among these companies will you find bulky layers of bureaucracy or bloated management committees. Orders do not come down to the front-line troops from lofty, isolated main offices in a far-off corporate headquarters. But there is a tendency, even in the largest of these firms, for constructive ideas to flow up as well as down; Ben & Jerry's new owner Unilever, for example, is considering ways to use some of the progressive compensation policies and environmentally sound packaging choices developed in Vermont in other businesses that it owns.

Additionally, all of the companies described within these pages practice an active policy of promotion from within. Since most of the managers have risen through the ranks, they usually believe in the same principles and tenets as the founders and are thus more likely to continue their companies' direction undeterred.

5. *The founders of these companies recognize that they are not perfect and have willingly brought in outside expertise when needed. At the same time, they do not hesitate to cut this expertise free when they feel it is unneccessary or counter productive.*

America Works is a perfect example of this. While it was moderately successful in the beginning under the exclusive management of its husband-and-wife founding team, the company eventually reached a point where it required another perspective and additional talents in order to grow. A retired manufacturing executive was invited to join the firm as a third partner, and he brought needed capital to the company as well as a sense of formal business operation that was lacking in the founding entrepreneurs. By pulling in the reins, implementing rigid accounting procedures, and emphasizing the firm's past accomplishments, he helped America Works successfully expand into new markets. When the founders felt the third partner was inhibiting growth, however, they bought him out.

Most of the other companies in these pages opted at some time for similar changes. Shorebank, Quickie and Ben & Jerry's all called in outside help when their founders recognized that they had reached their limits in certain areas. They went out and found experts in these areas who were in tune with their philosophies and principles and unhesitatingly turned over real responsibility and power to them. The results speak for themselves.

Patagonia, on the other hand, ended their relationships with high-level outside hires when the company realized these newcomers were pushing it in unwanted directions. This decision, likewise, proved to be a turning point.

6. *These companies truly encourage all of their employees to become part of a shared mission—offering them ownership stakes, encouraging them to learn all they can about its operations and finances, and urging them to take advantage of company-sponsored opportunities for growth in personal and business matters.*

The gospel of "empowerment" is preached these days at even the largest corporate institutions, but it has been a hallmark of these companies since day one. At Birkenstock, where everything from executive salaries to corporate donations was always discussed openly, this was ultimately taken a step further when employees actually became owners of the firm.

Free or subsidized classes for members of the workforce—touching upon a wide range of subjects— also are commonplace. Employees at these companies regularly have the opportunity to learn everything from personal finance and CPR to contemporary management techniques and improved communication skills. All of this leads to internal loyalty, decreased turnover, increased productivity and a more pleasant and satisfying work environment.

7. *These companies always pay equitably on all levels and usually offer benefit packages that raise total compensation rates to heights far outdistancing the competition.*

Upper management in companies with a conscience will never be accused of accepting exorbitant salaries and are in fact often underpaid in relation to their peers. They are paid fairly, however, and are sometimes eligible for bonuses and other incentives tied to company performance, a practice sometimes called "linked prosperity."

Lower-echelon workers at these businesses, on the other hand, will probably never get rich in their positions but still tend to make more than their counterparts in comparable companies. Bonuses, profit sharing, superior working conditions, advancement opportunities and superlative benefits—such as the excellent on-site child care facilities at Ben & Jerry's and Patagonia—raise the compensation packages to an even greater level.

8. *These companies are strongly people-oriented at every level, eschewing executive perks and often preferring an honest personal approach that is epitomized by all employees being on a first-name basis.*

Some visitors to firms profiled in the preceding pages are surprised at the uniformly democratic nature of their operations. Reserved parking spaces are non-existent. Titles are usually for outside use only, and telephone directories tend to be alphabetized by everyone's first name. On-site cafeterias regularly play host to company presidents along with hourly wage earners, who often sit together at the same tables.

Despite the skepticism occasionally directed by outsiders toward such policies, these egalitarian measures do not ring false here. The caring attitude is genuine, as owners and managers sincerely feel empathy toward their workers and genuinely treat them like members of their own extended families. That's why it is easy for them to institute programs like on-site child care that may decrease profits at the outset but build loyalty and productivity over the long run. In particular, firms like Greyston and America Works—which employ the very people they are working to assist—always go the extra mile to ensure that everyone under their umbrella is reaching their full potential in the workplace and in their outside lives.

9. *These companies constantly solicit input from their customers on all manner of subjects, ranging from product direction to corporate donations, and listen to what they are told.*

Much as they treat their employees, these firms treat their customers as they themselves wish to be treated. They offer a first-rate product and excellent service. Advice on the use of these products and services is freely provided. Repairs, exchanges, and refunds are all cheerfully made.

Long before the word "stakeholder" was commonly used to denote everyone (including consumers and suppliers) with a stake in a given company, these firms looked at those to whom they were connected as real people who were not to be treated any differently than their workforces. They were always considered a part of the corporation's family. Newsletters, catalogs, toll-free numbers and other outlets are constantly available for the company and its stakeholders to share information and views.

10. *Founders and upper-level managers at these companies exhibit a sincere interest in events outside their corporations, and act when they can to impact them.*

Spend a few minutes with any of the executives from these profiled companies, and chances are they'll want to talk about a lot more than just their own businesses. They're likely instead to share their thoughts on the local homeless situation, a regional environmental issue, or the nation's education policy. They're knowledgeable about an array of subjects that impact their constituents and their communities, and because they have a vehicle at their fingertips that can be used to enact change—their companies—this interest often leads directly to action. Patagonia, Stonyfield, Tattered Cover and Ben & Jerry's are among those who have pushed the envelop in this regard, even supporting cutting-edge social causes that occasionally threaten their commercial success.

Such commitment shows that companies with a conscience are dedicated to more than issues directly affecting their fiscal bottom lines. They care about the world around them and work earnestly to make it a better place in which to live.

11. *Employees throughout these companies take an active role in their communities, with real support from the organizations themselves.*

Apart from the generous corporate-initiated donations of cash and in-kind services that companies with a conscience regularly share with their neighbors, employees usually become deeply committed on their own to the issues that matter to them. The people at Stonyfield are passionately involved in environmental concerns that stem directly from their location and their industry, for example. Employees at Birkenstock have long helped local businesses develop recycling programs. Workers at Ben & Jerry's offer help to virtually any non-profit in their home state that requests it. Staffers at Quickie spend their weekends at athletic events for the disabled. Personal involvement in local affairs has been a constant at Shorebank and the Kansas City Chiefs right from the start.

And when such an interest is displayed, these companies back their workers all the way. Patagonia even operates an official internship program that permits eligible employees to take up to two months of paid leave to work with a non-profit group of their choice. Sometimes, with the company's blessing, those employees even decide to stay on with the non-profit instead of returning to Patagonia.

12. *These companies deal as often as possible with like-minded businesses, and encourage their employees to do the same.*

A mutually beneficial cycle of commerce and assistance has developed among companies with a conscience, which regularly exchange goods and services and ideas. Not surprisingly, most also refuse to do any business at all with companies whose policies and principles run contrary to their own.

The conscious sourcing of materials is the most obvious manifestation of this, such as when Ben & Jerry's buys its brownies from Greyston—and stops buying its cookies from a subsidiary of a tobacco firm. The sharing of information, such as when Shorebank assists another financial institution interested in starting a development bank, is another. The cyclical practices end up creating new business, sparking new ideas, and making new friends.

13. *These companies constantly look to the future but always pay attention to the past.*

Flexibility and a willingness to refocus are two common traits found at companies with a conscience, at least among those who truly have their focus on both the fiscal and social bottom lines. When changes around them call for new products, new methods of delivery, and new technologies to pull them off, they do what needs to be done without taking their eyes off the road that got them to this point. America Works shifted its training from office support to security positions as marketplace needs evolved; Patagonia moved exclusively to organic cotton when it learned how to produce an acceptable alternative to the natural fiber; Tattered Cover underwent two disruptive but essential computerizations in order to provide better customer service; Interface changed the very nature of its carpeting in order to remake itself and its industry. No planned obsolescence or stagnation is apparent here.

Much of this ever-changing activity stems directly from the philosophies and principles espoused officially in mission statements that govern how almost all of these businesses operate. These living, breathing documents are generally short on words—as they are supposed to be—but consistently long on ideals. And while they rarely offer specifics, they always provide the guidelines that spell out exactly what is expected of everyone in the organization—and of the organization itself.

Most significantly, perhaps, these mission statements are also subject to change. And they are changed whenever these companies recognize a need to expand their direction, refocus their energy, or redefine their very existence.

For, as was noted earlier in several different ways, every business that is profiled in this book really is a collection of stakeholders: owners, managers, employees, customers, suppliers, and neighbors far and wide who are affected by the firm's actions and reactions. Companies with a conscience recognize this fact and are always striving to make the alterations necessary to meet the evolving needs of the people they impact.

Bibliography

Adelson, Andrea. 1999. "Wedded To Its Moral Imperatives." The *New York Times*. 16 May.

Ain, Stewart. 1998. "A Dynamo in the Food Marketing Arena," The *New York Times*. 12 April.

Alcala, Carlos. 2000. "Outdoor Gear Companies Get Greener." The *Sacramento Bee*. 2 August.

Anderson, Ray C. 2000. "On Course: More on the Interface journey toward sustainability." *Green Money Journal,* Winter 2001.

Andrews, Nina. 1988. "Partnership Will Buy Celestial Seasonings." The *New York Times*. 13 September.

Arnold, Matthew. 2001. "Is Ben & Jerry's losing its bohemian appeal?" *Marketing*. 3 May.

Armstrong, Larry. 1998. "Patagonia Sticks to its Knitting." *Business Week*. 7 December.

Atchison, Sandra D. 1989. "Why Celestial Seasonings Wasn't Kraft's Cup of Tea." *Business Week*. 8 May.

Atchison, Sandra D. 1991. "Putting the Red Zinger Back into Celestial." *Business Week*. 4 November.

Atchison, Sandra D. 1993. "Herbal Teas in Hot Water." *Business Week*. 1 March.

Back, Brian. 2001. "Shorebank's expertise sought by World Bank." *Business Journal-Portland*. 13 July.

Barrett, Joyce. 1995. "Patagonia: only organic cotton from now on." *WWD*. 14 August.

Beilinson, Jerry. 1999. "Hurdles That Go Beyond the Slope." The *New York Times*. 31 December.

Bellafante, Ginia et al. 1995. "Doestoyevsky and a Decaf." *Time*. 5 June.

Ben & Jerry's Homemade. "Company Info." Available WWW: http://www.benjerry.com/co-index.tmpl

"Ben & Jerry's is Back." 1999. *Fortune*. 2 August.

"Ben & Jerry May Leave Ben & Jerry's." 2000. *Associated Press*. 20 November.

"Ben & Jerry's Learns Corporate Lesson." 2000 *Associated Press*. 30 November.

Benyus, Janine M. *Biomimicry*. 1997. William Morrow.

Bernstein, Elizabeth. 1996. "Two leading independent stores face cuts." *Publishers Weekly*. 5 August.

Bernstein, Emily M. 1991. "Brady gets new wheels in Fresno." The *Fresno Bee*. 8 June.

Bernstein, Sharon. 1999 "Sunrise Medical Founder Resigns in Effort to Right Floundering Firm." The *Los Angeles Times*.; 6 October.

Berry, Donna. 2000. "New Product Company of the Year: Stonyfield Farm." *Dairy Foods*. November.

Bessler, Chris. 1989. "Chouinard." *Trips*. July.

Bettelheim, Adriel. 1990. "Celestial targets bigger tea markets." The *Denver Post*. 28 July.

Breslin, Meg McSherry. 1998. "James Fletcher, CEO of South Shore Bank." *Chicago Tribune*. September 19.

Brigham, Courtney Claire. 1999. "Turning heads of Giants." The *Eagle Tribune*. 29 August.

Broadway, Bill. 2001. "Good for the Soul—and the Bottom Line; Firms Promote Spirituality in Workplace and Fine It Pays" The *Washington Post.* 19 August.

Brokaw, Leslie. 1996 "Guerrilla Marketing: Stonyfield Yogurt's Gary Hirshberg." *Inc. Online.* 12 November.

Caggiano, Christopher. 1999. "Celestial Seasonings' Mo Siegel on how he knew it was time to step down." *Inc.* April.

Cohen, Warren. 1999. "4 Ray Anderson." *U.S. News and World Report.* 4 January.

Conniff, Richard. 1991. "Welcome to the Neighborhood." National Geographic. May.

Cove, Peter. 2000. "Welfare Reform Is Hatching a Bureaucracy of Its Own." *Knight Ridder/Trubune Business News*, 29 August.

Davis, Bennet. 1999. "Profits from principle: Five Forces Redefining Business." *The Futurist.* 01 March.

Dean, Rick. 2002. "Lamar Hunt A Gentle Giant." *Football Digest.* February.

Deibel, Mary. 2000. "... But Some Companies Are Finding Happy Workers Cheer Bottom Line." *The Plain Dealer.* 23 January.

Devaney, Polly. 2001. "Ben & Jerry's gets a licking." *Brand Strategy.* April.

"Domini Moves Into Positive Investing." 2000. *Associated Press.* 14 June.

"Don't Monkey with a Good Thing." 2001. *Dairy Foods.* May.

Dorfman, Dan. 1991. "Manager credits God for heavenly returns." *USA Today.*

Dornblaser, Lynn. 2001. "A Cup of Tea, Mate." *Prepared Foods.* March.

Dubroff, Henry. 1989. "Celestial Seasonings Grows Up." *CFO.* October.

The New Encyclopedia Britannica, 15th edition. 1995. Chicago: *Encyclopedia Britannica.*

Executive Update Online. "The Whole Nine Yards." Available WWW:http://www.gwsae.org/ExecutiveUpdate/2000/December/nine.htm

Ezzard, Martha. 2001. "Sacrifice for your country: Cut energy consumption." The *Atlanta Journal and Constitution*. 21 October.

Ferguson, Tim W. 1991. "Disabled Still Denied Access to Accessories, Seller Complains." The *Wall Street Journal*. 4 June.

Fong, Tillie. 2000. "Bookstore Records Case To High Court." *Rocky Mountain News*. 29 June.

"Forsman, Theresa. 2000. "Both Economy, Ecology Boosted by Businesses Renewable Technology Praised." The *Record* (Bergen County, NJ). 19 April.

"Founder of outdoor wear company has unusual message: Buy less." 1999. *Associated Press*. 29 October.

Fredrickson, Tom. 2001. "Cityresidents grab jobs as number at work soars; Immigrants, former welfare recipients pump work ranks; will gains stick?" *Crains New York Business*. 9 April.

Fromartz, Samuel. 2001. "Greyston Offers People A Path, Not A Program." *Shambhala Sun*. July.

Getler, Warren. 1993. "Insiders at Celestial Seasonings Snap Up IPO Shares, but Snapple is Hotter So Far." The *Wall Street Journal*. 1 September.

Goldberg, Bruce. 1997. "Doing well by doing good." *Colorado Business Magazine*. September.

"The Good Guys." 1999. The *Sporting News*. 2 August.

Graham, Judith. 1994. "Wheelchair maker buys Boulder cushion firm." The *Denver Post*. 20 September.

Graham, Sandy. 1998. "MO better tea." *Colorado Business Magazine*. July.

Gram, David. 2000. "Ben & Jerry's sold to global giant Unilever." *Associated Press*. 13 April.

Greenmoney Journal. 1999. "Stonyfield Farms" Summer.

Guiding Principles. Greyston Bakery. Available at www.greystonbakery.com

Greyston Times. Available at www.greyston.org.

The *1998 Grolier Multimedia Encyclopedia*. 1998. Danbury, Conn.: Grolier Interactive, Inc.

Grzywinski, Ronald. 1991. "The New Old-Fashioned Banking." *Harvard Business Review*. May-June.

Gupta, Udayan. 1992. "Blending Zen and the Art of Philanthropic Pastry Chefs." The *Wall Street Journal*. 2 January.

Hain Celestial Group. "2001 Annual Report." Available at http://www.hain-celestial.com/ar2001/index.html

Hawken, Paul. 1997. "Magic Carpet: how to make a profit by reusing waste." *Mother Jones*. 13 March.

Haynes, Erin and Jennings, Peter. 1999. "Working Wiser." *World News Tonight with Peter Jennings*. 7 September

Hallett, Anthony and Hallett, Diane. 1997. *Encyclopedia of Entrepreneurs*. New York, N.Y.: John Wiley & Sons.

Hays, Constance L. 2000. "Investment Group Makes Bid for Ben & Jerry's." The *New York Times*. 10 February.

Hays, Constance L. 2000. "Ben & Jerry's Takeover Is Seen Close." The *New York Times*. 12 April.

Hays, Constance L. 2000. "Ben & Jerry's to Unilever, With Attitude." The *New York Times*. 13 April.

Hicks, L. Wayne. 1993. "Celestial's drug tests: Tempest in a pee pot." *Denver Business Journal*. 10 December.

Hope, Gayla. 2002. "Business Unusual." *CNN Financial News*. 4 March.

Hopkins, Jim. 2001. "Ben & Jerry's co-founder tries venture philanthropy." *USA Today*. 6 August.

Horn, Miriam. 1991. "Zen and the art of self-help." *U.S. News & World Report*. 2 September.

Horowitz, Carl F. 1997. "Saving Money and Doing Good." *Investor's Business Daily*. 10 December.

Horrigan, Jack and Rothet, Mike. *The Other League*. A Benjamin Company/Rutledge Book. 1970.

Hubbard, Burt. 2001. "Denver's Downtown Delight." *Rocky Mountain News*. 20 August.

"Can Business Still Save the World?" *Inc. Magazine*. April, 2001.

Industry Standard, The. "Tattered Cover Book Store." Available at http://www.thestandard.com/companies/dossier/0,1922,262906,00.html

"Investors Look To Save Ben & Jerry's." 2000. *Associated Press*. 4 February.

Jaffe, Thomas. 1991. "Will Sunrise Also Rise?" *Forbes*. 13 May.

Jevens, Lisa. 2001. "Investors put money where their hearts are; Direct dollars to socially responsible firms." *Crain's Chicago Business*. 17 September.

Kane, Courtney. 2000. "Stonyfield Farm tries to change the world and sell some yogurt." The *New York Times*. 6 September.

Kansas City Chiefs. Information available at www.kcchiefs.com.

Kass, Jeff. 2001. "Sporting Goods Sellers Aid Environments." *Rocky Mountain News*. 30 June.

Kiley, David. 1988. "Celestial Gets a Divorce." *Adweek's Marketing*. 19 September.

Kinkead, Gwen. 1999. "The Green CEO." *Fortune*. 24 May.

Kirkpatrick, David D. 2001. "Signs of Slow Holiday Sales Worry Book Publishers." The *New York Times*. 19 November.

Kiuchi, Tachi and Shireman, Bill. 2002. *What We Learned in the Rainforest*. San Francisco: Berrett-Koehler.

Kohler, Jermey. 2000. "Employers hard up for labor are turning to ex-convicts." *St. Louis Post-Dispatch*. 12 July.

Koller, Lynn. 2001. "ShoreBank says it's not easy keeping Chicago businesses and households afloat." *Bank*

Technology News. February.

Kramer, Louise. 1998. "Celestial Seasonings Tea Back on the Front Burner." *Advertising Age*. 7 December.

Kreck, Dick. 2001. "Nature's clarion call dwindles." The *Denver Post*. 7 December.

LaBarre, Polly. "Patagonia comes of age." 1995. *Industry Week*. 3 April.

Lehr, John A. 2000. "Clothing Maker's New Chief Vows to Stay Course." *Associated Press*. 13 March.

Leib, Jeffrey. 1993. "Perrier may be weak link in Celestial iced-tea chain." *Denver Post*. 24 October.

Leib, Jeffrey. 1994. "Celestial Poised for Big Splash." *Denver Post*. 11 February.

Leib, Jeffrey. 1994. "Tea Deal May be Dumped." *Denver Post*. 12 May.

Levering, Robert et al. 1985. *The 100 Best Companies to Work for in America*. Reading, Mass.: Addison-Wesley.

MacPherson, Doug. 2001 "Stonyfield Yogurt Gains a New Partner." New Hampshire Public Radio. 4 October.

Major League Baseball. "Detroit Tigers and Detroit Public Schools team up." Available at http://www.mlb.com/NASApp/mlb/mlb/news/mlb_news_story.jsp?article_id=det_20020322_DPS_pr&team_id=det

Major League Baseball. "Red Sox Exhibition to Benefit The Joey Fund." Available at http://www.mlb.com/NASApp/mlb/mlb/news/mlb_news_story.jsp?article_id=bos_20020320_joeyfund_pr&team_id=bos

Marcel, Joyce. 2001. "Ben Cohen: Educating business in marketing ethics." *The Vermont Business Magazine*. August.

Mazur, Laura. 2001. "The trouble with takeovers." *Marketing*. 8 February.

McClenahen, John S. 1998. "Modest man, ambitious mission." *Industry Week*. 19 January.

Meersman, Tom. 1999. "Manufacturer preaches environmentalist gospel; Carpet-maker says business can save planet and make profit." *Star Tribune* (Minneapolis, MN). 24 February.

Meersman, Tom. 1999. "A corporate green shift; Several companies that have tried to be 'eco-efficient' have discovered that saving the planet can also save them money." *Star Tribune* (Minneapolis, MN) 14 April.

Melillo, Sara. 2001. "ShoreBank partners up to give inner-city projects access to cash." *Crain's Cleveland Business*. 27 August.

Milliot, Jim. 2000. "Chain Sales Rose 11% in Fiscal '00 to $6.8 Billion." *Publisher's Weekly*. 27 March.

Milliot, Jim. 2000. "Tattered Cover Must Turn Over Records in Drug Case." *Publishers Weekly*. 30 October.

Morrow, David J. 1998. "Wheelchair Makers Are Trying to Expand Their Turf." The *New York Times*. 21 January.

Nissenbaum,Dion. 2001. "Sweatshops Get New Opponent." *San Jose Mercury News*. 19 August.

Nixon, Brian. 1987. "Chicago's Shorebank: The National Model." *Independent Banker*. April.

Norris, Floyd. 1992. "Low-Fat Problem at Ben & Jerry's." The *New York Times*. 9 September.

O'Brien, Maureen. 1993. "Huge expansion planned for Denver's Tattered Cover." *Publishers Weekly*. 8 February.

Osborne, David. 1989. "A poverty program that works." *The New Republic*. 8 May.

Osborne, David. 1996. "Welfare Reality Check." The *Washington Post*. 10 November.

Ottman, Jacquelyn A. 1998. "Stonyfield Farm Exemplifies New Green Marketing Model." *Marketing News*. 5 January.

Palmeri, Christopher. 1999. "It's in the tea leaves." *Forbes*. 6 September.

Pankratz, Howard. 2000. "Bookstore search on hold." *Denver Post*. 13 April.

Patagonia Inc. "About Patagonia." Available at http://www.patagonia.com/about/main_about_us.shtml

Paulson, Steven K. 2002. "Court: Police can't see book store records." *Associated Press*. 8 April.

Pelegano, Justin Quinn. 2000. "Remembering Derrick Thomas." Huddlin' with the Pros. www.huddlin.com. February 15.

Petruno, Tom. 1992. "Simple Plan Makes Sunrise Medical a Wall Street Star." The *Los Angeles Times*. 24 August.

Petruno, Tom. 1996. "Sunrise Scam Throws Light on Incentive Pay Programs." The *Los Angeles Times*. 15 January.

Phillips, Stephen. 1986. "Small Bank Revives Urban Area." The *New York Times*. 30 January.

Posnanski, Joe. 2002. Chiefs' Holmes Makes All the Right Moves." The *Kansas City Star*.

Proctor, Cathy. 2001 "Organic Growers Attract Corporations' Attention." The *Denver Business Journal*. 9-15 February.

Quint, Michael. 1992. "This bank can turn a profit and follow a social agenda." The *New York Times*. 24 May.

Reed, Carson. 1990. "(S)wamped by success, a Denver book store computerized." *Colorado Business Magazine*. February.

Reed, Robert. 1990. "Thinking Small." *Crain's Chicago Business*. 16 July.

"World Leader In Pollution Prevention Speaks at EPA Conference." Regulartory Intelligence Data. August, 4, 1998.

Richardson, Cheryl Jenkins. 1989. " Shopping plaza caps off revival of South Shore." *Chicago Tribune*. 15 October.

Rodrique, George. 1997. "New York paying company to find jobs and help clients keep them." The *Dallas Morning News*. 1 January.

Rogers, Doug. 1991. "Sunrise Medical Profits Propelled by Custom Wheelchairs." *Investors Daily*. 8 May.

Rose, Julie. 2002. Stonyfield: Did the Yogurt King Sell His Soul?" *Fortune Small Business*.January.

Rosenzweig, Billa. 1992. "The Republic of Tea." *Brandweek*. 22 November.

Rothman, Howard. 1996. "Under Pressure." *Business Ethics*. September/October.

Rothman, Howard. 2001. *50 Companies That Changed the World*. Franklin Lakes, N.J.: Career Press.

Ruggless, Ron. 1995. "Bookstores offer a new bestseller: restaurants." *Nation's Restaurant News*. 3 April.

Rundle, Rhonda L. 1995. "Sunrise Medical puts president, 2 others on leave pending inquiry into finances." The *Wall Street Journal*. 27 October.

Rundle, Rhonda L. 1996. "Sunrise Medical Only Limps Along After Fiscal Scandal." The *Wall Street Journal*. 31 January.

Rundle, Rhonda L. 2000. "Sunrise Medical Board Backs Buyout Bid." The *Wall Street Journal*. 18 October.

Santana, Arthur. 2001. "DC. Unprepared for an Influx of Ex-Convicts." The *Washington Post*. 21 July.

Scholl, Jaye. 1994. "Staying healthy." *Barron's*. 12 September.

Schmitt, Kate. 2002. "An Interview with Gary Hirschberg." *Green Living*. 27 January.

Schweiger, Tristan. 2000. "CEO of Stonyfield Farms tells the secret of his success." *Pennsylvanian*. 5 April.

"SEC Files and Settles A Suit Against Barton, Formerly of Bio Clinic." 1999. The *Wall Street Journal*. 25 February.

Shapiro, Joseph P. 1991. "Re-inventing the Wheel." *APF Reporter*. Summer.

Shorebank Corp. "2001 Annual Report." Available WWW: http://www.shorebankcorp.com/main/2001AnnualReport/

Shorebank Corp. "About South Shore Bank." Available WWW: http://www.sbk.com/livesite/aboutssb/ab_ssb.cfm

"Siegel Oversees Celestial Development, Exec Reorg." 2000. *Brandweek*. 2 October.

Slimak, Paul. 1991. "A taste for adventure." *Country Accents*.

January-February.

Sneyd, Ross. 2000. "Warning to buyers: Don't mess with Ben & Jerry's." *Associated Press*. 18 January.

Spurge, Lorraine. 1997. *Business Encyclopedia Illustrated.* Santa Monica, Calif.: Knowledge Exchange.

Steers, Stuart. 1994. "Tattered Cover to anchor 16th St. deal." *Denver Business Journal*. 22 July.

Stieghorst, Tom. 1998. "Summit Focuses on Welfare Reform." *Sun-Sentinel* (Fort Lauderdale, FL). 27 January.

Stonyfield Farm. 2000. *A Practical Guide to Understanding Organic*. December.

Stonyfield Farm. 1997. *Stonyfield Farm's Environmental Cookbook.*

Stonyfield Farm. 2002. "Stonyfield Farm and Environmental Responsibility." Available at www.stonyfieldfarm.com/Ido/WhatWeDo.shtml

Strauss, Gary. 1989. "Patagonia's rugged wear leads pack." *USA Today*. 11 January.

Sullivan, Carol Edmonds. 2001. "Intellectual Freedom." *Denver Post*. 2 September.

Sullivan, Robert E. "Just Desserts." *Rolling Stone*. 9 July.

Sunrise Medical. "About Sunrise." Available WWW: http://www.sunrisemedical.com/

Sweeney, Kevin. 1991. "Corporate Tithing in Good Times... and Bad." *In Business*. November-December.

Tattered Cover Bookstore. "Info Desk." Available WWW: http://www.tatteredcover.com/NASApp/store/IndexJsp

Thompson, Stephanie. 2001. "Ben & Jerry's keeps its folksy focus." *Advertising Age*. 12 February.

Thompson, Stephanie. 2001. "Ben & Jerry's puts Freese on global warming, sales." *Advertising Age*. 27 August.

Tucker, Doug. 2000. "Thousands Mourn at Arrowhead." *Associated Press*. February 15.

United Way of America. "United Way and the National Football League." Available WWW:

http://national.unitedway.org/nfl/ptnr_story.cfm

Vasquez, Beverly. 1996. "Celestial carves niche in Japan's tea market." *Denver Business Journal*. 15 November."

Vasquez, Beverly. 1998. "Celestial sips retail operations." *Denver Business Journal*. 28 August.

Vestar Capital Partners. "Sunrise Medical: Public to Private/Management Buyout, December 2000." Available WWW: http://www.vestarcapital.com/investments/cs_sunrise.html

Wallace, Bruce. 1999. "Hitting a sour note." *Maclean's*. 1 February.

Watson, Robert A. 2001. *The Most Effective Organization in the U.S.* New York: Crown Business

Weber, Larry. 2002. *The Provocateur*. New York: Crown Business

Wieffering, Eric J. 1991. "Trouble in Camelot." *Business Ethics*. January-February.

Wolf, Richard. 1999. "Welfare to Work Provides benefits beyond reducing rolls." *USA Today*. 27 April.

Index